African American
Foreign
Correspondents

Media and Public Affairs

Robert Mann, SERIES EDITOR

African American Foreign Correspondents

[A HISTORY]

Jinx Coleman Broussard

Published by Louisiana State University Press
lsupress.org

LOUISIANA PAPERBACK EDITION, 2026

DESIGNER: Mandy McDonald Scallan
TYPEFACE: Whitman

Library of Congress Cataloging-in-Publication Data

Broussard, Jinx C. (Jinx Coleman), 1949–
African American foreign correspondents : a history / Jinx Coleman Broussard.
pages cm. — (Media and public affairs)
Includes bibliographical references and index.
ISBN 978-0-8071-5054-2 (cloth : alk. paper) — ISBN 978-0-8071-5055-9 (pdf) — ISBN 978-0-8071-5056-6 (epub) — ISBN 978-0-8071-8839-2 (paperback) 1. African American press—History. 2. African American journalists—History. 3. Foreign news—United States—History. 4. Foreign correspondents—United States—History. I. Title.
PN4882.5.B595 2013
070.92—dc23

2012042691

This book is dedicated to

my husband, Robert Broussard Sr.,
who is my number one cheerleader . . .

my children and siblings, who kept me grounded . . .

and my late parents, whose dream I am living

Contents

Acknowledgments

This book began as a result of a conversation that John "Jack" Maxwell Hamilton and I had when he was working on his history of American foreign reporting. Jack, who was dean of the Manship School of Mass Communication at the time, asked if I had ever heard of John "Rover" Jordan, an African American foreign war correspondent for the *Norfolk Journal and Guide.* Of course I had not, but my research on Jordan led to the discovery not only of black war correspondents, but numerous others who reported from all over the world. Jack and I wrote and published an article in *American Journalism* on some who wrote from abroad during World War II. Following that, he suggested I write what has become this book. My thanks, therefore, goes first to him for starting me on this journey. I also thank the Manship School and the Reilly Center for Media and Public Affairs at Louisiana State University for resources and other support that enabled me to travel to conduct research and present my findings.

I am indebted to the graduate research assistants who spent numerous hours looking at microfilm, finding material about unheard of correspondents, locating and digesting news articles from abroad, and providing valuable input. A special thanks goes to Skye Chance Cooley, Benjamin Rex LaPoe, Cristina Mislan, and Masudul Biswas, who wrote articles with me based on our research, as well as Erica Taylor and Lyle Perkins. The *Chicago Defender* gave me access to the files of its foreign correspondents, and the archivists at *The Afro-American* and several libraries and research centers directed me to sources and assisted me after my visits. They include Michael Kluge and Beverly Cook of the Vivian G. Harsh Research Collection of Afro-American History and Literature of the Chicago Public Library, and the staff at the Moorland-Spingarn Research Center at Howard University, the Peabody Collection at Hampton University, Morgan State University, the Chicago Historical Museum, and the Schomburg Center for Research in Black Culture of the New York Public Library. I owe my gratitude to them and to Raymond Boone, a former editor and foreign correspondent for *The Afro-American* who now publishes the *Richmond Free Press.* Without his assistance, I would never have heard of or met William Worthy Jr., nor would I have learned so much about how and why the black press engaged in foreign news gathering.

Finally, I thank my family members for their support and cheerleading, and for trying to provide a sense of balance as I devoted years to this book.

African American Foreign Correspondents

Introduction

Mary Ann Shadd Cary was a self-assured and fiercely independent twenty-eight-year-old when she headed north to Canada almost one year to the day after passage of the Compromise of 1850, which strengthened the Fugitive Slave Act. The measure, aimed at minimizing regional strife as the United States expanded westward, appeased slave owners by allowing armed pursuit and capture of anyone suspected of being a runaway slave. It also penalized federal officials who did not aid in the process. Although Shadd Cary had been born to prominent free people of color in Delaware, she knew she was not safe from a rule that made no distinction between free blacks and slaves.

Shadd Cary left behind the work she had been doing as a teacher and a freelance journalist for the black press. Her decision could not have been easy, for she was committed to building her community and working with the press to advance her people. But she could not abide by the slave law she called "odious" and the danger it posed. She left her family behind and headed for a place that guaranteed freedom and opportunity for blacks. Not long after settling in her new homeland, Shadd Cary wrote a persuasive pamphlet aimed at spurring black emigration to Canada. Soon after, she became the first black woman to edit a North American newspaper, the *Provincial Freeman*. The weekly circulated in Canada and the United States.

What makes Shadd Cary distinctive is the fact that she became a foreign correspondent and helped define a role that was still very much in formation at the time. Her work is symbolic of the largely unrecognized genre of African American foreign correspondence, which has been treated as an anomaly. Traditionally, foreign correspondents have been portrayed as suave, daring men—and a few tough, aggressive women—who followed the story wherever it took them. Black writers and the publications for which they wrote have not fit into the picture. Nevertheless, their output testifies to the longevity and vast amount of black global reporting. Like their white counterparts, they represent the men and women who saw the world firsthand, related their experiences, framed issues on the world stage, and created context and meaning for people of color and other audiences worldwide.

This book is about people like Shadd Cary and the periodicals that invested their human and financial resources to tell the truth or, as they often wrote, to tell the other side of the story. Shadd Cary and Frederick Douglass, both abolitionists, became accidental foreign correspondents and gave birth to the genre of international news gathering by blacks. Although this work primarily addresses African American foreign correspondence in black print publications, where it was most prolific, it also gives attention to writings from abroad by blacks who worked for mainstream publications.

Foreign correspondence can be letters, official reports, news, and other information gathered abroad for dissemination at home; it is intertwined with the broad expanse of history. Foreign news gathering by U.S. media dates to colonial times, when accounts of news from England were rewritten for dissemination in the new land.[1] As the genre evolved, men and women often risked their lives to provide firsthand accounts of wars, insight into world personalities, and commentary on events.

Early international news gatherers were quasi correspondents, untrained in the profession, who worked in other primary occupations while reporting. They were gatekeepers who determined what news and information from abroad gained a place on the public agenda. These prestigious reporters often made their own assignments, gathering, presenting, and interpreting social, economic, and political issues and events abroad for audiences at home. The experiences of Americans living or traveling abroad provided the human-interest aspect of foreign reporting.[2]

Despite representing a vast output of editorial content for almost two centuries, black foreign correspondence remains almost invisible in media history. When the journalists appear in major works, they are little more than asterisks. Robert Desmond's award-winning work on foreign correspondence, for instance, names Edgar T. Rouzeau as the first black accredited correspondent to cover World War II and identifies Ollie Stewart, John Jordan, William Randy Dixon Jr., and Edward N. Toles as correspondents who covered various theaters of war. Desmond fails to mention more than twenty other blacks who covered the war, or that blacks reported from abroad at all.

Groundbreaking works on the black press pay scant attention to black international news gatherers. For instance, Roland Woseley's *The Black Press, U.S.A.* and Armistead Pride and Clint C. Wilson's excellent *A History of the African-American Press* contain no reference to African Americans who worked in this elite area of journalism. Two major books, however, provide more than a glancing view of reporting from overseas by blacks. John Maxwell Hamilton's *Journalism's Roving Eye: A History of Foreign Correspondence* and Hayward Farrar's *The Baltimore Afro-American: 1892–1950* both devote entire chapters to the subject.

The Black Press

To understand black foreign correspondence, it is instructive to first look at the medium that spawned it. This medium arose out of a need to provide visibility and truth in a world where the mainstream or establishment media systematically failed to acknowledge the existence of black people or, just as detrimentally, characterized them as deviant, immoral, and inconsequential. *Freedom's Journal*, the first newspaper published by blacks, vowed that race members would no longer allow publications such as Mordecai Manuel Noah's *New York Enquirer* to routinely vilify and degrade them. "Daily slandered," said the prospectus, "we think that there ought to be some channel of communication between us and the public, through which a single voice may be heard in defense of five hundred thousand free people of color."[3] Other periodicals followed the lead of *Freedom's Journal* by reacting and responding to the dominant society and the mainstream media. Abolitionist and black separatist Martin R. Delaney whitewashed houses to earn money to start *The Mystery* because he "so bitterly resented censorship of African Americans."[4] William Hodges began the *Ram's Horn* after the editor of the *New York Sun* made him pay for publication of a letter to the editor, a nonexistent requirement for whites.[5]

Many organs that were instruments of strident protests against slavery ceased publication during the Civil War, largely because of inadequate finances, lack of advertising, and sabotage by whites; but the medium grew quickly after Reconstruction. The passage of Black Codes in the South, and other repressive measures, systematically stripped blacks of the protections of the Civil Rights Act of 1866 and the Thirteenth, Fourteenth, and Fifteenth Amendments.[6] The black press became the eyes, ears, and champions of the race. Pride and Wilson explain, "The newspapers brought home to their readers the instances of flouting the law, the lynchings, the brutality, and the outrages that occurred almost daily. The African American reader was kept aware of the need for alertness and for challenges to repression—objectives that Negro newspapers have pursued to this day."[7]

In New York, T. Thomas Fortune's *New York Globe* reflected how this vocal medium navigated a society rife with injustice. The weekly gained a national circulation as it adopted a militant and defiant tone that pressed for civil liberties and countered white stereotypes of blacks as subhuman and unworthy of constitutional protection. Other black editors and publishers were advocates who spurred movements for social reform. In 1891, for instance, Edward P. McCabe took a page from Shadd Cary's book, establishing the *Langston Herald* to promote settlement in the all-black town. In 1898, a fiercely militant Ida B. Wells used her newspaper, *Free Speech,* to urge Memphis blacks to leave that city following the lynching of three black businessmen.

As the black press proliferated at the turn of the twentieth century, publications of a religious, sectarian, fraternal, and political nature sought to strengthen the racial bonds by chronicling blacks' activities. Periodicals continued to educate the community on matters of black achievement and progress, and they served up an ideology of racial self-help, productivity, and race pride. The emergence of a more educated populace and a growing black middle class further contributed to the growth of the black press and the expansion of its mission. For example, the *Voice of the Negro,* which was published from May 1904 to October 1907, ran articles that focused on black achievement and literature, as well as political, educational, social, and economic issues. Some of those articles originated abroad. With Max Barber as its editor, the periodical vowed to "stand as the vanguard of a higher culture and a new literature," to be "a force of race elevation," and to reflect "current and sociological history so accurately" so as to "become a kind of documentation for the coming generations."[8] Again, the goal was to tell the real story—the other side—and to tell the truth.

The desire for a truer representation of the race and the quest for civil and social justice contributed to the continued growth of the black press during the first fifty years of the twentieth century. Circulation increased as the medium took the country to task for its mistreatment of blacks. As a result, some changes occurred. The government felt pressured by the black press and race leaders to integrate the workforce, to allow blacks to fight in both world wars, to end lynching, and to create a just and equitable society. Marcus Garvey's *Negro World,* which was published from 1920 to 1924, told readers repeatedly that black was beautiful and that the road to success involved entrepreneurship. Buoyed by such messages, tens of thousands of blacks embraced Garvey's Universal Negro Improvement Association (UNIA) and his Back-to-Africa movement. From the *Chicago Defender,* readers learned that the North offered redress from the dehumanizing treatment they suffered in the South. Many poor blacks took publisher Robert S. Abbott's advice and became a part of the Great Migration. Readers followed with rapt attention Joel Augustus Rogers's accounts of the Italian-Ethiopian War in the pages of the *Pittsburgh Courier* from October 1935 through April 1936. And they followed the exploits of black military personnel during World War II, brought to them by thirty black men who reported from various theaters of war. With the cry of "victory at home and abroad," black publishers and editors sought the right for blacks to fight for their country and the right of black journalists to cover the war from abroad. At home, they pressed for passage of legislation to end segregation in all aspects of American life.

The still successful *Ebony* magazine came on the scene at the halfway mark of the twentieth century and continued to educate, inform, and entertain readers and to bring them news from abroad. Other magazines and newspapers came and went during the ensuing decades. With the end of legal segregation, the fate of the black press was almost sealed. The medium had always faced financial hardships; that factor, coupled with the loss of many of its best journalists to mainstream media, had a detrimental impact on the black press. Yet black media organizations continue today, with more than two hundred publications registered as members of the National Newspaper Publishers Association (NNPA).

In its surveillance function, the black press monitored society and the mainstream press and developed a public sphere of its own. As R. N. Jacobs noted, this alternative or parallel sphere enabled blacks to discuss and debate issues and make sense of their lives and world.[9] *Chicago Defender* publisher John H. Sengstacke said on the occasion of that paper's fiftieth anniversary in 1955 that the black press had "given voice to the basic aspirations [of blacks]" and given them dignity.[10] Enoch Waters, whose career in the black press spanned more than thirty years, provided another perspective, arguing that the output of the medium was "addressed more to the conscience of whites who controlled the levers of power than to powerless blacks who had but little access to the publications and who, because of enforced illiteracy, were unable to read."[11] Historian Maxwell Brooks offered the opinion that the medium "provided the raw material" that molded public opinion.[12] Black foreign correspondence was and is a part of that raw material.

Black Foreign Correspondence

Black foreign correspondence evolved and grew as the black press grew. Gathering news from abroad was central to the mission to create an alternative reality of African Americans and people of African descent worldwide. Words such as "tell the truth" or "the other side of the story" or "our story," or "see for ourselves" appeared repeatedly in dispatches from abroad, becoming a mantra of black foreign reporting. Some writers ventured out alone, without official backing; others were dispatched by prestigious publications such as the *Chicago Defender, The Afro-American*, the *Pittsburgh Courier, Ebony*, and the Associated Negro Press (ANP) news service. These organizations often had to plead and protest to gain the right to cover occurrences abroad. Black foreign correspondence was not confined to the black press. For instance, Douglass's writings from Great Britain found a home in abolitionist newspapers, while the reporting of William Worthy Jr., Roi Ottley, and other black correspondents intermittently ran in mainstream newspapers.

Black foreign correspondents were like the quasi correspondents in the general media who earned their living primarily in fields other than journalism. Although that role changed after completion of the transatlantic cable in 1858, which enabled the faster transmission of news, black foreign correspondents overwhelmingly remained part-time stringers until World War II. While reporters for the mainstream media learned the languages, cultural nuances, and social systems of the countries from which they reported, black writers rarely lived in foreign lands. They engaged in episodic news gathering.[13]

African American foreign correspondents and others who wrote for the medium went where black news was, where the news coincided with events at home. Rarely did the writers conduct interviews with official U.S. sources or other whites. They were intent on getting the black side of the story because they believed the mainstream media too often reported in an untruthful and demeaning manner.

This book challenges the traditional concept of foreign correspondence as a mainstream media enterprise. It introduces readers to black foreign correspondents who were emblematic of various periods in history or whose contributions warrant special recognition. Its focus is on *what* the correspondents reported, not so much on how they did so, because that information often was not available. Despite the difficulty of obtaining information about the lives and work of black foreign correspondents, this book goes beyond merely giving the names and affiliations of correspondents, culling information from news accounts, oral histories, and papers to bring them alive to readers.

What drove individual reporters in the black press, and those who eventually worked in integrated media, to engage in foreign correspondence? How did they do their jobs? What challenges did they face? To what extent did African American foreign correspondence challenge assumptions about black people around the world, channel black discontent, and confront the dominant systems at home and abroad? Did the correspondents address the issue of class?

While illustrating the vast amount of editorial content from abroad, this account highlights the intersections of race and media and of media and government. It also provides insight into the black perspective by exploring how African American journalists reporting from abroad saw the world, related their experiences, and framed global issues, providing context for people of color and other audiences worldwide.

War coverage receives special attention, for the black press, like the white press, was especially prolific during those periods. From World War I to the Vietnam War, African American foreign correspondents followed black troops and told their stories, giving them visibility and credibility. From World War II on, correspondents were embedded with the troops they covered.

Although foreign reporting took different forms at different times, it coalesced around shared racial and cultural identity, transnational white supremacy, and representation of darker peoples. The very name of Marcus Garvey's *Negro World* alludes to a Pan-African community that transcended national boundaries. News from abroad overwhelmingly linked African Americans and their counterparts in the Americas, the Caribbean, and Africa, and it provided the basis for comparing the black experience in the United States with that in other countries.

While this book seeks to rescue an important genre from obscurity, it also breaks new ground in several ways. First, it argues that slavery and the status of free people of color in American society during the antebellum period led to the birth of black foreign correspondence and determined its subject matter.

Oppressive conditions throughout the world ensured the continuation of the genre. Both Douglass and Shadd Cary left the land of their birth in the 1840s and 1850s, with the goal not of reporting but of escaping repressive conditions. Forced out of the United States, they used their vantage point and their words to push for social change—something they could not achieve at home. The issues of slavery and emigration dominated foreign coverage. George Washington Williams, W. E. B. Du Bois, and other intellectuals understood that they were part of a larger community and that ways of subjugating people based on gender, race, and class cut across borders. Williams went to Africa in the late 1800s to report the real story of King Leopold's Belgian colony of the Congo. Du Bois had the backing of the National Association for the Advancement of Colored People (NAACP) when he traveled overseas after World War I to help convene a Pan-African Congress and to try to affect the future of postwar Africa. Correspondents understood the larger nature of liberation struggles. Thus, when African nations were throwing off the yoke of colonialism after World War II, writers for the black press were on the scene to chronicle their progress.

Second, this book argues that reporting by blacks is important as an antidote to the elite media. Correspondents saw the world primarily through the race lens. In 1904, for instance, the *Voice of the Negro* and the *New York Times* both supported Japan in the Russo-Japanese War, but the magazine viewed Japan's victory as a triumph of a kindred race over a European power, while the newspaper interpreted Russia's occupation of Manchuria and expansion into Asia as "hostile to American interests."[14]

The mindset of black international reporting also guided the quest to provide more accurate coverage and to expose evils at home within the context of race relations abroad. Correspondents challenged America to mirror how foreign nations treated nonwhite others. The short-lived *Moon Illustrated Monthly,* for example, founded by Du Bois in 1905, promised to be a "high class journal" that would "interpret the news of the world to them and inspire them toward infinite ideals."[15]

Third, news from abroad sought to elevate the standing of people of color by highlighting their accomplishments and refuting the negative stereotypes in mainstream media. Some two decades after *The Afro-American* sought to redefine Pan-African identity that also became part of *Ebony*'s mission. The magazine largely presented good news, for, as publisher John H. Johnson wrote, too few positive stories about blacks were published. Linda Johnson

Rice wrote on the magazine's fiftieth anniversary in 1995 that her father had founded the magazine when "Africa was still viewed as the 'Dark Continent' occupied largely by 'savage' tribes and ferocious jungle beasts. Little, if anything, was written in the U.S. press about the ravages and exploitation visited on Africa and its people by greedy European colonialists, and even less about the valiant struggle waged by Africans to free themselves."[16]

Even after black journalists joined elite media organizations and became foreign correspondents, however, many were still committed to telling the untold stories of their race. Thomas A. Johnson of the *New York Times* reported on the experiences of African American soldiers in Vietnam, and Howard French, another *Times* foreign correspondent, looked for stories of hope from Africa during the 1990s, even as he filed objective accounts of chaos on the continent.[17]

Today black foreign correspondents appear on television and have bylines in mainstream publications. Like their white counterparts, they usually engage in parachute journalism, going abroad to cover a specific story. Although foreign correspondence has decreased significantly since the golden age of the genre during World War II, it has been almost nonexistent in the black press for the last half century. With the advent of integration, many top journalists of color joined the staffs of mainstream media, thus depriving the black press of the stars who had traditionally been assigned abroad. Ongoing financial woes contributed to an inability to field reporters overseas. As in the early days, individual newspapers try to obtain firsthand coverage. *The Afro-American* sent a reporter to Iraq during Operation Desert Storm to tell the story of blacks fighting there. The newspaper also dispatched a reporter when the United States invaded Afghanistan. Both journalists, however, spent only two weeks in the Middle East.

A race-centered perspective that did not echo the elite media's international news gathering or the government's agenda characterized African American correspondence well into the twentieth century. The editorial output challenged inequities that consigned the race to an underclass in the United States and oppression abroad. The coverage educated readers about a wider world and the lives of oppressed and marginalized people. As it advocated, criticized, and cajoled, black foreign correspondence strove to bring about global social and economic change, but little changed for the black community in America as a result. Racism and its attendant codes were too entrenched.

Black international news gathering often veered from objectivity into advocacy. Today, as most black foreign correspondents work for mainstream media outlets, their dispatches do not have a race-centered worldview but reflect the journalistic norm of objectivity. While the correspondents may report on events that affect people of color throughout the world, they do not advocate change or challenge the mainstream. Almost without exception, they are simply reporters presenting the facts.

[1]
The Genesis

Frederick Douglass: First Sojourn Abroad

When former slave Frederick Douglass boarded the *Cambria* steamship for Great Britain on a hot August day in 1845, he was on his way to becoming the first African American foreign correspondent. Douglass was well aware that the issue of slavery transcended national borders. His travels and speeches in the United States had left him hungry to take his message farther. Great Britain was a natural extension. Although England had been involved in the slave trade in colonial America, the country had since abolished human trafficking. Reformers across the ocean called on America to do the same. When the Hibernia Anti-Slavery Society in Europe invited Douglass to speak, friends at home began raising travel funds for him. A number of leading abolitionists opposed the idea, believing the cause was better served by having Douglass remain in the United States.

But Douglass paid little attention; his mind was made up. He could be called an accidental foreign correspondent because his reasons for going abroad were to escape the reach of slavery and to publicize America's treatment of blacks. He hoped to call attention to the subjugated status of his race and bring pressure from abroad to end slavery. He left his wife Anna and their three young children and headed overseas in the company of James Buffman and the Hutchinson Quartet, fellow antislavery proponents who often shared the stage with him at abolitionist events.

With sixty dollars his associates had raised and three hundred fifty dollars from sales of his autobiography, Douglass began a two-year sojourn in Great Britain and Ireland. Audiences eager to hear about his personal experience with America's peculiar institution awaited him—as did a new life. Just seven years after his escape, he was for the first time free to live without looking over his shoulder for pursuers. He would enjoy the type of liberty that eluded even free black men and women in the United States. He arrived in Liverpool and then traveled to Dublin and other places in Ireland and Great Britain.

He used his speaking and writing skills to tell the story of blacks in America. On September 29, 1845, he wrote from Dublin that his book, released overseas, had sold one hundred copies in short order. He noted that he was welcomed "side by side with white speakers" and was "received as kindly and warmly as though my skin were white."[1]

Many letters Douglas sent home were published in the *Liberator,* William Lloyd Garrison's well-regarded abolitionist newspaper, founded in 1831 to push for emancipation.[2] Douglass was committed to eyewitness reporting. "I am not going through this land with my eyes shut, ears stopped or heart steeled," he wrote. "I am seeking to see, hear and feel [a]ll that may be seen, heard and felt . . . and . . . disclosing the result of my observations."[3]

His writings from abroad differed from the mainstream media's foreign correspondence, which in 1846 focused primarily on the Mexican-American War. Professionalization of reporting in the mainstream media occurred at this time. As the United States pursued its westward expansion, Douglass did not address the conflict. He was not a professional journalist, nor did he have the backing of a newspaper. He was a solitary man acting on behalf of his race.

Douglass's social commentary juxtaposed his country's racial discrimination with the United Kingdom's attitude toward race.[4] The following excerpt from the January 1, 1846, issue of the *Liberator* is representative of Douglass's foreign correspondence:

> I have no end to serve, no creed to uphold, no government to defend; and as to nation, I belong to none. I have no protection at home, or resting-place abroad. The land of my birth welcomes me to her shores only as a slave, and spurns with contempt the idea of treating me differently. So that I came an outcast from the society of my childhood, and an outlaw in the land of my birth. "I am a stranger with thee, and a sojourner as all my fathers were." That men should be patriotic is to me perfectly natural; and as a philosophical fact, I am able to give an *intellectual* recognition. But no further can I go. If ever I had any patriotism, or any capacity for the feeling, it was whipped out of me long since by the lash of the American soul-drivers. . . .
>
> I can truly say, I have spent some of the happiest moments of my life since landing in this country [Ireland]. I seem to have undergone a transformation. I live a new life. The warm and generous cooperation extended to me by the friends of my despised race—the prompt and liberal manner with which the press has rendered me its aid—the

glorious enthusiasm with which thousands have flocked to hear the cruel wrongs of my down-trodden and long-enslaved countrymen portrayed—the deep sympathy for the slave, and the strong abhorrence of the slaveholder, everywhere evinced—the cordiality with which members and ministers of various religious bodies, and of various shades of religious opinion, have embraced me, and lent me their aid—the kind hospitality constantly proffered to me by persons of the highest rank in society—the spirit of freedom that seems to animate all with whom I come in contact—and the entire absence of everything that looked like prejudice against me, on account of the color of my skin—contrasted so strongly with my long and bitter experience in the United States, that I look with wonder and amazement on the transition. In the Southern part of the United States, I was a slave, thought of and spoken of as property. In the language of the LAW, *"held, taken, reputed and adjudged to be a chattel in the hands of my owners and possessors, and their executors, administrators, and assigns, to all intents, constructions, and purposes whatsoever."*—Brev., Digest, 224. In the Northern States, a fugitive slave, liable to be hunted at any moment like a felon, and to be hurled into the terrible jaws of slavery—doomed by an inveterate prejudice against color to insult and outrage on every hand. (Massachusetts out of the question)—denied the privileges and courtesies common to others in the use of the most humble means of conveyance—shut out from the cabins of steamboats—refused admission to respectable hotels—caricatured, scorned, scoffed, mocked and maltreated with immunity by any one (no matter how black his heart,) so he has white skin. But now behold the change. Eleven days and a half gone, and I have crossed three thousand miles of the perilous deep. Instead of a democratic government, I am under a monarchial government. Instead of the bright blue sky of America, I am covered with the soft grey fog of the Emerald Isle. I breathe, and lo! The chattel becomes a man. I gaze around in vain for one who will question my equal humanity, claim me as his slave, or offer me an insult. I employ a cab—I am seated beside white people—I reach the hotel—I enter the same door—I am shown into the same parlor—I dine at the same hotel—I enter the same door—I am shown into the same parlor—I dine at the same table—and no one is offended. No delicate nose grows deformed in my presence. I find no difficulty here in obtaining admission into any place of worship, instruction or amusement, on equal terms with people as white as any

I ever saw in the United States. I meet nothing to remind me of my complexion. I find myself regarded and treated at every turn with the kindness and deference paid to white people. When I go to church, I am met by no upturned nose and scornful lip to tell me, *"We don't allow n——s in here."* . . .

. . . Thank heaven for the respite I now enjoy! I had been in Dublin but a few days, when a gentleman of great respectability kindly offered to conduct me through all the public buildings of the beautiful city, and a little afterward, I found myself dining with the Lord Mayor of Dublin. What a pity there was not some American democratic Christian at the door of his splendid mansion, to bark out at my approach. *"They don't allow n s in here!"* The truth is, the people here know nothing of the republican Negro hate prevalent in our glorious land. They measure and esteem men according to their moral and intellectual worth, and not according to the color of their skin. Whatever may be said of the aristocracies here, there is none based on the color of a man's skin. This species of aristocracy belongs pre-eminently to "the land of the free, and the home of the brave." I have never found it abroad, in any but Americans. It sticks to them wherever they go. They find it almost as hard to get rid of it as to get rid of their skins.[5]

While this letter contained very little reporting in the traditional sense, it was typical of early African American foreign correspondence, which provided information about a country's history, landscape, and culture. The correspondent sometimes provided no topical news, instead enlightening readers about places to which they had little access. Douglass's description of how other nations treated blacks compared to the United States would become a major theme of other African American correspondents.

Douglass seized the opportunity to reach a larger, perhaps whiter audience by sending his letters to newspapers other than the *Liberator.* After Horace Greeley's *New-York Tribune* published Douglass's January 1 letter to Garrison, Douglass wrote to thank the editor, who was also an advocate of emancipation.[6] He assailed organized religion both at home and abroad for turning a blind eye to poverty and oppression, for allowing slaveholders to worship in the name of Christianity, and for compromising on the issue of human bondage. Observing the wretchedly poor on the streets of Ireland, he believed the church and the government were morally bound to address their plight. In a letter dated March 27, 1846, he described the conditions of the working class in England, Scotland, and Ireland and called upon abolitionists in the United States to care about those across the ocean. In Douglass's words, "He who really and truly feels for the American slave cannot steel his heart to the woes of others; and he who thinks himself an abolitionist, yet cannot enter into the wrongs of others, has yet to find a true foundation for his anti-slavery fate."[7] Criticism of other institutions for their complicity in the oppression would become a recurring theme in African American foreign reporting. By April 1846, Douglass had participated in many antislavery meetings and shared his observations with *Liberator* readers. In the May 15 issue, he reported that Scotland was "in a blaze of anti-slavery agitation" and that discussions there mirrored those in the United States.[8]

After friends in Great Britain raised enough money to pay his slave master for his freedom, Douglass returned to the United States a free man in April 1847. Foreign correspondents for the black press would continue to embrace and extend the paradigm Douglass originated, focusing not only on blacks at home but on other marginalized people overseas.[9]

Not long after Douglass returned to New York, he began publishing the *North Star* newspaper with the help of supportive whites. This dismayed Garrison, who saw no need for a black newspaper that addressed only black concerns. He believed the *Liberator* and the abolitionist press could fulfill that role, and he feared Douglass's venture would dilute black support. Friction developed between the two men. Nevertheless, on November 1, 1847, the *North Star* began publication in Rochester; it continued for four years before financial woes led to its merger with the *Liberty Party Paper*. The new venture was renamed *Frederick Douglass' Paper*.

As a free man of color, this former slave, eloquent orator, and successful journalist made subsequent trips to Canada, Scotland, and England to plead the abolitionist cause and bring pressure to bear against human bondage. He later became an ambassador to Haiti. Less than a decade after Douglass went abroad, the continuing plight of slaves and the precarious perch of free blacks in American were the impetus for Mary Ann Shadd Cary to cross the border into Canada and generate her own brand of foreign correspondence.

Mary Ann Shadd Cary: You Belong in Canada!

Like Frederick Douglass, Mary Shadd Cary was an accidental foreign correspondent—a designation that did not even exist in the black press. Her motivation for going to Canada had more to do with the position of blacks in

American society. The sense of self and racial identity and a commitment to racial uplift and self-reliance were the impetus for Shadd Cary's foreign correspondence. As the rights of free blacks were steadily chipped away in the years leading up to the Civil War, free people of color, abolitionists, and black nationalists engaged in a vigorous debate about the course blacks should take to escape oppression. Some activists urged colonization in Africa, others favored emigration to Canada, and still others urged immediate emancipation in the United States.

Shadd Cary had traveled to Canada even before she made her permanent move. She and her father Abraham Shadd were among fifty-three persons who attended the Great North American Anti-Slavery Convention on September 11, 1851. The only woman present, Shadd Cary was familiar to the group of emigration advocates, for she had ignored the gender roles of the day and joined the ongoing debate on the future of her race. She had attended many male-dominated meetings, some held in her home with her father presiding. Upon her return to the United States, her notes of the proceedings were published in abolitionist newspapers.[10]

Shadd Cary argued for emigration to Canada, a position diametrically opposed to that of Douglass, who argued immediate emancipation in the United States. To Shadd Cary, colonization was "racial bigotry."[11]

While Douglass has been immortalized in the history of blacks in America, Shadd Cary's name and work are not well known, although some vital information is on the record. She was born in 1823, and her family "existed in a quasi-free status in which they enjoyed considerable privileges compared with the majority of black Americans." Like other free people of color, she "enjoyed the rare opportunities to obtain an education, practice several professions, travel extensively, engage in politics, and make independent choices about how to live her life."[12] That life had been assured by the circumstances of her birth.

Mary Ann was the first of thirteen children born to Abraham Shadd and his wife Harriet Parnell of Delaware. They were free-born blacks whose mixed-race ancestry classified them as mulattoes, or colored, with privilege and status based on complexion. Although some family members could easily have passed for white, Abraham and Harriet chose to identify as "persons of color, and to cast their lot with the darker members of the race."[13]

By the 1830s, life for free people of color in Delaware had become precarious. The state's black population had grown since the late 1700s as a result of the slave trade and immigration from Maryland. As a consequence, the state's white power structure adopted some of the policies that southern states were enacting. Although Delaware had constitutionally barred the importation of slaves in 1776, and had given blacks the franchise, it now passed Black Codes that revoked that right, barred them from holding public office, required them to produce identification or risk being jailed or enslaved, and made them obtain a license to carry firearms. Blacks who left the state were not allowed reentry, and other blacks were prohibited from emigrating there.[14]

The repressive atmosphere in Delaware precipitated Abraham's decision to take his family to West Chester, Pennsylvania, twenty miles from Philadelphia. Radicalized by discrimination and segregation, Abraham became a leader in the abolitionist movement, sold subscriptions to the *Liberator*, and even made his house one of the stops on the Underground Railroad, all the while working as a successful shoemaker.

Abraham's advocacy undoubtedly sowed the seeds of activism in Mary Ann and shaped her racial ideology. Teaching was virtually the only economic opportunity for blacks, and Shadd Cary absorbed her father's belief that education was the road to self-sufficiency for African Americans. In 1839 she completed her six-year education at a private Quaker boarding school in West Chester and opened a school for African American children in Wilmington. She continued to work as a teacher in Delaware, Pennsylvania, and New Jersey for ten years, striving to combat ignorance and use education as "the frontline of the racial battlefield."[15]

Adept at writing and lecturing, Shadd Cary published articles in abolitionist journals while still in her twenties. One of the earliest examples of her activist, straightforward, even strident tone was a twelve-page pamphlet, *Hints to the Colored People of the North*, which she published in 1849. Excerpts from it ran in the *North Star* as part of a letter from someone whose job was to distribute the pamphlet. Signing the letter with only the initials, J. B. Y., the writer began by stressing the difficulty of getting readers to embrace the pamphlet's content:

> I had a number of them [pamphlets] in my possession to dispose of; but I have not been able *to* sell more than three or four in about two months. As a reader of the *North Star*, I have been watching very carefully, for the last six months, for some of our able and distinguished writers in this city to take notice of this little document, but have

> watched in vain. It has been widely circulated in this city, but I believe very little money has been paid for it. In fact, some have said that had they known that the work contained some things which it does, they would not have had it as a gift; but what the objectionable part is, I have yet *to* learn, unless it be it tells too much truth—particularly in setting the condition of our people in its true light.[16]

Shadd Cary's pamphlet alienated blacks in Philadelphia, for she emphatically told the professional class to shun short-term gratification and the trappings of a materialistic white culture and focus on gaining emancipation and combating crushing discrimination. Suggesting that blacks wanted to impress each other and whites, Shadd Cary questioned whether their extravagances improved their "condition as a people." Whites would conclude that African Americans single-mindedly "attend *to* their exterior!" and that they "set more value on the outside of their heads than on what the inside needs."[17]

A letter published in the *North Star* gave readers further insight into Shadd Cary's views of the role African Americans should play in gaining their liberty. She chastised race members—herself included—for their failure to progress despite fifteen years of meetings, programs, organizing, planning, and "whining over our difficulties and afflictions, passing resolutions on resolutions."[18] The black church was equally responsible for the downtrodden condition of the race, she wrote; as a powerful institution in the community, it sapped African Americans of whatever resources they had and fostered "ignorance as a duty, superstition as a religion."[19] Shadd Cary was unyielding in her belief that her people should act instead of merely talk.

By the autumn of 1851, the situation for African Americans in the United States had become even more intolerable. Shadd Cary could not abide the subjugated position of her race. Less than a decade after Douglass had sent correspondence from Great Britain, a determined Mary Ann Shadd walked away from the relative comfort of her life in Delaware and headed north to take up the cause of her fellow blacks. She settled in Windsor in Upper Canada, a small farming enclave of less than two hundred that was the first stop for African Americans seeking a safe haven. With financial support from the American Missionary Association, she opened an integrated school.

Like Douglass's foreign correspondence, Shadd Cary's developed as a direct result of her escape from oppressive conditions at home. She was convinced that her freedom was at stake and that abolitionists would fail to stir the conscience of America to change the status quo. Also like Douglass, she acted alone, without the backing of the black or abolitionist press. But unlike Douglass, who went overseas to enlist international pressure on the United States to end slavery, Shadd Cary was not trying to influence the dominant society. She went to Canada to tell a different story from what slaveholders were proffering and what some in the black press were writing about the negative aspects of immigrating to Canada. "None of the papers published by our people, in the states, answers our purpose," she explained. "They either pass us [emigrationists] by, in cold contempt, ignore us altogether, keep themselves or their readers, or both, ignorant of what Canada is, or in some other way, by opposition or neglect, disparage us."[20]

When she arrived in her new homeland, Shadd Cary almost immediately began to travel extensively and to gather data, which she soon published as a forty-page pamphlet that unfavorably juxtaposed the American experience for blacks with the promise of Canada. She wrote in *A Plea for Emigration,* "[F]riends, ignorant on this point [the geography of Canada] appeal to fears having no foundation whatever, when the facts are fairly set forth."[21]

Authentication was a crucial goal for Shadd Cary. Her readers had to believe in the reliability of her information on every aspect of Canadian life—its laws, culture, religion, and geography—because her goal was to allay the fears of blacks and convince them to make the life-changing decision to leave the familiar for the unknown. She used footnotes, tables, maps, and direct quotes in her almost encyclopedic piece. Her firsthand observations and eyewitness accounts based on numerous conversations with persons who had lived in the province for many years led her to state with conviction that there were no impediments to emigration and that blacks could live and prosper in Canada. To counter those who argued that the weather was too harsh, she used tables that illustrated climatic conditions and temperature ranges for various regions.[22]

Such eyewitness news gathering and use of supporting data from credible sources would become routine in African American foreign correspondence—just as it was in the mainstream media. Because Shadd Cary and those who followed her were telling an alternative story, it was crucial to show that trusted people attested to veracity of their information.

The title of the pamphlet conveyed Shadd Cary's urgency and began to make her case. She was determined to inform, encourage, and convince blacks to leave the United States and move to Canada. She cautioned them not to believe the propaganda spread by slaveholders and colonialists, designed to discourage exodus to Canada. Those forces had unsavory motives—to maintain the status quo or, failing that, to remove blacks to distant Africa. Neither option was acceptable to Shadd Cary.[23]

Canada was attractive because slavery was virtually unknown there and the form that existed was less oppressive than slavery in the United States. The laws protected all people; blacks would have human rights and equal protection. Additionally, except for those in Quebec, Canadians spoke the same language as their neighbors to the south, and the land was free. Indeed, Canada was "highly conducive to mental and physical energy"; anyone, no matter how destitute, could succeed there. "I firmly believe that with an axe and a little energy, an independent position would result in a short period!" Shadd Cary wrote.[24] As proof, she pointed out that blacks could work in trades in Canada that they were denied access to in the United States. "If a coloured man understands his business, he receives the public patronage the same as the white man. He is not obliged to work a little better, at a lower rate. There is no degraded class to identify him with, therefore, every man's work stands or falls according to merit, not as is his color."[25]

Two years after her arrival in Canada, Shadd Cary embarked on another venture that would become a major vehicle for her international journalism and a platform from which to materially impact the status of her race. With several backers she started the *Provincial Freeman* newspaper. It carried a mix of local news, editorials, letters, and reprints of stories from the United States and abroad. The one issue published in 1853 paralleled a theme that predominated in the African American press and that would become a major tenet of black global journalism—debunking myths about people of color. The newspaper pledged to "represent Canada's black population as independent and autonomous 'freemen' rather than as dependent and oppressed 'fugitives,' as portrayed by the opposition."[26] The newspaper was also a resource for anyone contemplating emigration. A year later, a headline in the newspaper blared: "ATTENTION!!!" "Self-reliance is the True Road to Independence." The article that followed proclaimed that "persons abroad want reliable information of Canada, *from* Canada," and that the *Provincial Freeman* would provide it.[27] Emigration advocates would be better able to compare Canada with other countries, and African Americans would see the benefits of an exodus to the north.

Readers were asked to send copies of the four-page paper to others, to find "one, two, or three or fifty subscribers" at one dollar and fifty cents per year and to submit articles for publication. One agent for the paper was Abraham McKinney, whose goal was to sign up one thousand subscribers in New York,

Pennsylvania, and New Jersey in 1854.[28] From its original base in Windsor, the publication also circulated in the United States through sales Shadd Cary made when she returned there to lecture, through subscriptions, and through a network of individuals and organizations. Shadd Cary kept readers abreast of her travels and activities. A blurb in the November 11, 1854, issue, for example, identified her as a general agent for the newspaper who was on a business trip to Michigan and Ohio, among other places, to "seek to extend" the paper's circulation. She would also "lecture by invitation, on the practicability of an en masse *Emigration* of Colored Americans to the Canadas, and other British Provinces, north of the United States."[29]

Shadd Cary tried to keep her position as editor of the newspaper a secret because the norms of the day frowned upon women undertaking endeavors outside the realm of domesticity.[30] Samuel Ringgold Ward, a cofounder of the paper, was listed as its editor. He had immigrated to Canada some years earlier and was a traveling agent for the Anti-Slavery Society of Canada. But Mary Ann's role was clear to her contemporaries and was attested to on several occasions. For instance, shortly before the paper's demise in 1858, a petition by seven Canadians who sought support for it noted that Isaac Shadd and his sister had been publishing the *Provincial Freeman* in the interest of blacks and had "unflinchingly held up the standard to incite the colored people to progress, both mentally and morally."[31]

As she had done in *A Plea for Emigration*, Shadd Cary cited sources that would lend credibility to her foreign correspondence in the *Provincial Freeman*. Signing the following article with only an *S*, the writer explained:

> A white gentleman who never was known to take any interest in colored people before now, told me that he was going to Canada this summer, expressly to see the fugitives and colored people of Canada, and wanted me to give him letters of introduction to some colored fugitives there. I know of nothing that is doing more good than the general stir about *emigration*. It is indicative of enterprise, say the whites, and they seem doubly willing to do something for us. They are satisfied that we now mean something more than talk, and that we are really dissatisfied and mean to better our condition.[32]

Contrasting the conduct of the United States with other nations' policies was a consistent theme in the *Provincial Freeman*. Shadd Cary's article of January 20, 1854, for instance, noted that no European nation cherished Negro slavery as the United States did. In her homeland, she wrote, "the servile condition of the colored people has given rise to a prejudice such as always exists where there are such antagonisms as the positions of master and slave; and the fact that persons of African, or partly African descent only, are included in the servile class, naturally causes prejudice to become intensified; so that when the slave becomes a *freeman* the color is a bar to his progress."[33]

The *Provincial Freeman*'s foreign correspondence reflected the editor's advocacy of integration and racial assimilation and her ferocity in battling for them. Commenting on the establishment of new black newspapers in the United States, Shadd Cary noted that "without exception" the editors were "advocates of the old, long tried and long condemned policy of remaining in the United States, at all hazards, almost to a man, to *make* white America give to them equal political and social privileges, in the face of the contrary policy with respect to whites, so long tried by their opponents, and with such admirable results."[34] She was especially venomous toward activists who supported immigration to other countries. The newspaper offered the following commentary on April 15, 1854.

> The supposed crusade by John Mitchell of convict notoriety, against Canada, has called forth disclaimers from both the press and private citizens of these provinces in no way flattering to the prospects of annexationists in the U. S. . . . Emigrants to the Tropics, you will find as much as you will be able to manage, fostered and strengthened by the Negroes themselves. A man's dark color is no proof against prejudice. Should you labor for a livelihood, complexional identity will not save you! You will find colored nabobs as thick as hope, who will dispute every inch of ground with you, on the score of your pecuniary "inferiority." Colored men are as merciless as other men, when possessed of the same amount of pride, conceit and wickedness, and as much, if not more ignorance. They make just as bad masters as the worst of the whites, in their best moods, and infinitely worse in their worst. . . . You *cannot* be a whole African Nation here brethren, but you can be *part* of the Colored British nation. This nation knows no one color above another, but being composed of all colors, it is evidently a *colored* nation. An integral part of this nation you can be, looking as tall or as short as your aims or efforts make you—nothing under the sun to prevent you. . . . We of Canada wish success to you, but why need we attend?

> We have emigrated—we know that this country is all any reasonable person would ask; as you are not so certain. . . . Now is the time for those who love more than the name of Liberty to realize their wants.[35]

Shadd Cary equally castigated fellow blacks abroad and those who had preceded her to Canada, on issues ranging from integration to their collection of funds on behalf of the race. The latter individuals were guilty of malfeasance and of establishing separatist initiatives that kept the black race in an inferior position, she argued. Her worldview was that through hard work and tenacity, African Americans would assimilate and advance in a more color-blind British society.

Shadd Cary's efforts to generate news from abroad were not without pitfalls. In one instance, she wrote that "after a hurried and rapid journey by steamboat, railroad and wagon, without being able to stop at Hamilton" she had finally reached her destination, a "settlement called Dawn."[36] During its lifespan, the *Provincial Freeman* had moved with its editor from Windsor to Toronto and then to Chatham in search of more readers and more money. Plagued by lack of financial resources, the newspaper ceased publication in 1858. Richard Almonte notes that *A Plea for Emigration* was ignored by both Americans and Canadians. And Jane Rhodes suggests that Shadd Cary believed her views on gender roles were responsible for the *Provincial Freeman*'s inability to become financially stable.[37] Arguably, her acid tongue antagonized friends and potential supporters alike.

With the demise of the newspaper, Shadd Cary's foreign correspondence essentially ended. But for five years, the *Provincial Freeman* had been the most prominent black newspaper in Canada and had developed a following in the United States. Some 15,000 free and fugitive blacks made Canada their home during that period, but the extent to which Shadd Cary influenced them is unclear. After almost fifteen years in Canada, the expatriate moved back to the United States. The Civil War had ended and blacks were free. While in Canada, Shadd Cary had been a teacher, editor, lecturer, traveler, activist, mother, and the wife of Thomas Cary for four years before his death in 1860. Equally important, she had been a tenacious and pioneering foreign correspondent. Upon her return, she picked up where she left off, becoming a teacher and principal in Detroit for one year before moving to Washington, D.C., and enrolling in law school at Howard University. She continued to write for black publications. Fourteen years after enrolling, she completed her degree, becoming the first black woman to earn a law degree in this country. She continued her activism on behalf of her race and women's rights. A few years before her death in 1893, another black journalist was endeavoring to engage in foreign news gathering.

George Washington Williams: Divergent Perspectives

When George Washington Williams delivered his commencement oration at Newton Theological Seminary in 1874, he revealed an interest in Africa that would take him to the continent twice in the next fifteen years and lead him to become a foreign correspondent. On his first trip in 1884, Williams met with King Leopold II of Belgium to gather information about the monarch's policies in the Congo Free State, the African colony that was his personal fiefdom. The continuation of slavery and the slave trade on the African continent greatly concerned Williams. He hoped King Leopold would give Africans in his colony the opportunity to work as free men to develop the region into a model other colonial powers could embrace.[38]

Leopold was pleased to meet with this African American, born into slavery, who had urged the U.S. Senate Foreign Relations Committee to recognize as a friend the International Association for the Exploration and Civilization of the Congo. The committee did, and Williams believed he was partly responsible. He wrote in the *Boston Herald* that Leopold was "one of the noblest sovereigns in the world," adding that the king's goal was to "promote the best interests of his subjects, ruling in wisdom, mercy, and justice."[39] Williams believed the king's explanation that Belgium's motive was to Christianize the Africans without expectation of financial gain. Williams considered Leopold a friend to Africa, but he would change his view a few years later.

The world had undergone tremendous change during the years leading up to Williams's journey. The Indian wars from 1875 through 1885 were coming to an end in the United States; European nations waged small proxy wars to gain territories elsewhere; and the conquest of both Asia and Africa began in earnest. By 1895, virtually all of Africa, with the exception of Ethiopia, was under white colonial rule. Europe was in turmoil, mounting conflicts and entering binding treaties with other nations. In the United States, by 1880, African Americans were almost two decades removed from institutionalized slavery. But they were still in what historian Lerone Bennett called "internal colonialism, a system that reproduced the old relationships of dominance and subjugation under new names and new formulae."[40]

Africa was on Williams's mind when he set sail in September 1889 for Brussels, where seventeen nations were to hold the Antislavery Conference of the European Powers in November. He had hoped to be a delegate to the conference, even lobbying the U.S. government to allow him to represent the country, but to no avail. Williams was able to travel, however, because he obtained a commission from S. S. McClure to write articles about Europe and Africa for the Associated Literary Press newspaper syndicate. With that assignment, Williams became a bona fide foreign correspondent, a "journalist-reporter" employed by a mainstream media enterprise.[41] He hoped to share his views with a wide audience back home. For two months, he talked to Belgian officials and filed articles.[42]

William's biographer John Hope Franklin called him a wanderer and adventurer. The pattern may have begun early, for his parents, Thomas and Ellen Rouse Williams, moved frequently. Thomas was a free person of color. One year after his son's birth in 1849 in Bedford Springs, Pennsylvania, he moved the family to Johnstown, Pennsylvania. The family eventually wound up in New Castle. The young Williams received very little early education. By the time he reached adolescence, his father sent his rebellious son to a refuge home for undisciplined children to learn a trade and possibly become a barber.

But George Washington Williams had other things on his mind. At fourteen, he ran away to join the Union Army and fight with the U.S. Colored Troops in the Civil War. He was initially rejected because of his age but later was allowed to serve. Although he was injured and received an honorable discharge, he reenlisted following his recovery and fought in several battles. Soon after that conflict ended, Williams headed to Mexico to fight with the Republican army against French colonialists, rising to the rank of lieutenant colonel in the First Battery from the state of Tampico. His next adventure was a stint as a cavalryman with the U.S. regular army, where he saw battle in the Comanche campaign in 1867. After a short time at Howard University in Washington, D.C., he enrolled in Newton Theological Seminary in Cambridge, Massachusetts, where in 1874 he became the first African American graduate. He pursued a variety of careers, including serving as minister of the Twelfth Baptist Church in Boston.

Williams understood that the press was the key to racial advancement, so he left his post in Boston and moved back to Washington in 1875 to start a newspaper he hoped would be a voice for blacks and "a powerful agent for reorganizing the race."[43] According to the *Commoner*'s mission statement, it would "be their teacher, their friend, their mirror."[44] It encountered the same obstacles that perennially plagued the black press—an inability to secure sufficient numbers of subscribers, advertisers, and capital. Three months after its debut, it ceased publication. Williams moved to Cincinnati, Ohio, in 1876 and became pastor of Union Baptist Church.

Williams became a lawyer in 1881 and two years later published his two-volume *History of the Negro Race in America*, followed by the *History of the Negro Troops in the War of the Rebellion*.[45] Although these works were not financially successful, they earned the author the distinction of being the first major African American historian. Williams was active in Republican politics throughout the 1880s, after first being elected to the Ohio legislature in 1879 and serving one term.[46] The same spirit that had prompted this "man of burning ambition" and "boundless energy"[47] to seek out new places and experiences compelled him to seek firsthand information about Africa by traveling to the continent. Variously described as a blue-eyed, light-complexioned mulatto or as dark-skinned with dark hazel eyes,[48] Williams set out at the turn of the twentieth century to be an eyewitness to events in Africa. Although he suffered from chronic respiratory problems and had been especially ill in 1889, he ignored the advice of his physician to recuperate in a warm climate.[49] He was set on being part of the conference that would affect a people with whom he shared a transnational identity.

Williams fancied himself a truth-seeker and wanted to ascertain whether famed *New York Herald* foreign correspondent Henry Morton Stanley was telling the truth about Africa. His research for his books had shown him a different place and people from those depicted by Stanley and other white explorers. He wanted to discredit negative myths about the African people. Finally, he wanted to use his findings to call for an end to human trafficking and other abuses. Hence, Williams's travel to the continent is as much a story of Stanley and his version of Africa as it is a saga of Williams's desire to get the facts. He and other blacks distrusted mainstream reporting.

Stanley gained immense acclaim for further opening up Africa and conveying its importance to the industrialized world. According to some accounts, *New York Herald* publisher James Gordon Bennett dispatched Stanley to Africa in 1871 to search for famed explorer Dr. David Livingstone, who had not been heard from in almost five years.[50] For approximately ten years, beginning in 1854, Livingstone crisscrossed most of Africa looking for the source of the Nile River. His detailed accounts of his travels opened up the continent to the

Western world and gained him stature as "the greatest propagandist for Africa the European world had yet known."[51]

Livingstone's disappearance and Stanley's journey to find him are legendary. But Stanley had another reason for going to Africa. "I knew what had been accomplished by African explorers," he wrote, "and I knew how much of the dark interior was still unknown to the world." He read more than one hundred books about Africa and studied them "with zeal."[52] He wanted to discover and write about parts of Africa that were still untouched.

After finding Livingstone in November 1871 and remaining with him for months, Stanley returned to the United States with data about areas of the continent that had not been mapped. Livingstone's exploration had ignited world and media interest in Africa. Curiosity became even more intense as the *New York Herald* chronicled Stanley's trips to the mouth of the Congo River, where he arrived in September 1877. The reports resulted in Leopold's decision to cultivate Central Africa and, with Stanley's assistance, to organize the International Association for the Exploration and Civilization of the Congo. Stanley returned to Africa in 1879 to work for Leopold. He remained for five years, signing treaties with more than 450 African chiefs who gave their land to the king. Thus the groundwork was in place for the founding of the Congo Free State.[53]

Stanley's coverage awakened the world to Africa and made it ripe for exploitation and evangelization. His accounts framed the continent's inhabitants in pejorative terms, influencing the dominant society's perception of this largely unknown land and people. Portraying it as the "Dark Continent"[54] made it easier for countries to justify their presence there. After all, the Africans with whom Stanley had clashed in 1876 belonged to a "species of human vermin that puts its uncompromising savagery in the way of all progress and all increase of knowledge," the *Herald* proclaimed in September 1877. Stanley's reference to blacks as pagans arguably provided a pretext for evangelists to embark on missions to convert the "heathens." In the words of historian Norman R. Bennett, the actions of the missionaries "would permanently change the character of the African life Stanley had found."[55] As the missionaries did their work, governments took their political and economic organization to a land they viewed as devoid of structure. By the last quarter of the nineteenth century, European nations had engaged in a series of imperialist actions that led to the colonization of African nations—and to expansion in lands occupied by other nonwhite populations.

While Stanley's foreign news gathering hastened African colonization, it also was important because of its impact on the media. Through their characterizations, the *New York Herald* and its star correspondent constructed a myth of blackness that persists today, applied not just to Africans but also to those who descended from them. Beverly Ann Deepe Keever has noted that the mainstream media's framing of racial minorities in America created stereotypes about blacks as violent savages characterized by a lack of restraint, sexual prowess, and physical strength, or as the "sambo who is also ignorant, lazy, carefree, good humored."[56] Such stereotypes made it easier for whites to reconcile holding people in captivity. This argument is applicable to Stanley's work.

Stanley's foreign-affairs reporting also redefined the role of the press in gathering news, adding the new dimension of coverage of Africa. Stanley's dispatches for the *Herald* on December 22, 1871, acknowledged as much. "An African exploring expedition is a new thing in the enterprises of modern journalism," Stanley wrote.[57]

Not every newspaper was impressed with Stanley. The *New York Sun*, among others, characterized his exploit as a hoax. As John Maxwell Hamilton noted, "Those rivals impugned his character, an endeavor facilitated by a wealth of good material, and questioned the veracity of his work."[58] Other newspapers praised Stanley and the *Herald*. The *Buffalo Express* called the assignment "the most extraordinary newspaper enterprise ever dreamed of."[59] The *Herald* also promoted itself, practically gushing that its "journalistic enterprise struck the first blow against the slave trade of the Nile basin."[60] Arguably, this posturing was disingenuous because slavery continued and the negative stereotypes the newspaper published seem to have done more damage than good for Africans.

Williams sought backing from Belgium for his journey to the Congo, but his requests were denied. "Officials who formerly greeted me cordially, now avoided me," he wrote.[61] With little money, he sidestepped the roadblocks that King Leopold and Belgian officials placed in his way and made a tortuous journey to the land of his ancestors. He left Liverpool in January 1890 and arrived in Boma, the capital of the Congo, fifty-three days later. On the almost 3,300-mile journey, he gathered firsthand information during stops in Liberia, Sierra Leone, the Ivory Coast, and locales under French or Portuguese domination. Williams later recounted the grueling four months he had spent traveling from the mouth of the Congo River to the Atlantic Ocean at Loango, just as Stanley had done.

Using information he had uncovered, Williams became one of the first persons to challenge King Leopold's reign of terror in the Belgian Congo. In a separate report to Collis P. Huntington, the railroad magnate who had helped finance his African travels, Williams also disputed Stanley's contention that it was possible to build a railroad in the Congo. Calling such advice "irresponsible," Williams maintained that a railroad could not be built for the amount of money or within the time frame Stanley advocated.[62]

> When he describes things and persons he displays the ability of an able correspondent. But the moment he attempts to deal with figures and trade, he becomes a romancer. . . . Modern history records nothing equal to the speculation of Mr. Stanley . . . And while I have an interest in the civilization of Africa equal to any person's, I cannot be silent, or suffer to pass unchallenged statements calculated to mislead and deceive the friend of humanity and civilization.[63]

These words both challenged a mainstream version of reality and illustrated why blacks engaged in foreign correspondence. Williams's report criticized the manner in which the company surveyed the Congo, as well as other work conducted. The writer informed Huntington that the company did not lay even one mile of road or railroad, but had instead exploited the land and resources.

Williams did not stop with his open letter or his "Report on the Congo Railroad." He also tried to convince the United States to intervene in the colony, but President Benjamin Harrison ignored his October 1890 report on the violence and disregard for humanity in the Belgian colony. The black explorer eventually met with the president to discuss his plans to go to the Congo. He promised that he would rely on international law to prepare a memorandum on whether the United States should ratify the Berlin Act that had facilitated Leopold's acquisition of the Congo Free State.[64]

Williams published a chilling assessment of Leopold's atrocities in his "Open Letter to the King of the Belgium Congo." The monarch was "deficient in the moral, military and financial strength to govern a territory of 1,500,000 square miles," Williams proclaimed in one of twelve charges he leveled at both Leopold and Stanley, who was now an iconic foreign correspondent and Leopold's primary representative in the Congo.[65] Williams noted that he did not find one hospital in the almost 1,500 miles he traveled in the Congo; instead, there were "only three sheds for sick Africans in the service of the State, not fit to be occupied by a horse."[66] An even harsher assessment of how whites tricked African chiefs into giving up their land was a major point in the missive.

> There were instances in which Mr. HENRY M. STANLEY sent one white man, with four or five Zanzibar soldiers, to make treaties with native chiefs. The staple argument was that the white man's heart had grown sick of the wars and rumours of war between one chief and another, between one village and another; that the white man was at peace with his black brother, and desired to "confederate all African tribes" for the general defense and public welfare. All the sleight-of-hand tricks had been carefully rehearsed, and he was now ready for his work. A number of electric batteries had been purchased in London, and when attached to the arm under the coat, communicated with a band of ribbon which passed over the palm of the white brother's hand, and when he gave the black brother a cordial grasp of the hand the black brother was greatly surprised to find his white brother so strong, that he nearly knocked him off his feet in giving him the hand of fellowship. When the native inquired about the disparity of strength between himself and his white brother, he was told that the white man could pull up trees and perform the most prodigious feats of strength. . . . By such means as these, too silly and disgusting to mention, and a few boxes of gin, whole villages have been signed away to your Majesty.[67]

While Williams's letters and reports from abroad were few, they were significant. His accounts differed from those of a highly credible foreign correspondent whose reports in the mainstream media were widely accepted. Williams traveled the same areas as Stanley, interacted with the same inhabitants, and assessed the same resources and conditions. He did not agree with Stanley and other white explorers who saw Africa as a Dark Continent inhabited by barbarous people whom they could control through Christianization. Africa also was synonymous with tremendous resources readily and easily available to Europe and America. Stanley's decidedly Eurocentric perspective was widely accepted because people had very few reference points about Africa. Williams voiced an alternative view of colonial Africa that called attention to the dehumanization and exploitation of its people and resources.

As a foreign correspondent, Williams was in a different position from mainstream overseas reporters. The *New York Journal* had already sent reporters abroad to interview Pope Pius IX, funded and covered at least two hostage-rescue operations, and sent Nellie Bly around the world in 1889–90 to break the record set in Jules Verne's novel *Around the World in Eighty Days.*[68] This prominent black historian and journalist acted virtually alone to publish information he hoped would spur policy changes at home and abroad. Williams went to England to write a long piece on the abuses he found in the Congo. His chronic illnesses led to his death on August 2, 1891, in Blackpool. He was forty-two. Thus an important voice that tried to change the public face of Africa and speak for the oppressed was silenced. Leopold continued his numerous abuses in the colony and stripped it of resources until 1908. When he finally ceded control over the colony, more than half of its approximately eighteen million natives had perished.

Almost fifteen years would pass between Williams's reports and the next foreign correspondence generated by the black press.

[2]

Changing Landscape

No Longer an Individual Endeavor

T. Thomas Fortune traveled to Manila in February 1903 on a special assignment for the Department of the Treasury. His friend Booker T. Washington had convinced President Theodore Roosevelt to select the veteran journalist and race leader to gather information about trade in the Philippines. "I did not find one of them begging bread in Manila or in the provinces of Luzon,"[1] Fortune wrote in one of four in-depth articles that ran from March to May 1904 in the *Voice of the Negro,* a new periodical that appealed to an increasingly literate black population. Although Fortune was editor of the influential *New York Age* newspaper, his foreign reports appeared in the *Voice of the Negro* a year after his return. His accounts helped the periodical change the landscape of black foreign correspondence. No longer would such reporting be solely an individual endeavor, as with pioneers Frederick Douglass, Mary Ann Shadd Cary, and George Washington Williams. Now the black press acted on its commitment to explore the shared identity of all people of color and to inform the reading public of world events. The *Voice of the Negro* enlisted travelers and freelance writers to gather news from South America, Europe, and Africa.

It is unclear why Fortune wrote for the magazine and not for his own newspaper. It was probably because of his close ties with Booker T. Washington, the preeminent race leader of the day, who subsidized both publications directly and through advertising. Fortune's reporting challenged the stereotypes of darker races as inferior and unable to shape their destinies. He also used the words of Filipinos to challenge America's racial policies.

Fortune had the credibility to tell these stories. The executive director of the National Newpaper Publishers Association (NNPA) in 1974 called Fortune "the most brilliant editor and facile writer of the final decade of the 19th century."[2] Born in 1856 to a father who eventually became a leader in Republican politics, Fortune enrolled at Howard University in Washington, D.C., in 1876.

But he left after two years to get married and become a journalist. He worked for the *Rumor*, a black publication that became the *New York Globe* in 1881. Three years later, the *Globe* became the *New York Freeman;* Fortune was its owner until 1887. Fortune worked for Charles Dana's *New York Sun* and freelanced for other publications before rejoining the *Freeman,* now called the *New York Age,* in 1891. His publications were vehicles of agitation, vociferously challenging laws and traditions that solidified inequities in American society.

Blacks had made some gains, primarily in the industrialized North, but the South had systematically eroded the progress made during Reconstruction. Influential blacks held the Republican Party accountable for its failure to act on behalf of the race. In 1890, for instance, the *Age* called for support of the Afro-American League, an organization that Fortune and one hundred blacks from around the country formed to fight segregation and oppression.[3]

Fortune challenged white supremacy and the hypocrisy of nations that engaged in imperialism. A few years before he went to the Philippines, he blasted Rudyard Kipling's "The White Man's Burden," pointing out the poet's preposterous assumption that whites had the "burden" to colonize people of color. "Nobody has asked the whites to rob and enslave the black and yellow races of the earth," he wrote. "The burden, if such it be, was assumed voluntarily and without the consent and desire of the victims, who preferred and still prefer their land and liberty and freedom from the tyranny of white men."[4] George Washington Williams had expressed similar sentiments when reporting from Africa a few decades earlier. The subject was still important in the black national conversation.

Fortune's straightforward and aggressive posture made him a powerhouse in the black press as it gained the attention of the mainstream press and white society. Black editors and publishers knew that whites read their publications; they wanted to inspire white leaders to support equal rights and racial harmony. As historian William G. Jordan noted, "[T]o the extent that black journalists forced white people to pay attention, they succeeded in poking holes in the veil, making themselves visible, and forcing whites to reconsider their assumptions about blacks and race."[5]

By the end of the 1890s, 600 black newspapers existed nationwide. The number would increase by 150 during the next 20 years. Among them was the *Indianapolis Freeman,* the country's first illustrated newspaper for blacks, which circulated nationwide. The *Voice of the Negro* was one of at least five news organs that began during the first decade of the 1900s.[6]

The *Voice of the Negro*

The *Voice of the Negro* was the first black publication to methodically engage in foreign news gathering. It began publishing in January 1904 in Atlanta as the first black magazine in the South edited by black journalists. Austin N. Jenkins, a white businessman who owned a publishing company, financed the venture. He enlisted two black students from Virginia Union University to participate. John A. Hopkins became the sales agent. J. Max Barber, editor of the school newspaper, became editor of the *Voice of the Negro* shortly after nominal editor John Wesley Edward Bowen relinquished the position.[7] The *Voice of the Negro* soon became the premiere black magazine.

Although it published for only three years, it covered broad facets of black life and illuminated the achievements of the race, content that was sorely lacking in the white press. Recognizing that blacks were becoming cultured and educated readers, Barber vowed in the first issue to place the *Voice of the Negro* in the forefront "of a higher culture and a new literature."[8] It would be a vehicle for racial uplift, not just a magazine for the race. "We expect to make of it current and sociological history so accurately given and so vividly portrayed so as to become a kind of documentation for the coming generations."[9] The young editor wanted the magazine to reposition blacks in the public psyche as worthy of respect, dignity, and basic human rights. He exposed readers to the arts, religion, politics, education, and social and economic issues.

The *Voice of the Negro*—and black leaders—were keenly interested in news and commentary about international issues relevant to the African American community at home and to members of the African Diaspora. The rationale for foreign news gathering was simple: the United States was becoming an imperial power, and blacks were troubled by the ramifications of U.S. policies in its new possessions that were populated largely by people of color. With the signing of the Treaty of Paris at the conclusion of the Spanish-American War in 1898, the United States took possession of the Philippines and Puerto Rico and placed Cuba alongside the Caribbean Islands already under American political and economic control. In response to changing world dynamics, mainstream media sent correspondents overseas, but the black press often lacked the money to do so.

But the *Voice of the Negro* found ways to report on developments from abroad. It examined race relations in other countries and compared them to America's color problem. In three years the magazine ran thirty-four articles and commentaries generated abroad. That was impressive, given the costs of foreign news gathering and the chronic lack of funding that plagued the medium.

Barber was less concerned with cost than with his desire to describe world events and explore commonalities between nonwhites abroad and African Americans at home. The magazine used a variety of methods to obtain information. Prominent people of color traveling overseas often sent information home. Other stories bore the bylines of prominent black journalists such as Mary Church Terrell and William Pickens, a founding member of the National Association for the Advancement of Colored People (NAACP). No stories were generated from Africa, primarily because blacks were not traveling there. Fortune's pieces were the first foreign reporting in the magazine.

Fortune's first treatise shed light on the *Voice of the Negro*'s perspective. He supported Japan's strike on Russian forces at Port Arthur, a strategic location at the southern tip of Manchuria. The February 8 attack that began the Russo-Japanese War was just another salvo as countries maneuvered for primacy in the Far East. The *Voice of the Negro* declared Russia the "aggressor" and charged that it had prepared for war while saying it wanted peace. Japan had grown weary of waiting for diplomacy to work and "decided to strike for her life."[10]

Japan won the war in May 1905, and its victory effectively prevented Russia's expansion. The African American press and blacks in general empathized with Japan while it colonized China in the early 1900s. Blacks and liberal white Americans even created a black internationalism movement based on their view that world politics was determined by color or race. They viewed the Japanese as a darker race, and they believed the victory over Russia signaled the end of white dominance.

Unlike the white media, the *Voice of the Negro* was unable to cover the war. Correspondents for the Associated Press, the *New York Herald*, and other media were in Tokyo when the war began and fought Japanese censorship to cover the war. According to media historian Michael Emery, mainstream correspondents provided a "link between the story and home" that first revealed Japanese imperialism to Americans.[11] Owing to lack of resources and access, the *Voice of the Negro* and black newspapers could only report on the conflict from afar. The *Voice of the Negro* and at least one establishment newspaper, the *New York Times*, saw the conflict and the world differently. Although both publications supported Japan, the magazine framed Japan's victory as the triumph of a kindred race over a European power; the *New York Times* viewed Russia's occupation of Manchuria and expansion into Asia as "hostile to American interests."[12] Russia was "an anomaly and a political anachronism in modern Europe" that repeatedly broke its promises to allow the United States access "concerning commercial facilities in Manchuria," the newspaper charged in an editorial on New Year's Day 1905.[13] A March 1 editorial reminded readers of Russia's broken promise to pull out of Manchuria and concluded that such actions made it "clear to the American people that they had nothing to expect from Russia in the way of commercial privileges."[14]

These articles portrayed Russia negatively and conceivably molded public opinion. The *Voice of the Negro* characterized Russia as the "aggressor," consistent with its critique of European colonialist "aggressors." The magazine planted a seed, suggesting the black community perceive world affairs as a fight between white oppressors and nonwhite others. This view would persist in African American publications for decades. Eight years later, one of the leading black newspapers articulated an almost identical perspective, depicting the Japanese as allies of the black community in a common struggle. A 1913 editorial in the *Chicago Defender* looked back at the Russo-Japanese War and parodied stereotypes of Asians in reaction to the Japanese victory. "The world looked on and listened with amazement. Will the little yellow man dare attack the great white giant? Will heathen Japan be so audacious as to be hostile towards Christian Russia? Will not the yellow pigmy be instantly devoured by the great Russian bear? These were the questions virtually asked by the world."[15]

Fortune not so subtly compared opportunities for success in another country with the lack of opportunity for his race in the United States. By highlighting successful people of African descent in the Philippines, Fortune raised questions about the possibility of a better life when a society judged people based on factors other than skin color. One Fortune piece related the experiences of four hundred black veterans who had remained in the country or returned there after the Spanish-American War. Robert Gordon Woods told the journalist he had returned to the Philippines after the war because he wanted "to grow up in the country."[16] Woods was now gainfully employed; in fact, he was Fortune's guide for a portion of his trip. Many other American blacks were working in the private sector or in civil service jobs.

In his first article, Fortune wrote that race relations suffered from the way whites treated the natives. "The Filipino hates the white man as the devil hates holy water, and will never learn to love him, because the white man will never learn to love the Filipino," he argued, adding that it was "impossible for a white man, whether he be Spaniard or American, to treat an alien people on terms of equality."[17] In another article, Fortune explored race relations by describing how the darker races also wanted no contact with blacks. A "weakness of human nature led them to curry favor with those who, for the time being, are dominant in the environment," Fortune maintained.[18] He demonstrated keen insight into the complexity of race relations when he wrote, "Even the Red Indian, without a shirt to his back, wrapped in an army blanket black tax-payers help to pay for, and being too stolid and indolent to master the elements of modern civilization, thinks himself better than the American black man, and refuses to associate with him in any way, except as man and servant."[19]

Fortune also criticized the media for biased coverage. He maintained that before he even arrived in Manila, more than a dozen American newspapers castigated him and other blacks, and continued the attacks until he returned home. The Filipinos could not understand it all, Fortune wrote, and he offered the following explanation:

> The white Americans started out to have and to hold all of the advantage of whatever sort that were possible to be gotten out of the Spanish War, with its ill-starred conquest and forcible annexation of Porto Rico [sic], Guam and the Philippine islands. They did not want any black people in the game, and even in Cuba, they were kept out, even as in the other possessions, as far as possible, and are kept out even now, by official connivance; for the War Department at Washington requires of every applicant for a civil position in the islands that he send his photograph with his application: if his face be black, his application is turned down. But, despite all hindrances, civil, military and other, there are a large number of Afro-Americans in the Philippine Islands and in the character and standing of them, both as civil employees and independent business men and laborers, they bear favorable comparison with their white fellow citizens, who do not love them and who give them no more chance in the race of life than circumstances compel them to. Indeed, all in all, the Afro-Americans in the Philippines stand the climate better and are on terms of better and more helpful understanding with the Filipinos than are white Americans, who suffer terribly from the climate and do not get along with the natives, and they never will.[20]

Fortune picked up the theme of white exploitation, just as George Washington Williams had done. He wrote that he "had not seen a white man working with his hands," adding "they were all working with their mouths. Why do you expect the Filipino to do what you will not and cannot do?" He went on: "the white man in the Orient expects natives to labor as they labor in this country and Europe, and because the natives refuse to do it, as it would mean death to him, he is abused and denounced as a worthless creature."[21] Finally, he charged that power and greed were the reasons for America's presence in the Philippines. Neither was "sufficient anchorage in the government of an alien people or in the successful colonization of their country, for the purposes of domination and exploitation."[22] Through Fortune, the *Voice of the Negro* framed the United States negatively, a view black readers embraced.

While Fortune set the tone for foreign correspondence in the *Voice of the Negro*, others also wrote from abroad. U.S. involvement in the Dominican Republic and Haiti was the focus of articles in the April 1904 issue. Both countries were enmeshed in numerous revolutions as they attempted to maintain independence from colonial interests. From the Dominican Republic, Archibald H. Grimke ruefully speculated that the United States might one day intervene there to protect its investments in Santo Domingo, including ownership of most of the large sugar plantations. "Every pound of sugar produced on Dominican soil, except what is retained for home consumption, finds a market in the United States," Grimke wrote.[23] According to Grimke, the United States had gained control of Santo Domingo's natural resources via concessions by the Dominican government that allowed a foreign corporation to collect and disburse public revenue; internal dissatisfaction with those arrangements had led to government instability.[24]

Mary Church Terrell addressed race relations in the magazine while traveling in Europe. Terrell was a journalist, race activist, and leader in the black women's club movement when the Berlin International Congress of Women invited her to deliver an address. Terrell wrote that women she met in London and Paris, as well as at the conference, supported women's rights and equality for black people.[25] The magazine revisited the subject of race in a November 1905 story by Theophilus Steward. American race prejudice was almost nonexistent in Puerto Rico, Steward wrote; instead, social stratification was based on blood, birth, and family.[26] In the sixth year of the U.S. occupation of the Philippines, he criticized the United States, noting that he had not found any natives who were "ambitious to conquer and follow the American method of living and behaving."[27] Such articles set the themes and tone of black foreign reporting for decades to come.[28]

Significantly, seven years after George Washington Williams had documented inhumane treatment of Africans in the Belgian Congo, the *Voice of the Negro* urged passage of a resolution calling for the United States to intervene in the colony. The piece suggested that the world was finally "waking up to the shocking truth that King Leopold's pretended philanthropy in the Congo is in reality a ghastly lie." Leopold was a "human monster," who for private gain "recklessly exploited" the entire country. This short item was also a commentary on race relations in the United States; the magazine urged that a commission be appointed to investigate the role of the South in "this stench in the nostril of civilization."[29]

In articles reminiscent of Mary Ann Shadd Cary's pieces on Canada, the magazine wrote about the Philippines, Haiti, the West Indies, and other areas under American domination.[30] It overwhelmingly viewed the countries and their inhabitants in a positive light while challenging white colonialists to rise to a higher standard that respected rather than oppressed nonwhites.

By the time the *Voice of the Negro* ceased publication in October 1907, it had become the organ of the Niagara movement and had aligned itself with W. E. B. Du Bois's ideology of racial uplift. The magazine had made an enemy of Booker T. Washington, satirizing him by claiming that he slaughtered the English language and embraced the view that a college education was evil and the plow was beautiful. Editor Max Barber angered whites when he blamed "dishonest, unscrupulous, ambitious politicians" for the Atlanta riot of 1906. With a price on his head, the editor fled to Chicago. Fortune bought the debt-ridden magazine in 1907 and moved it to New York, but was unable to keep it going. Still, the publication had reached a maximum circulation of 15,000.[31]

The *Voice of the* Negro had whetted the appetite of readers who craved news from overseas; black global journalism would not be silent for long. As the world's major powers led the United States into World War I, the African American press would be in the forefront of reporting. The *Chicago Defender* and *The Afro-American* soon picked up the mantle, and the black press continued to provide news of foreign affairs.

[3]

The Quest to Cover Our Fighting Men

In August 1914, Carl James Murphy boarded the steamship *Bremen* in Baltimore, bound for the University of Jena in Germany. Soon after he arrived, he turned his attention to the tense situation in Europe, where the world was on the verge of its first major war. *The Afro-American* ran his letters home as front-page stories. Murphy was not a journalist but a traveler and an instructor of German. As the son of John H. Murphy Sr., the former slave who founded and published the newspaper,[1] he had the resources to travel abroad to further his education.

Murphy's articles took the reader to Old World cities as he traveled by rail through Germany.[2] They learned that he was treated well everywhere he traveled. They also read his views of the impact of developments in Europe on people of color, including the participation of darker peoples in the brewing conflict. In one story, Murphy wrote that he and other "prominent personages" of color were among the 150,000 Americans whose travel in Europe was restricted.[3] In September, *The Afro-American* reported that soldiers of color were fighting valiantly for France and England.

When Murphy returned from Germany, he had an interesting take on the war in Europe. In an article published on October 4, 1914, he stated that Germany would "ultimately win this war" and that media reports did "not fairly represent Germany."[4] He based his assertions on the fact that Germany had ten million men "ready to fight," stating that the Indian people under Great Britain's rule "would revolt against England, if they knew the real conditions."[5] As had black correspondents before him, Murphy criticized the subjugation of a darker nation by a European power. This theme would continue in African American foreign correspondence for decades.

Based in Baltimore, *The Afro-American* was an influential publication when the war began. The weekly newspaper had made a commitment at its inception in 1892 to be a voice for blacks and to uplift the race. Four years later, the Supreme Court's ruling in *Plessy v. Ferguson* established the doctrine of separate but equal and effectively made segregation the law of the land. In the face of ongoing racial exclusion and degradation, *The Afro-American* challenged inequities and sought to advance the race. Its pages brimmed with news and commentary about the condition of blacks and criticism of the dominant power structure.

The newspaper recognized the impact of international affairs on the black community in the United States, signaled by the prominence it gave to Carl Murphy's articles. Four years would pass before another black journalist reported from abroad, but that was not because the press had lost interest.

As soon as the United States entered World War I, *The Afro-American* focused on black servicemen as they prepared for war. The emphasis was on how troops were faring at army training camps now that the U.S. military allowed them to serve. The publication advocated for African American rights and protested American policies. A July 7, 1917, piece compared the United States unfavorably to France because America did not allow blacks in military academies but had bowed to pressure and established a segregated training camp. In another editorial the newspaper argued that the "success of the cause of the Allies should not only be [blacks'] fervent wish, but also the triumph . . . of the real principles of democracy."[6]

Letters from "Our Boys"

When black troops finally went to war, *The Afro-American*, the *Chicago Defender*, and other black publications were unable to report directly from overseas. They reprinted articles from white dailies that had correspondents on the ground, or they printed the letters of black soldiers. (Some soldieries wrote directly to the newspapers; others wrote to loved ones who sent their letters to the publications.)[7] Foreign coverage overwhelmingly highlighted the accomplishments of soldiers. On May 24, 1918, *The Afro-American* reprinted an article from an unidentified newspaper highlighting "the fine heroism of two Negro soldiers who, although wounded, beat off a raiding party of twenty-five Germans, killing and wounding five of them in a fierce hand to hand fight."[8] Two months later, another reprinted dispatch revealed that black troops in France had "held their lines well" when they "participated in the American defense against the big German offensive."[9] These articles probably came from the mainstream media, suggesting that blacks were neither completely invisible nor always portrayed negatively. The fact that black soldiers were assisting America in winning the war helped make the point that blacks at home deserved equity.

Letters from African American soldiers were the main source of direct information for blacks. A special column titled "Stirring Letters from Over There" announced on August 9, 1918, that *The Afro-American* would run letters from "Our Boys," who were in France.[10] It printed one soldier's account of how he felt overseas—as if he was in a "new world instead of an old one."[11] Publisher John Murphy believed in publishing the letters for they carried "their own message of safe arrival, good health and splendid treatment, and set at rest any fears that all might not have gone well with them."[12]

The Afro-American did not embellish the soldiers' experiences; some letters were merely soldiers' accounts to their families. Pvt. Dorsey wrote to his mother that he was in a hospital "with a machine gun wound in [his] left shoulder, but [was] getting along pretty good."[13] Another soldier mused, "When one sits down as I am now—alone, with nothing but his thoughts, his memories, his hopes—he is seized with a sort of melancholia, which is inevitable. We know we are face to face with death. While all of us are inspired by the same lofty sentiments as any other soldier—that dying-for-your country stuff—there is no one of us who wants or is ready to die just now."[14]

The soldiers' experiences framed race relations from the perspective of the men on the ground. Lt. Osceola McKaine wrote that "in France [the soldiers] were learning what it means to 'be really free, to taste real liberty, to be a man.'"[15] The *Chicago Defender* also published letters from black soldiers who shared their experiences and thoughts on the war. Clarence C. Hudson, a regimental sergeant, wrote that he viewed the war as a quest for democracy and that his inspiration to fight came from within. Lt. Stanley Norvell said that he found France, even in its war-torn condition, "an infinitely more agreeable place for [him] to live than [his] own country."[16] One can imagine the impact of such words on readers: a black soldier preferred risking his life in France to peacetime life in the United States.

Other letters viewed the United States positively. Sgt. E. A. Tooke wrote that France was a beautiful country, but he had never realized "just how good it was to be an American until he got 'over here.'"[17] War was not a good experience for Tooke. The *Defender's* agenda was to support both the war and the black troops, and simultaneously to suggest that the war was a new beginning for black America. The hope was that social justice and civil rights for blacks would prevail when the dominant power structure and white Americans saw the courage and loyalty of race soldiers.

While black newspapers tried to keep readers abreast of developments abroad, another major publication, *The Crisis,* presented the perspective of African Americans on national and international affairs. The official organ of the National Association for the Advancement of Colored People (NAACP), the magazine sought to expose prejudice against black people. *The Crisis* had begun publishing in November 1910 under the editorship of W. E. B. Du Bois, one of the nation's foremost black intellectuals and race leaders. An increasingly literate black population was the prime audience for the magazine's news and commentary about politics, education, and race achievements. An abundance of literary works further illuminated the intellectual and artistic abilities of blacks and contributed to race pride. Historians note that the growth of *The Crisis* "paralleled the growth of its editor's stature within African American leadership and intellectual circles."[18] Within a year of its launching, the magazine's circulation rose from 1,000 to 16,000. By the end of World War I, its circulation was 120,000.

After the U.S. entry into the war, an entire issue was dedicated to black soldiers from the United States, as well as from Africa and India, who were fighting for the Allies. Alluding to the oneness of "people of Negro descent," *The Crisis* editorialized, "You are not fighting simply for Europe; you are fighting for the world, and you and your people are a part of the world."[19] Coverage in the mainstream press and the black press sometimes followed a similar track. The March 1917 issue of *The Crisis,* for instance, paralleled the *Washington Post* in speculating that both Germany and Russia could become menaces.[20] An Associated Press story on page 1 of the *Washington Post* discussed Germany's plans for war and noted that the country had promised to give Mexico control of the former Mexican territories of Texas, New Mexico, and Arizona, which were now part of the United States.

Like *The Afro-American, The Crisis* saw the war as an avenue through which black people could advance. Their support and involvement would demonstrate their patriotism and abilities—proof that they deserved liberation after their service ended. Du Bois wrote, "This war is an End and, also, a Beginning.

Never again will darker people of the world occupy just the place they have before. . . . Out of this war will rise, too, an American Negro, with the right to vote and the right to work and the right to live without insult. These things may not and will not come at once; but they are written in the stars, and the first step toward them is victory for the armies of the Allies."[21]

Lukewarm Support

Most African American leaders supported the war and championed the right of their race to serve. Almost as soon as the United States entered the war on April 6, 1917, blacks had a visible presence and played a crucial role, although the first black troops did not go overseas until the spring of 1918.[22] The black press expressed pride in its men and women who wanted to assist in the war effort and praised U.S. involvement in the war, yet it charged that the United States practiced discrimination at home while fighting for freedom for people in other countries. This position was not unusual; the black press had a long history of loving the country blacks had helped build while abhorring many of its actions.

Black discontent with the war was a source of concern for government officials, who feared losing the crucial support of the African American community for the war effort. One of the U.S. government's first acts to shore up black morale was the appointment of Emmett J. Scott, a close ally of Booker T. Washington, as special advisor for race relations to Secretary of War Newton D. Baker.[23] Several factors accounted for Scott's appointment, including the intervention of Dr. Robert Moton, Washington's successor as principal of the Tuskegee Institute in Alabama. Moton advised Baker of the need to have in the department "a colored man in touch with Northern and Southern white people and colored people, who could advise whenever delicate questions arose affecting the interests of the colored people in the United States."[24] In a letter to white liberal philanthropist Julius Rosenwald, a founder of the NAACP and member of the advisory board of the Council of National Defense, Scott offered to assist in any capacity. In other letters, he asserted the willingness of blacks to fight for liberty and highlighted the exemplary service of race soldiers in previous wars.[25]

Soon after his selection in October 1917, Scott invited black leaders to the Conference of Negro Editors and Leaders, seeking their support for the war.

The government also wanted to counter the German propaganda machine that sought to thwart African American support by chronicling lynching and other forms of violence and pointing out that their country did not deserve their loyalty.[26]

Apparently *The Afro-American* knew that such a meeting was in the works months before it occurred and acquiesced to the government's attempts to mold black public opinion. The newspaper reported that the War Department and a division of George Creel's Committee on Public Information (CPI) had assigned a special committee of black leaders to speak to blacks "to create an opinion and sentiment among them that will be behind the national government in its prosecution of the war."[27]

The thirty black editors and publishers who accepted the government's invitation had high expectations that their discussions would bring about meaningful change in America and elevate the race. They saw World War I as an opportunity to lift up the black community. At home, they believed, things could not get much worse. Discrimination and segregation brought economic, political, and societal inequities. Jim Crow laws consigned blacks to an unending cycle of dependency and fear. Lynching parties would take the lives of least thirty-eight blacks in 1917, the year the United States entered the war. Fifty-eight black men and women would meet the same fate the following year.[28]

Frank discussions occurred during the meeting about blacks' support of their country and their leaders' antipathy regarding the state of their race.[29] The editors informed government representatives that they were not content to base accounts of the war on letters from soldiers or infrequent clips reprinted from the mainstream media. They objected to misinformation in the mainstream media that went unchallenged. Such misrepresentation of the race was pervasive and detrimental to its progress.

On at least one occasion, the *Chicago Daily News* had perpetuated negative stereotypes. In April 1918, the *Chicago Defender* reprinted and criticized an excerpt from a piece in the *Daily News* that used a pejorative term and made fun of two blacks. "It is a sad reflection on any newspaper that permits the use of the term 'Niggah' or any of its kindred expressions," the *Defender* declared. "Can you imagine the glorious people of France ridiculing their loyal Race soldiers in these terrible times? France would not think of such. Even despised Germany accepts men at their true worth, and America cannot do less and survive. . . . This war has no 'Lighter Side' for us. All that we have is faith and hope and love; in wealth and service and spirit, are given unstintedly and gladly—in face of all the dirty and inconsistent deeds of injustice and discrimination—the cause of right may triumph."[30]

Black leaders believed the only way to counter such negative characterizations was for the government to appoint a black journalist to go overseas to tell the stories of the sons, husbands, brothers, and friends of their readers who hungered for information. A major outcome of the conference was A Bill of Particulars that, among other items, defined the proposed relationship between blacks and their government and reaffirmed race loyalty and willingness to do their "full share in helping win the war for democracy," the *Chicago Defender* reported in early July. In return, the leaders expected their "full share of the fruits thereof."[31]

The resolution acknowledged that blacks did not expect to have race problems solved immediately, and it reassured the U.S. government that blacks would not be swayed by Germany's attempt to influence African Americans. Propaganda was useless, but the country's indifference to the plight of black people posed a danger. Although the conferees did not get action on their call for the Red Cross to use black nurses in the war effort, they succeeded in having a black journalist appointed to report about black soldiers on the home front and the war front. That person, they believed, would tell another side of the story.[32] Ralph Waldo Tyler, a well-known and respected journalist and public servant who was present at the gathering, was chosen. He was going to see for himself and tell the true story of the soldiers' experiences.

Soon after the meeting, Du Bois composed an editorial clarifying the prevailing black perspective of the war. He set aside his often scathing and bitter criticism of America's discriminatory policies and urged black people to put aside their quest for civil rights for the time being and "close ranks," standing firmly behind their country. He framed his rationale in the context of global politics, the links among racial minorities, and the impact of the war on all of them. A German victory would "spell death for the aspirations of Negroes and all darker races."[33]

Ralph Waldo Tyler: An Unusual Role and Agenda

In announcing Ralph Waldo Tyler's appointment as both a correspondent and an accredited representative of the government's Committee on Publication Information (CPI), chairman George Creel explained that the veteran newsman was uniquely qualified to become the first black "regular" war correspondent for any government in the world because of the experience he had acquired and the "intimate contacts" he had made in seventeen years of working for the mainstream media.[34] Tyler would be able to obtain news about black soldiers that "no other colored correspondent could secure,"[35] according to the CPI.

Tyler's departure for France in September 1918 marked another major milestone in the evolution of black foreign correspondence. The Columbus, Ohio, native had worked in management positions for black newspapers, including a stint as city editor for the Columbus edition of *The Afro-American* newspaper chain. He and three friends had even published their own newspaper, the *Free American*, before he joined the mainstream *Evening Dispatch* in 1888—not as a reporter, but as a janitor, the only position open to him.[36]

With the support of William D. Brickell, owner of the *Dispatch*, Tyler studied bookkeeping and shorthand in night school, eventually becoming the newspaper's head cashier and society editor. Although employed by a white newspaper, Tyler kept his finger on the pulse of the black community, editing a column on black news for the *Dispatch* and freelancing for black newspapers around the country. He later worked for another mainstream newspaper, the *Ohio State Journal*.

Tyler was no stranger to national or African American politics. He was as much a political appointee as a journalist, and he divided his time between the two professions.[37] His involvement in Republican politics in Ohio meant that he served as a spokesman for African Americans in his state. Perhaps Tyler's most important asset was his shared friendship with Emmett J. Scott and Booker T. Washington. The latter had founded the Tuskegee Institute and, with Du Bois, was one of the foremost race leaders and spokesmen of his time. The association with Washington led President Theodore Roosevelt to appoint Tyler to the coveted post of auditor of the navy, a position he held until Woodrow Wilson became president. When the United States declared war, Tyler left his job as an organizer for the National Negro Business League and became secretary of the National Colored Soldiers' Comfort Committee. He directed the group's efforts to raise money for black soldiers and their families. Just as Scott had done earlier, Tyler offered his services to the new administration.[38]

The Afro-American's report of Tyler's appointment echoed the bulletin issued by the Creel Committee. Tyler, the first black war correspondent, would "specialize on the conditions surrounding the colored troops in France"[39] and report daily on their activities[40] to the "anxious millions of colored Americans in this country" and tell the true "story of the valor by one of their own blood and kindred."[41]

The fifty-eight-year-old Tyler arrived in France on September 28, less than two months before the armistice. Despite the time frame, he filed several pieces that urged blacks back home to support the soldiers. His dispatches furthered the ideology of racial elevation and social justice with stories of black gallantry, accomplishments, and nationalism.

Six weeks after Tyler's arrival, his first dispatch appeared in *The Afro-American.* He operated under an intricate arrangement. While war correspondents for the *New York Times,* the *Chicago Daily News,* and other papers worked for their news organizations, Tyler worked for the CPI. His deployment limited him to the staff of the commander-in-chief of the American Expeditionary Forces (AEF), Gen. John Pershing. Letters Tyler wrote to the CPI's Carl Byoir in early October further illuminated his dual status as a correspondent for the black press and as a conduit through which the government sought to boost black morale.

On October 9, Tyler reported to Byoir that he expected to join the black combat troops soon, although "activities at the front" had delayed arrangements.[42] Two weeks later, the correspondent told Byoir that "per the advice of headquarters" he was leaving Paris to be with the Ninety-second Division. "I hope I am coming up to your expectations," he wrote, adding, "I certainly am working hard, and alert."[43] The letter also sheds light on his financial arrangement with the CPI. Because of the "high cost of living" in Paris, Tyler noted, the army had deposited one thousand dollars into his account in Washington. But Tyler believed the work he was doing made "the expense but negligible."[44] When he returned to the United States in January 1919, Scott thanked the army chief of staff in Brest, France, for facilitating the correspondent's "mission." Scott noted that he and Tyler had "been working together to keep a high morale among the Negro people of the United States."[45]

Tyler faced significant constraints in trying to execute his assignment. The U.S. government censored his accounts, as it did with those of mainstream correspondents. After an initial review, white correspondents' dispatches went directly to their newspapers, while Tyler's reports received additional scrutiny from the CPI to determine whether they contained information that would negatively affect black morale or alienate whites. Once the dispatches cleared the rigid censorship, the CPI sent them to Scott for further review and, finally, dissemination to black newspapers. Even the route to accreditation differed. Mainstream correspondents with the AEF received their accreditation by filing a two thousand-dollar bond and one thousand dollars for maintenance. Mainstream newspapers also posted a ten thousand-dollar bond that they forfeited if their correspondents did not adhere to federal guidelines. As an employee of the Creel Committee, Tyler paid no such fee. Reporters for the mainstream press were assigned to cover all aspects of the war, while Tyler's specific charge was to focus solely on black soldiers.

On at least one occasion Scott reminded his friend that his status differed from that of correspondents for the white press, who had no such race-specific responsibilities. He candidly told Tyler that "the press authorities of the War Department have regarded it as expedient that some of your letters be 'expurgated' in a measure, to conform to strictly military policies."[46] Tyler joined the Ninety-second Division in October and remained with it for several weeks. The division, organized in November 1917 from the first contingent of African American draftees, comprised six hundred black soldiers from nearly every state in the country.[47] In an article published November 8, 1918, Tyler wrote of his arrival in France after a ten-day voyage: "Former reporters seemed to have made an especial effort to make me forget, which I did, that my skin was several shades darker than theirs, and by so doing, to convince me that this 'world democracy' for which the Allies are fighting is neither a barren ideality nor a rainbow vision, but an actual probability whose advance courier is discernible with the naked eye."[48]

Later in the article, Tyler complimented the troops, announcing that he was "off to the front where . . . colored soldiers are stationed . . . [and] to the front with the same absence of fear that characterized the colored troops who sailed for France on the ship with me."[49] The following week, he described a successful raid led by black soldiers: "Splendid endurance and valiant fighting of the colored soldiers continue to come in," he wrote. "[T]he race back home should be proud of their colored soldiers over here, whose unyielding spirit and bravery is making history for the race."[50]

On November 29, 1918, the correspondent described the conditions at a casualty camp for wounded officers. He wrote that a general had assured him that there was "absolutely no discrimination because of color tolerated at [the] camp, either in the barracks or other assignments" and that blacks under his command "were splendid soldiers."[51] While he fulfilled the government's agenda, Tyler was also careful to cite credible sources to buttress the facts he presented.

While these articles were running, Tyler advocated on behalf of soldiers who were discriminated against overseas. His November 5 letter to Scott began, "For our soldiers over here, this war is a tragedy in more ways than one. You will recall that our conference of June 19th to 21st. incl., we petitioned that the 'dead line' for Colored officers be abolished. The farther I go over here the more evidence is assured that the 'dead line' is a reality."[52] Tyler enclosed five memoranda labeled Exhibits A through F that proved discrimination against black soldiers and confirmed that their morale was low. "That rank prejudice is prevalent, I submit [to] you . . . two of many hundreds that might be supplied."[53] One memorandum from a white officer stated that he would not allow blacks to serve as officers in the Ninety-second Division owing to the need to "to supply efficient officers."[54] The officer wrote, "There will be colored officers insofar as they can be obtained, but colored officers who are incompetent will not be retained simply because they are colored, nor will their own estimate of their fitness be accepted. Examinations, practical tests, and their observed conduct in war must decide such questions."[55]

Although black soldiers were constrained overseas by the same type of Jim Crow practices that prevailed at home, and Tyler faced his own peculiar restrictions, his correspondence accomplished the goal of the black press, to tell the story of black troops and to counter negative misrepresentations of their role in the war.

Tyler's dispatch on the front page of *The Afro-American* on December 6, 1918, contradicted the argument that blacks were incompetent. He asserted that Americans could feel "proud of the [Ninety-second] division in France" that had amassed a record as a "gallant fighting machine."[56] He reached a broader audience than the blacks who read his accounts. The mainstream media also read the black press and no doubt took note of Tyler's articles.

Although some of Tyler's stories from overseas did not get past the censors, information about racism—especially prejudice in the AEF against the Ninety-second and Ninety-third Divisions—made it into print and caused fallout from black editors and the CPI. Tyler defended himself in a December 6 letter to Scott, denying that he had sent uncensored stories home. He had sent duplicate copies of a personal letter to the editors of the *Washington Bee* and to his former paper, the *Cleveland Advocate.* Tyler wrote that he did not think the letters would be published. He would have liked to submit exclusive material to the *Advocate,* but he had refused out of deference to the CPI and a sense of fairness to other race newspapers. He successfully navigated between his fellow black editors and publishers, who wanted their country to do what was right, and the government that decided what he should tell his readers.

The *Chicago Defender* Tries to Go It Alone

The *Chicago Defender* was not pleased about the arrangement that sent Ralph Waldo Tyler overseas, although publisher Robert Abbott was present at the meeting. Independent and competitive, Abbott decided to send Roscoe Conkling Simmons to Europe immediately after Tyler received his assignment.[57] Simmons was a nephew by marriage of Booker T. Washington, but he was also a leader in his own right. In addition to being a *Chicago Defender* columnist, he was a renowned orator with ties to the Republican Party.

According to Abbott's biographer Roi Ottley, Simmons remained encamped in Paris, distracted by its allure and its women. The newspaper nevertheless trumpeted Simmons's return and took credit for having fielded a foreign war correspondent. Articles with Simmons's byline appeared in the newspaper in April and May 1919.[58] "The Colonel has got the goods," an April 12, 1919, article announced; it described Simmons as an "orator, journalist and idol of a nation of followers" who had been to Paris and back. Simmons had traveled "at the instance [sic] of an entire people." He was now back and "loaded down with documents and photographs that probably no other man could have got in Paris."[59] A week later, the *Defender* ran a series of blurbs announcing that Simmons would give his first address since his return from Paris. A month after that, the newspaper promoted another Simmons speech "for the purpose of giving the citizens of Chicago an opportunity to hear from the lips of Colonel Roscoe Conkling Simmons, special representative to the war-stricken countries, the story of the part the darker races played in the Titanic struggle that recently came to a close and something of the great constructive measure mapped out."[60]

Carl Murphy took the helm of *The Afro-American* eight years after his return from Europe and guided it to success and sustainability for forty-five years before his death in 1967. In its halcyon days, the weekly newspaper became a chain that published editions in Virginia, Washington, D.C., and eleven other cities. During that time, *The Afro-American* chain dispatched numerous correspondents overseas to cover a variety of stories. The *Chicago Defender,* the Associated Negro Press (ANP), and the *Pittsburgh Courier* also increased their commitment to foreign news gathering in the ensuing decades.

[4]
Compelled to Scour the World
The Interwar Years

With fifteen hundred dollars from the National Association for the Advancement of Colored People (NAACP) to cover his expenses, William Edward Burghardt Du Bois sailed for France on December 1, 1918. "I did not talk—I went,"[1] the editor of the organization's magazine *The Crisis* noted years later. Du Bois had acted swiftly when he learned of an unexpected opportunity to work in France as a foreign correspondent after World War I. In the immediate aftermath of the Great War, and during the interwar years, Du Bois and the black press engaged in enterprise reporting, digging up their own stories. According to longtime *Chicago Defender* foreign editor Metz Lochard, the black press came out of the war "full-grown" and "self-supporting"; its journalists were "full-time careerists" whose editors "wanted their papers to be like the white dailies."[2] These journalists placed the color-line problem "within the framework of a thorough understanding of the national economic, social, political scene."[3] They were sometimes rebuffed in their efforts, as Du Bois was, but they found ways to obtain information and tell their stories.[4]

Du Bois's action was consistent with his refusal to accept the status quo and his commitment to fight entrenched racism. After all, black soldiers had helped ensure victory in the Great War. After the war, interest among educated and influential blacks in nonwhite races worldwide was so great that black editors were committed to obtaining firsthand information about foreign affairs.

In September 1918, once it was clear to Du Bois that the Allies were going to win World War I, he and fellow NAACP board members agreed that the organization should play a role in deciding the future of Africa. Because of Du Bois's stature, the NAACP agreed that he should convene a Pan-African Congress in Paris, the location of the upcoming peace conference.[5]

Du Bois sought a meeting with President Woodrow Wilson in November

1918 to make the case for African Americans to be present at the postwar peace negotiations. "It would be a calamity for the two hundred million black people to be absolutely without voice or representation at this great transformation of the world,"[6] Du Bois wrote in a letter to Secretary of War Newton D. Baker. In response to one of Du Bois's other entreaties, the president's secretary, Joseph P. Tumulty, sent Du Bois a letter stating that a meeting with the president was impossible. Wilson, he explained, needed to devote the time before his departure for Europe to "what must be done, and done carefully, by way of preparing for his absence."[7] Wilson had no interest in allowing black Americans to attend the Paris Peace Conference, where they would have the opportunity to place America's race problem on the international agenda.

Undeterred by his dismissal, Du Bois made plans to leave, but he had difficulty gaining permission from the French government to hold the Pan-African Congress. With the help of Blaise Diagne, the black deputy in the French Parliament who represented Senegal, Du Bois persuaded Prime Minister Georges Clemenceau to allow the congress to convene. Du Bois later wrote that Clemenceau needed votes from the black members of Parliament and the support of the 280,000 African troops who had fought in the Great War.[8] Du Bois went abroad almost immediately after the signing of the armistice, before receiving an affirmative response to his proposed meeting.

His first article, in the February 1919 issue of *The Crisis*, lightheartedly recounted his shipboard experience. He did not get seasick, he shared a room and private bath with three roommates, and he and other reporters waited for hours to obtain press credentials from George Creel.[9] Du Bois was among more than six hundred correspondents from around the world covering the conference, including two hundred journalists from the United States.[10] From Paris, Du Bois sought to place the future of Africa and the issue of race and imperialism on the international agenda. In the January 1919 issue of *The Crisis*, he explained his threefold mission: to convene a Pan-African Congress, gather information for a historical account of blacks in the war, and collect "first-hand material."[11]

As both the convener of the congress and the magazine's editor, Du Bois had a dual role similar to that of other black foreign correspondents and to that of prominent white correspondents. He both reported the happenings and was part of them. The congress was vital to the future of continental Africans, for whom Du Bois and the NAACP wanted self-governance absent the yoke of European colonists at the war's end. He would try to pressure delegates at the peace table to respond to the interest of people in America and around the world.[12] Du Bois insisted on basic rights and a new world order.

Fifty-seven delegates representing Europe's Africa colonies, South Africa, Egypt, Haiti, and the Dominican Republic attended the congress and passed resolutions calling on the League of Nations to ensure that their fellow members of the African Diaspora be treated fairly and given a voice in their own governments. Their actions, however, gained no standing with the world's great powers.

Du Bois expressed his disappointment in the Paris Peace Conference in the May issue of *The Crisis,* writing that British and French officials had agreed to consider the congress's resolutions, and Portugal and Belgium had "offered complete co-operation," but the United States had torpedoed all efforts to guarantee rights for people of color.[13] Du Bois charged that people of color had received little attention at the conference, which he characterized as "just a few men in a small room" who decided Africa's "future and mankind's destiny for the following century."[14] The colonization of Africa that began in 1885 with the approval of the United States would continue with America's support. The issue of social justice in the world did not sway those in power after the war. People of color essentially remained in a state of submission, much like blacks in America.

While the Pan-African Congress was a major focus of foreign correspondence in *The Crisis,* the magazine also ran other dispatches from Du Bois. The March 1919 "Overseas" issue ran his firsthand accounts of the war's devastating impact on France. The environment was gloomy and smoky, he wrote, and many cafés and businesses in once booming areas had closed.

While his coverage was similar to correspondence in the dominant media, Du Bois was watching the peace process from a different vantage point. His reporting addressed a common theme in black foreign correspondence—placing race in a global context and juxtaposing race relations abroad and in his country. "Vive La France" expressed the writer's amazement and excitement about a day-long French celebration that honored "black and 'yellow' servicemen" who had died during the war. Comparing France to the United States, Du Bois exclaimed, "How fine a thing to be a black Frenchman in 1919—imagine such a celebration in America!" Indeed, the "civilized French" did not understand American "Nigger-hatred."[15] This was far afield from the government's agenda.

The *Washington Post,* on the other hand, primarily reflected the government's agenda. Articles in February and April 1919 addressed President

Wilson's trip to the Paris Peace Conference and his push for the League of Nations.[16] A February 7 dispatch elaborated on the status of the League of Nations treaty and concluded that the organization had accomplished one-third of its task. The following day, a front-page article stated that Wilson was trying to ensure the adoption of the league's constitution before returning to the United States. On February 9, another dispatch reported that Wilson was leaving Paris with the fate of the enemy unsettled.[17] The only reference to Africa was a map of the European nations' partitioning of the continent—a fragmentation Du Bois hoped the Pan-African Congress would prevent.

Coverage in the first and third weeks of April in the *Washington Post* was similar. News about the league often dominated page 1 and addressed postwar developments in Japan, Arab nations, and other countries, but not in Africa. There were no stories about or photographs of Du Bois or the Pan-African Congress; people of African descent were essentially rendered invisible. Such reportage confirmed the charge the black press frequently made and served as an impetus for the medium's global journalism.

Du Bois's foreign correspondence provided an audience of highly literate blacks, and white supporters, with a perspective they did not get in the mainstream media. In the months immediately after the Great War, Du Bois managed to go abroad without the support of the government, just as his predecessors had. He did not cover the peace conference in the manner of the mainstream media's foreign correspondents. There is no indication that he spoke to official sources, covered any conference sessions, or received news from the U.S. press department in Paris.

The Associated Negro Press Begins

While W. E. B. Du Bois was overseas, another venture into black foreign correspondence began. The Associated Negro Press (ANP) had the potential to pursue the same agenda as *The Crisis* and to reach an even more diverse audience. The news service debuted in Chicago on March 21, 1919, the year violence and discrimination against blacks escalated into race riots that rocked the nation. At least twenty-six race riots erupted from April to October 1919 in such places as Beaumont, Texas; Chicago; Elaine, Arkansas; Washington, D.C.; and Charleston, South Carolina. Black people were even more concerned that their precarious state would not improve and that their country would continue to deny them access and opportunity. Rather than concentrating only on national issues, African American journalists looked outward, hoping that information about race relations abroad would effect change at home. Claude Barnett envisioned bringing to fruition the efforts black newspapers had tried to sustain decades earlier. He had studied the strategies Robert Abbott used to shepherd the *Chicago Defender* weekly newspaper to national prominence. Realizing that small weeklies were hungry for national news, Barnett believed the time was right for a national news service. He sought the support of larger black weeklies, but Abbott and other leading publishers withheld their support.[18] Nonetheless, Barnett pressed forward, using capital from a cosmetics firm he had cofounded.

The news agency filled a crucial niche in international news gathering. Although some black foreign correspondents had tried going it alone, that was not economically feasible given the precarious financial situation they chronically faced. The black press was far behind the mainstream media in establishing a news service. In 1838, the *New York Herald*'s James Gordon Bennett had organized America's foreign news service, using correspondents who were natives of the countries from which they reported. Until the twentieth century, the black press had neither the means nor the opportunity to access international news on a routine basis. White dailies tended to decrease international coverage during times of relative calm in the world, as they did after World War I. But blacks intensified their foreign reporting in the 1920s. The issues that affected people of color overseas, and the activities of blacks abroad, were relevant to blacks at home because they faced similar challenges. The new press association led the way in reporting that connection.

The ANP sought to exemplify professional journalism by offering fair, objective, and balanced news about the national black community. It shunned the formula of Abbott's and other black newspapers that blended sensationalism and racial uplift. The 1920 ANP annual report stated that it wanted to be viewed as responsible in its national and international coverage. It would work to advance the race, to explore and present the shared identity of people of African descent worldwide, and to win the respect and support of both blacks and whites who could advocate for African Americans at home.

Barnett's initial focus was national in scope, but he was equally compelled to "scour the world" for race news and build a "world-wide service" as a starting point for "Race Journalism."[19] He recognized the parallels between black Americans and people living under colonialism abroad. He believed the key to gaining influential white support was to contrast the treatment of ethnic minorities worldwide with the treatment of blacks at home. The ANP would make a political statement about racial injustices that it hoped would bring about positive change.

The going was rough for the infant agency. A major obstacle was the failure of the eighty black weeklies that signed up for the service to abide by the terms of their agreement. They were to receive weekly packets of press releases for a fee and, in return, supply stories from their areas to the agency. But they often did not pay, nor did they generate articles. Because the ANP had no funds to pay a permanent professional reporting staff and was unable to obtain stories from the weeklies, the news service clipped and rewrote articles from mainstream dailies and relied on part-time journalists and influential persons in areas heavily populated by blacks. According to historian Lawrence Hogan, the ANP obtained the service of "hardworking, talented correspondents by appealing to the feelings of many blacks that the time was right for 'a race news agency,' and by putting work for the ANP in the context of service to one's people."[20] These correspondents included Roy Wilkins and William Pickens, both NAACP executives, and Enoch Waters and Percival Prattis, who went on to prominent careers as full-time journalists. Pickens worked for the ANP as a regular correspondent from its beginning until 1945. The ANP also rewrote and distributed news from Africa, Europe, and the West Indies that originated with the establishment media. Part-time stringers and travelers abroad also reported for the ANP.

The *Negro World's* Appeal

While the ANP and black periodicals served blacks who wanted to learn about people in distant lands, the *Negro World* also had great appeal during the 1920s. With international news the cornerstone of its coverage, the official organ of Marcus Garvey's Universal Negro Improvement Association (UNIA) helped create a black identity and shape black consciousness.[21] The weekly newspaper, which began publishing in 1918, transcended national concerns and racial politics.

Lawrence Levine stated that the 1920s was a time when the country turned its back on blacks and crushed their aspirations.[22] They watched as the progressive movement reformed many areas of American life but excluded them, ensuring their continued grinding poverty. Scholars describe this period as a time in which free blacks had a few years in the sun before being conscripted again. This nadir led to a black militancy manifested in both protests of grievances and pride in the race. Within that context blacks seized the opportunity to create a society free of endemic racism. That opportunity came via two seminal movements: Garveyism and the Harlem Renaissance, of which Du Bois was one of the primary architects.

Racial and cultural identity and the oneness of people of African descent undergirded Garvey's philosophy. Garveyism espoused racial advancement through race pride, unity, self-reliance, and economic freedom through entrepreneurship—all without reliance on the dominant society. As James Cones wrote, Garvey's ideology held that white people would never "place black people on a par with them."[23] The *Negro World* transmitted the message of black nationalism: focusing on developments at home was useless because the fate of black people lay beyond those boundaries, in the land of their ancestors—Africa. Garveyism did not try to convince America to grant blacks access to public accommodations or to remove the yoke of segregation or to provide a quality education. Instead, it promoted the idea that black people could flourish in Africa.

The *Negro World* made international affairs a cornerstone of its coverage, relying on a small army of unpaid stringers in the West Indies, sub-Saharan Africa, the Caribbean, and other locales to supply a steady stream of news, commentaries, letters, and poems that highlighted the positive aspects of black life worldwide. Special sections of the sixteen-page weekly focused solely on Spanish and French news. Women were valued correspondents for the newspaper. Amy Jacques Garvey, the wife of Marcus Garvey, created a special page, "Our Women and What They Think," to give a voice to females in the Garvey movement.[24] Her mission was "to encourage Negro women to express their views on subjects of interest to their communities, and particularly affecting our struggling race."[25]

The paper expressed great interest in international affairs. The negative impact of white imperialism and the exploitation of Africa was a predominant theme. The weekly reported on the vast natural resources in Africa and the West Indies and asserted that whites had robbed those lands of their bounty and stripped the people of their livelihood. In Garvey's view, the major cause of World War I was the European nations' desire to keep their populations poor and ignorant while removing their wealth in order to rebuild the Western nations' infrastructure and "maintain European superiority."[26] Du Bois expressed a similar view in the *Atlantic Monthly*, maintaining that the intent of France, Germany, and England to gain supremacy in Africa, coupled with racial prejudice, had precipitated the war.[27] Chagrined that African officials entered into agreements with whites, Garvey said that the UNIA stood ready to engage in cooperative entrepreneurial ventures with those countries.

Foreign correspondence in the *Negro World* promoted the UNIA as complaints swirled around its controversial leader. One story warned against regarding "Garveyism as merely a crude unwashed racialism" and concluded that it was folly to dismiss "Marcus Garvey as a smooth tongued charlatan, shallow, noisy and insincere."[28] The dominant media, and even some black newspapers, characterized him that way, but stories from abroad revealed unyielding support for Garvey, even as he prepared to serve a jail sentence. He had been convicted of mail fraud in connection with his Black Star shipping line, which was intended to transport blacks to Africa. Pieces about UNIA meetings and activities were filed from Nicaragua, Cuba, Honduras, and Central America.

Problems continued to plague the *Negro World* as its controversial leader's troubles escalated. Its chronic money woes increased after Garvey's conviction, but the weekly remained influential thanks to the leadership of Amy Jacques Garvey. At the movement's apex, the *Negro World* maintained its immense appeal to the masses; tens of thousands of people of African descent worldwide joined the UNIA. John Hope Franklin estimated that between 600,000 and 6 million people read the newspaper.

J. A. Rogers: A Full-fledged Foreign Correspondent

When Joel Augustus Rogers was a young man, he worked as a Pullman porter with the express purpose of traveling to different cities and visiting their libraries. He paid white conductors to check out books because libraries were for whites only. He wanted to know about kindred peoples because, when he was a child, his Sunday school teachers had told him that the black man bore God's curse of inferiority. Rogers would spend his life traveling to more than sixty countries, gathering data to disprove that myth.[29] While on his trips, some of which lasted three years, Rogers wrote freelance articles for the black press and sometimes for the mainstream press. Yet he is not commonly thought of as a foreign correspondent. African Americans primarily saw him as a noted, self-taught historian, anthropologist, and writer.

During a career that spanned almost sixty years, Rogers educated, informed, and shaped the opinions of readers about events, places, and people of which they had scant knowledge. He became one of the foremost black journalists, writing approximately three thousand articles from 1917 until 1966, the year he died.

Born in Negril, Jamaica, in 1883, Rogers left there in 1906 and stayed briefly in Chicago before moving to Harlem, where he spent most of his life. He became a naturalized citizen in 1917. He maintained a longstanding relationship with fellow Jamaican Marcus Garvey, and he wrote a regular column for the *Negro World.*

Rogers's works challenged notions of white superiority and highlighted Africa's glorious past and present. He researched black history in six languages. He wrote sixteen books and lectured extensively. In 1935, he became the first black correspondent that the African American press dispatched abroad, covering the Italian-Ethiopian War for the *Pittsburgh Courier.*

A decade before that assignment, Rogers wrote articles about race relations in England that ran in the *New York Amsterdam News.* His articles about blacks and whites in England who gained distinction in their fields followed the pattern of previous African American foreign correspondents, observing the status of their race abroad and highlighting its achievements.[30]

In 1925, Rogers went to Europe to conduct museum research for one of his books and to learn about Africa and its people.[31] A September dispatch in the *Pittsburgh Courier* described his arrival in Paris,[32] and in October he wrote about Italian dictator Benito Mussolini.[33] His articles from abroad did not appear in the newspaper again until 1927.

Throughout 1927 and 1928, the *Pittsburgh Courier* and other African American publications ran Rogers's weekly dispatches from France, Italy, Belgium, Holland, Morocco, Gibraltar, and Switzerland. His stories contextualized race relations by exploring the status of people of color in different countries. In such articles as "I Find Italy a Land of Art," "Rogers Meets 'Homesick' American Negroes in Marseilles, France," and "Ethiopia and Egypt Made Nordic Civilization Possible," he gave a positive perspective on people of African descent.[34]

A piece that ran in the *Chicago Defender* in 1927 described a brawl started by an aristocratic Cuban after he saw black musicians playing in an orchestra and observed other blacks in the company of white women. In Rogers's words: "The dark Nordic blood of Senor Valdes boiled at the scene. . . . Law enforcement, subsequently, arrested the Cuban man, and when he appeared in court the next morning, he exhibited such a change of heart, one would have thought he had read *Uncle Tom's Cabin* overnight." The señor's attorney told the judge he came from a land that barred black people from such places. "How could he know, your honor, that in Paris, a black man is a king?"[35]

In an article about homesick African Americans in Marseilles, Rogers began by observing that America was still young compared to Europe. The French city was 2,500 years old, once part of Julius Caesar's Roman Empire. His next piece was a bleak assessment of the black population in Marseilles. They hailed from the United States, the French and British West Indies, Africa, and Madagascar, among other places. There were so many, Rogers wrote, "One almost fancies himself back in a Negro neighborhood in America."[36] Many came to the seaport city hoping to find a ship to take them home. "One young man from Virginia was in a state of rags equal to that of a Casablanca Arab. 'Would you like to get back to America' I asked him. 'Would I?' he replied, 'If I could swim it [the Mediterranean] I'd start back tomorrow.'"[37]

Rogers was telling his readers that, despite problems at home, the condition of black people in one foreign city was so bad they wished they were back in America. Many asked him for help. "I have never wished so hard before that I was rich," he wrote.[38] Rogers did not attempt to portray Marseilles as a utopia. Instead, he reported the good and the bad and explained why certain situations existed. His depiction of blacks abroad suggested that class was the major factor affecting their status in one French city. This view differed from the prevailing sentiment of the black press, that whites exploited darker peoples to gain material wealth. The media's Afrocentric perspective did not focus on the economic status of poor whites. Championing the cause of blacks was the goal. Rogers would follow that approach as his foreign reportage took center stage during the following decade.

[5]

Robert Abbott Finds a Racial Paradise

As a Negro and a product of North American traditions, my natural, logical reaction was the desire to reach some clear, positive conclusions as to the real depth and extent of the Brazilian democratic spirit or to what degree it was truly inclusive of the Negro. And this, I feel I have done.

—ROBERT ABBOT

This was Robert Sengstacke Abbott's explanation for why he had traveled to South America in 1923 to gather news.[1] He began his journey with an agenda, a hypothesis he was intent on proving even if the facts did not support it. His theory was that other countries treated people of color with respect and dignity; therefore, they lived a much better life than their brethren in America. Abbott knew he had the power to influence an enormous black audience through his weekly newspaper the *Chicago Defender*, and he was keenly aware of its white readership. He knew that some white readers had empathy for suffering blacks, but he also knew that his message of equality and progress angered some racist white southerners. Thus he went abroad to collect information that he hoped would help mold public opinion and ultimately change societal dynamics for blacks in America.

When Abbott began his newspaper, his office was the kitchen of the rooming house where he lived on State Street in Chicago. He was the entire staff, serving as reporter, editor, and peddler of his weekly.[2] "American Race Prejudice Must Be Destroyed" was the first of nine points in the *Defender*'s platform, and it left no doubt that the newspaper was going to champion black rights against an unjust society.

Abbott had developed his worldview long before he began the newspaper in 1905. According to his biographer Roi Ottley (who later became a *Defender* executive and a foreign correspondent), Abbott's half-white stepfather, Rev. John H. Sengstacke, had instilled in the boy a belief that the black race needed a "public defender" and that a newspaper was one of the strongest weapons an African American could have to defend his race. Abbott, whose father died when he was two, so admired his stepfather that he took Sengstacke as his middle name. Abbott loved his country, but he held it accountable for its consignment of blacks to a marginal status.[3]

He created the newspaper, he wrote, "to give encouragement to [the black person's] ambitions, voice his longings and clothe him in dignity." Abbott's nephew John H. Sengstacke, who succeeded him as editor and publisher of the *Defender,* wrote on the newspaper's fiftieth anniversary in 1955, "It has emphasized his obligations as a citizen, and supported his faith in America."[4] Sengstacke was continuing the work his uncle had started: "recording and interpreting one of the most amazing phenomena of our time; the political and economic coming of age of the Negro in America."[5]

Abbott used his business acumen to capitalize on trends and create an influential publication. He even tapped into yellow journalism, diligently studying and imitating successful white newspapers that fed readers a steady diet of sensationalized news. To that mix he added news of his race and strident criticism of the status quo. Metz Lochard, a longtime editor at the *Defender,* believed the newspaper was successful because it glamorized African American personalities and ran series on the "Negro problem" and columns by prominent blacks.[6] The weekly was the first black newspaper to run a health column and full-page comic strips.

The entrepreneurial publisher outwitted the dominant power system in the South that banned circulation of his paper; he hired national representatives to generate circulation, solicit advertising, and gather news. He enlisted Pullman porters to throw copies of the newspaper from trains. Poor African American field workers were among the tens of thousands who either read or had the *Chicago Defender* read to them. They believed its contention that life was better in the North, and they headed to cities the newspaper wrote about. According to Sengstacke, his uncle crystallized black "aspirations as complete integration into American life" and aroused blacks "to individual achievement and fuller participation in the affairs of our country."[7]

Scholars confirm that the *Defender* was largely responsible for the Great Migration of perhaps a million blacks; it also assisted them when they arrived in places as foreign to them as another country, helping them find housing and employment. The newspaper's initiatives "came like manna from heaven for the poverty-stricken, hopelessly constricted blacks of the southern country,"[8] media historian Armistead Pride noted. It even "schooled its bewildered newcomers in the rudiments of social conduct."[9] In the 1920s, the *Defender* was one of the most influential black newspapers, with a circulation of 250,000. Because an estimated four people read each paper, the readership was actually about one million.[10]

A factor in the newspaper's influence was its crusade against lynching. An unpublished history states that Abbott's "descriptions of the unbelievable brutality of the mobs awakened the national conscience, and fostered a unity among Negroes that otherwise might not have been possible."[11] In 1919, spurred by the Chicago race riot of that year, Abbott planned to build a printing plant to ensure that he would be able to publish without obstacles. Two years later, the *Defender* rolled out of his printing press on Indiana Avenue.

The *Defender* had been publishing for almost twenty years when Abbott decided to engage in personal journalism and write about foreign affairs and race relations abroad. In January 1923, accompanied by his wife Helen, he left Chicago for South America. He spent three months there and was the first African American to report from that part of the world. The newspaper reported on January 13 that Abbot would "make minute investigation into conditions that affect the Race and write a series of profusely illustrated articles from each city."[12]

The end of World War I did not terminate the *Defender*'s goal of engaging in independent foreign reporting. The weekly had grown significantly before and during the war, making Abbott a millionaire. The *Defender*'s expansion and enhanced status renewed Abbott's determination to independently collect information. He was not content to depend solely on news from the relatively young Associated Negro Press (ANP); he wanted more, and he wanted his audience to know how and why he was going to South America. The *Defender* promoted the venture in articles and advertisements while Abbott was abroad and after his return. Two months after the trip began, a blurb on page 1 promoted his venture: "15,000 Miles for First-hand Info: Robert S. Abbott, LL.B. Is Now Touring the Countries of South America and will give a . . . Review of Conditions as regards the progress and the general development of the darker races in a Series of Articles . . . . Watch for Announcement of Date of Opening Articles."[13]

When Abbott returned to Chicago in May 1923, Roscoe Simmons gushed in a column, "Your advocate, *Defender*, forerunner, Robert S. Abbott, builder of this newspaper, your ONE newspaper run according to the rules, is back home."[14] Simmons explained that Abbott "was told about South America, its wealth, opportunities, [and] its freedom. Freedom is Abbott's religion."[15] Abbott's tour took him to Chile, Uruguay, Argentina, and Panama, but he spent most of his time in Brazil, where people of African descent accounted for more than 50 percent of the population. Abbott, like black foreign correspondents before him, faced obstacles as he traveled abroad. A millionaire, he did not lack financial resources; racism was the culprit. He had difficulty booking passage on various steamships; after he secured passage, the Brazilian government initially refused to allow him entry. He finally succeeded in entering the country with the persistent intervention of Senator Medill McCormick of Illinois.[16] Bigotry cropped up again while Abbott was onboard the ship. In Abbott's presence, an Episcopal chaplain invited others to attend a shipboard service, but he did not extend that courtesy to the publisher. In protest, four of the five white men refused the invitation, Abbott later explained. He faced more discrimination on his trip: he was denied access to four hotels in Rio de Janeiro—all run by Americans—and one in Chile. Although the practice was against Brazilian law, Abbott still could not stay at the hotels because the country did not enforce the statute. Chile enforced its law, alleviating a housing problem for Abbott and his wife.[17]

These incidents so affected the publisher that he recounted them in his first speech after he returned home; he addressed them again in August when his articles began to run. "We arrived at the Gloria Hotel," he wrote. "But behold! Even here we are met by that incubus monster who, like a legendary sea serpent, it seems, has tracked our courses down the South Atlantic way and proposes to find an abode in Brazil."[18]

Abbott provided a skewed perspective when he discussed race relations abroad. There was often a disconnection between what actually occurred and Abbott's interpretation of it. Even as he described incidences of racism, he still wrote that intolerance did not exist in South America. He charged that the racism he encountered was rooted in American influences, thus absolving Brazil of any culpability. He wrote in his second article, "Even in the fair land of Brazil, whose heart pulses, whose every fiber is vibrant with the democratic tradition of the great French revolution, the slimy thing of American colorphobia would presume to assert itself."[19]

In subsequent articles, he wrote of positive race relations and equal opportunity for people of color elsewhere in South America. Of his time in Montevideo, Abbott asserted, "A black skin seemed to excite no ill feeling or comment and our few days stay was marked by a perfect spirit of cordiality and kindly grace."[20] He believed people of African descent gained status if they were successful, and he offered as evidence a description of a "new aristocracy" in Sao Paulo, Brazil, that was not based on an individual's blood, but on "true culture, patriotic usefulness and high moral principles."[21] He ran several photographs, including one of a black police officer directing traffic, one of a police officer on a motorcycle, and one of a mechanic who was a member of a trade union.[22] At the time, African Americans in the United States could not join trade unions. Unions used such measures as literacy tests and skill requirements to exclude blacks from obtaining jobs reserved for whites.

Abbott wrote about being asked to leave the Palace Hotel in Sao Paulo in the middle of the night because of his race, and he recounted the prejudice a black music student encountered at a predominantly white school. But he seemed to suggest that such treatment did not matter because he had met prominent black people, including the minister of the interior for the state of Sao Paulo.[23] He undoubtedly excused blatant racism because to write about it would have debunked his premise that the United States compared unfavorably to other nations in its policies and actions toward African Americans. This view would continue in black foreign correspondence well into the 1990s.

In his articles, Abbott included information about the climate, geography, and beauty of the places he visited. He elaborated on the accomplishments of people of African descent, as well as the economy, culture, population, and history of countries in South America. Through his reportage, the *Defender* contextualized race relations and racial progress in South America, juxtaposing them with the lack of rights for blacks in the United States. Abbott was "more determined than ever to fight to make sure our country, like Brazil, like Argentina, lands of true democracy rather than a country of mock democracy."[24] He hoped to pressure the United States to grant equal standing to African Americans at home. His foreign correspondence clearly had a political agenda. He wrote that he "was made to feel ashamed . . . of the spirit of some so-called Americans," and he relished "a spirit of common brotherhood" in Brazil, where everyone worked together. "There are no 'Negroes' in Brazil; there are only Brazilians," he wrote.[25] Foreign correspondents for other black periodicals would also visit Brazil in years to come with the same mission that guided Abbott.

His reporting from South America led to a major change in the *Defender*'s editorial policy.[26] The publisher had always asserted that blacks were equal to whites, but he had been unable to demonstrate this fact. He found the evidence in South America, a place where blacks were professionals, financiers, and tycoons. Armed with this confirmation, Abbott stepped up his call for reforms in Chicago's public sector and argued in print that blacks were better suited than whites to represent themselves in Congress. The Brazilian adventure also led the publisher, who had focused so much on sensationalism, to devote more space to coverage of black achievement.[27] The newspaper made a commitment to invest in additional foreign reporting. For six years it solicited articles that related to the "American scene" from prominent Brazilian journalists, ensuring that readers would continue to get news from that part of the world.[28]

The *Defender* went a step further, adding a foreign news desk during the 1920s.[29] Stories from the Virgin Islands provide an example of the geopolitical nature of its coverage. The first of a two-part series by Carlos Hechos in 1924 asserted that the United States had acquired the Virgin Islands a week before entering World War I in order to secure the Panama Canal and to ensure its national security.[30] U.S. imperialism did not sit well with the *Defender*, which conveyed its discontent with the headline: "Story of the Virgin Islands of the United States: Land Where Dark People Dwell and Are Ruled under the American Flag Yet Are Not Considered US Citizens." A second dispatch called for the United States to remove its "undemocratic naval administration from the islands."[31]

Off to Europe: Abbott Finds Racial Utopia

The decade of the 1920s was ending when Abbott again went abroad to see for himself. He expected this trip to be as successful as his previous one six years earlier. This time Europe was his destination. He and Helen sailed in June 1929 and spent five months traveling throughout the continent. The journey started in Paris and took them to Belgium, Holland, Germany, England, Austria, and Italy.[32]

Abbott wanted "to meet, talk to and rub elbows with the upper classes in Europe, both white and Negro, and to compare the social and cultural progress of Negroes in the Old World with that of the Negro in the United States and perhaps . . . discover the reason for the striking differences."[33] He did not file his articles from Europe, just as he had not filed from South America, because the newspaper did not belong to the press associations and had no access to transatlantic or telegraphic cable. Abbott wrote thirteen articles about "My Trip Abroad" when he returned. His first piece noted:

> [T]here is one thought that has remained uppermost in my mind during . . . my trip. Many . . . things that I saw would keep bringing it back to me. . . . All of my life, even from my earliest childhood I have felt in the depths of my being that the theory that color makes the man was one of the biggest lies ever told. Now, after months of daily contact with the white man on his own soil, I am more firmly convinced than ever that I am right. Better, I firmly believe now that such a theory could have originated only in a madhouse among lunatics.

In subsequent installments, Abbott wrote about black achievements in the arts, government, and politics; about life in France; and about how the races interacted.[34] His articles about England were less positive. He described it as "a country of queer contradictions as regards the Negro."[35] He saw black men married to white women and living in upscale neighborhoods "without being tormented like they would have been in America."[36] But thirty London hotels had denied lodging to Abbott and his wife because of their race.

Some of his later pieces read like travelogues. He was amazed that Rome had not fallen after the war; instead, it had "risen to a state" that far surpassed anything it "might have been in the days of the Caesars."[37] Abbott's only mention of Africa was in an article about a visit to the Congo Museum outside Brussels. He found it "a welcome sight" after his visits to "dozens of museums and cathedrals, all pretty much alike."[38] The Congo had been a Belgian colony under the rule of King Leopold II and colonists had stripped it of much of its wealth. A substantial bounty, no doubt, had found a home in the Congo Museum, where Abbott marveled at African art and musical instruments. This reporting educated readers about the history of the colony and the impact of colonialism there.

Because Abbott's goal was to engender economic and social change at home, he painted a skewed picture of Europe. Just as he had in his previous foreign correspondence, he glossed over the racism he encountered. He held on to his view of racial tolerance in France, although he reported that people of African descent were primarily entertainers—stereotypical roles—and that universities enrolled very few black students.[39] Just as he had excused racism in South America, Abbott acknowledged bigotry in England, noting that the "color bar" could be as "cruel in some parts of the old world as at home." But he minimized the unpleasant episodes and focused on the fact that he and Helen had stayed in the home of "good friends" who entertained them in one of London's "most exclusive neighborhoods."[40]

In a piece about an African prince who had renounced his throne to stay in France, Abbott blamed Americans for the prejudice the prince encountered. The prince told Abbott that a nightclub that had always welcomed him had recently made him and his party leave after he danced with a white French woman. With biting criticism, Abbott charged, "Americans swarming to Paris to inaugurate their vulgar display of wealth accumulated during the days when France, England, Germany and the rest of the world were suffering, had taken complete charge of the nightclubs and places of amusement. Finding that France receives all men on their merits, these Americans with no sense of decency had bribed some of the nightclub owners and employees to refuse service to black men."[41]

The writer praised French authorities for issuing a statement that the country would not tolerate "American prejudice" and for telling people from the United States that they were required to respect "French laws and customs while they are on French soil."[42] Upon his return home, Abbott wrote about a visit to Chicago, where he shook hands with "a chimp in the zoo." It was, he reported, "the most hearty welcome" he received in America.[43]

Abbott lauded Europe as a continent that was "not the place for the man or woman who does not believe in . . . complete social equality with no strings tied to it."[44] Interestingly, his wife saw things differently. Helen Abbott told her sister that she hated the terrible experiences they had in South America and Europe, where she and Abbott were treated as "racial freaks."[45] Europeans had continually stared at the light-complexioned woman of stately bearing, whom they mistook as white, and her short, very dark husband, who sported an ivory-tipped cane. According to Abbott's biographer, Helen understood "the fact that there was indeed a deep strain of racial prejudice toward Negroes running through the fabric of the continent, often so subtle that it was not always seen by the naked eye." The Abbotts escaped "the more nauseating aspects of Europe's racial prejudice because American blacks enjoyed a unique status while abroad" primarily because there were so few of them and they were not "in competition with white men socially or economically."[46]

Although many of Abbott's experiences abroad proved that people of color were discriminated against and treated in a stereotypical fashion, his mission was to show unsympathetic white readers that people in lands far away understood that persons of color were equal. But he did his people a disservice by painting a picture of a utopia abroad that did not exist. Despite his distorted perspective, however, Abbott's foreign correspondence solidified a pattern of personal journalism from abroad by African Americans. He and other blacks would step up their reporting from abroad during the following decade.

[6]

The 1930s

A Defining Decade

In 1932, Homer Smith became the *Chicago Defender*'s correspondent from Russia. Using the pen name Chatwood Hall, he filed primarily from Moscow but also from Kiev, Odessa, and other locales. The *Defender* had made foreign coverage routine by establishing the foreign news service in the 1920s. Publisher Robert S. Abbott wanted the *Defender* to be the leader in the black press during the defining decade of black global journalism. A desire to provide firsthand information and to acquaint "America's millions of race members with their scattered brothers in other sections of the world" were among the reasons the *Defender* cited for obtaining reports from Italy, England, France, Germany, Ethiopia, Brazil, the West Indies, Africa, and the Soviet Republic, making it a leader in black foreign reporting. Its reports often had no bylines. The *Defender* supplemented its foreign news coverage by clipping and rewriting articles from dailies and giving those publications credit. By 1934, dispatches about the impending Italian-Ethiopian conflict were running almost weekly. The newspaper boasted in early 1936 that it had undertaken a "new task" during the previous decade that had made it the pioneer in "race journalism."[1]

The newspaper was not the only black media organization providing global coverage. The Associated Negro Press (ANP) news service, the *Pittsburgh Courier, The Afro-American,* and the relatively new *Atlanta Daily World* continued their autonomous pursuit of foreign news. Among the ANP correspondents whose byline appeared in black newspapers during this defining decade was entertainer Rudolph Dunbar. While living and performing in Europe, he was listed on ANP dispatches as its first exclusive correspondent. British socialite Nancy Cunard, who was committed to social justice, filed reports about wars from Europe and Africa. To cover the Italian-Ethiopian conflict in 1935, the ANP also tapped African American aviator Col. John H. "Johnny" Robinson, who went to Africa to aid Ethiopia's air force. In 1937, California journalist Fay

Jackson, who covered Hollywood for the ANP, headed to England to report on the coronation of King George VI. Ralph Matthews reported on the coronation for *The Afro-American.*

Black newspapers that used the ANP service also acted independently. The *Pittsburgh Courier* ventured into foreign news gathering in 1931 when it sent star journalist George Schuyler to Africa. He filed reports on conditions in Liberia and wrote a series of articles on the continued existence of slavery there and in Ethiopia. The weekly took center stage in the middle of the decade with exclusive reports about a war that threatened the African nation of Ethiopia. Although the newspaper became a major black publication because of its coverage of the Italian-Ethiopian war, it was not in the forefront of foreign news gathering on a regular basis. Its global journalism was event-driven, as when publisher Robert Vann reported on the 1936 Olympics.

The Afro-American's coverage was also event-driven. Editor and publisher Carl Murphy and managing editor William Jones provided weekly reports from Africa and the Diaspora during the 1930s. Murphy reported from Haiti, while Jones filed stories from the League of Nations and from Africa. Some accounts state that Fay Jackson was the sole African American reporter at the coronation, but *The Afro-American*'s Ralph Matthews also covered the event.

These prestigious publications filled a void left by the mainstream media because they reached a more literate and involved black populace and were circulated in such places as India and the Philippines. This robust period was in many ways similar to the golden age of the genre in the mainstream media. In fact, black international news gathering grew exponentially, and the genre came into its own. Reports from Europe and the West Indies covered a wide range of topics and issues during the turbulent decade leading up to World War II. Reports on race relations abroad, European colonialism, and the historic interconnectedness of blacks globally were mixed with coverage of lynchings, discrimination, and social problems in black publications. Black achievement and talent, and America's domination of people of color, were covered. Thus, while the black press could not always field correspondents or generate as many stories as white dailies, black publications provided ample coverage.

Metz Lochard, who for years was the *Chicago Defender*'s foreign editor and editorial-page chief, wrote that the black press had seized the opportunity and exploited "to the fullest" the fact that the world was watching the United States to see how it dealt with its "sore spot," the "negro problem," as it supported democracy around the world.[2] In 1931, the African American press not only continued to demand full rights for its race, it told blacks to *expect* equality. Lochard stated that the black press wielded influence because fewer people controlled the medium. Thus it promoted "a greater unanimity of thinking" that led to "group-action" aimed at bettering the condition of blacks in America. Black newspapers had the "opportunity to prick, hit, hammer and blast the conscience of white America that had nurtured fascism at home."[3]

Providing foreign news took grit and determination. The ANP, which supplied news to more than one hundred member newspapers, constantly solicited them for membership fees to fund foreign news gathering. Director Claude A. Barnett tried to persuade member newspapers to help finance foreign news gathering efforts, but those organs lacked the resources to run their own operations. Through cajoling and convincing arguments that stressed the need to join the struggle, the ANP enticed more than a dozen people to cover foreign affairs for little or no pay. Black publications struggled to stay afloat during the Great Depression. "Things are desperate," Abbott wrote to his nephew John Sengstacke in February 1934.[4] The publisher had not taken a salary for more than three years and had had to lay off his most highly paid female worker. How Abbott was able to pay Hall is unclear. The year before, the directors of his publishing company had directed Abbott to repay two hundred fifty thousand dollars that he had placed in his personal account in 1931 and 1932, while the corporation was in the red to the tune of sixty-six thousand dollars.[5] Despite its hardships, the *Defender* continued to engage in global journalism while highlighting mass unemployment, lack of adequate housing, and lack of jobs for blacks at home. As Lochard stated, "Black editors were smarter as a result of the experience in the last war and the post-war years in which discrimination was not only continued but increased. Their newsgathering facilities had expanded to follow their men around the globe. Their protests were couched in terms of global responsibility and merged with the problems of subjugated people everywhere. Their reading public, with its advancing education, greater race pride, and greater unity, was ready for group action."[6]

By the end of the decade, correspondents for the prestigious African American press were reporting from far-flung places. Chatwood Hall was especially proud that he was not a stringer but a salaried correspondent, not only for the *Defender* but for the *Pittsburgh Courier* and *The Afro-American*. He even had cable facilities.

Chatwood Hall's View from Russia

Homer Smith, writing under the name Chatwood Hall, provided a major service with his reporting from the Soviet Union. This expatriate was seeking equality. That was especially interesting to blacks who wondered whether communism was a viable alternative for blacks relegated to second- or third-class citizenship in America. The *Pittsburgh Courier*'s Robert Vann was a major exception. His biographer Andrew Buni writes that Vann was the "only vehemently anti-communist black editor," although Vann was a product of capitalism and "viewed collectivism as a threat to his own position."[7] Buni found this "perplexing" because Vann's success had come via fellow blacks and "owed nothing to the national system as a whole."[8]

Hall knew that all too well. The twenty-two-year-old aspiring journalist could not find employment commensurate with his talents at home and he was fed up with racism in the United States. The fact that Hall had a degree in journalism from the University of Minnesota (where he first began using his pen name) was of little consequence in Jim Crow America. The best he could do was to write freelance articles while working full-time for the post office, a route many educated blacks took. Fed up with rampant discrimination and entrenched racism at home, Hall sent a letter to Russian officials offering his services as a consultant to the Moscow post office. He received a positive response and was on his way. He wrote in his 1964 memoir, *A Black Man in Red Russia:* "I yearned to stand taller than I had ever stood[,] to breathe total freedom in exhilarating gulps, to avoid all the hurts that were increasingly becoming the lot of men (and women) of color in the United States. The solution seemed simple to me: Russia was the only place where I could go and escape color discrimination entirely. Moscow seemed the answer."[9]

Hall's road to foreign reporting was the result of oppressive conditions for African Americans in the United States. He did not go to Russia only to file reports but to earn a living commensurate with his talents. As soon as he was sure he was headed overseas, he approached the *Chicago Defender* and several other newspapers with his proposition. In Moscow, he implemented practices that made the Russian postal system more efficient. As he learned about his new home, he started his global reporting. The Soviet Union enthusiastically accepted him. Within three days of his request, he had an expansive office on the first floor of the old czarist post office, three assistants, and two typewriters, one with an English keyboard and one with a Russian keyboard.

Hall joined prominent blacks who had already moved to Russia, including Harlem Renaissance poet Claude McKay; black activist and attorney William L. Patterson, who had defended the Scottsboro Boys; author Richard Wright; and noted singer and actor Paul Robeson. These expatriates shared Hall's view of communism and its utopian ideals that eschewed racism and colonialism. Several hundred blacks were living in the Soviet Union by the 1930s. Maxim Matusevich wrote that blacks were "ideological allies of the Soviet Union" and "cultural links" between Russia and the rest of the world.[10] "A black person walking down the street in Moscow or Leningrad immediately assumed political and cultural significance far beyond their otherwise quite modest station in life. . . . [They] were symbolic of Soviet claims of internationalism, one of the cornerstones of new Soviet identity."[11]

Like previous black foreign correspondents, Hall wrote while also doing his primary job. Writing did not become his main endeavor until 1935, when he chose not to renew his contract with the post office. Now he could do what he was unable to do in America—be a "full-time journalist."[12] His first three years in Russia enabled him to become a correspondent in the same mold as mainstream global journalists. He immersed himself in the country, learning about its people and politics, traveling, observing, making contacts, and becoming accepted. He even married a Russian woman. He was in the Great Kremlin Palace, official press card and special pass in hand, when the new Union of Soviet Socialist Republics Constitution was ratified.[13] During the fourteen years Hall lived in Russia, his stories ran not only in the *Chicago Defender* but in other black newspapers. The ANP also distributed his dispatches.[14] The foreign correspondent produced a steady stream of information about life in the Soviet Union, its government, its people, and their views. Race relations figured prominently in the *Defender*'s correspondence from Russia. In fact, Hall's first article, written while he was en route to Russia in July 1933, reported that discussion of the Scottsboro case was banned onboard the steamship *Europa*. Subsequent stories and Hall's "Column from Moscow," which ran regularly from March 1933 through August 1935, gave African Americans insight into the life of Russian natives and compared life for blacks in Russia with life in Jim Crow America. Hall observed that Russian mothers did not allow their children to behave negatively toward or discriminate against "our brothers, our friends."[15] On April 2, 1938, the *Defender*'s foreign news page ran a large picture of an expansive housing development in Russia with Hall's story that announced "Jim Crow Is Unknown in Russia." In one story about race, Hall wrote:

> When the Soviet government came into power following the revolution of 1917 it found in its lap, as a heritage from the czarist regime, an acute race problem, upon the swift liquidation of which depended a great degree the success and consolidation of the victory.
>
> Central Russia, that is, Russia proper, under the czars looked upon other sections of this vast land as colonies, much the same as England considers India or as the U. S. A. considers the Philippines and Haiti. The inhabitants of these "backward" regions were treated as the population of all colonies—oppressed, exploited, considered inferior, denied determination, subjected to Jim Crow laws and many other forms of humiliation.
>
> What did the Soviet Government do in this dilemma? Did it go into a huddle and call "interracial meetings," have "exchanges of pulpits," appeal to public opinion, conscience and heaven, and yell that "You can't change human nature"? Did it cavort about the rear appendage of the race problem "bull" or did it look the beast squarely in the face, grasp him by the horns and ladder him for the "count of 10"?[16]

Hall wrote that the Soviet Union had eliminated economic and cultural discrimination by providing development opportunities. As a result, "the race problem is today a dead issue on at least one-sixth of the surface of the earth. Privileges once enjoyed by certain groups have been abolished; complete equality of rights and privileges exist for all citizens, not in theory but in fact, regardless of race, color, rank or wealth."[17]

In a February 2, 1935, article Hall compared "Red" Russia with "White America." Blacks and whites in Russia could use the same public baths, he wrote, but in America the races could "hardly bathe in close proximity in huge Lake Michigan or the Atlantic Ocean without the imminence of precipitating a race riot."[18] In another article, he found the Soviet agrarian system superior to America's. With the Depression taking its toll in the United States, Hall covered a convention of Russian collective farm workers. He pointed out that the Depression was the worst "agrarian crisis on record," that it was "hanging like a pall of despair and hopelessness over the toiling black farmers . . . and their white agrarian brothers."[19] The Russians had "forever abandoned individual farming, with its ultimate enslavement of the individual farmer, to the landlord, the 'kutak' and the capitalist."[20] Hall also linked people in other lands to blacks when he added that the workers had a "keen interest in the plight of their Negro agrarian brothers in America" and they knew about the "general terror and exploitation to which the toiling race farmers in the South are subjected."[21]

The *Defender* carried Hall's reportage on black entertainers in Russia. He reported on a group of actors who had traveled to Russia amid much fanfare to make *Black and White*, a motion picture about race relations there. He recorded their disappointment with the many delays and, finally, their disgust when the film did not materialize. He conveyed the frustration of the actors, three of whom publicly blamed the Russians for caving in to American pressure. He wrote about a black actor who had been selected to play Othello and about a young singer who had moved Moscow to pursue her career.[22]

Although Hall showed that black entertainers were achieving a modicum of success, his dispatches and columns did not paint a completely rosy picture of race relations in Russia. Six months after his arrival, he wrote that blacks were a novelty in Russia, but Russians were perhaps more knowledgeable about the color-line problem than whites in America. He reported that American whites were cordial to blacks on Soviet soil, "but in the United States these same hospitable 'comrades' would not even notice a dusky American, would feel themselves contaminated to greet a Negro."[23] Hall's use of the word "novelty" echoed Helen Abbott, who used the same word when she wrote to her sister in 1929 about how Europeans reacted to her and her husband. While white correspondents often worked in conjunction with the government,[24] the views of the black press were the polar opposite of the government's. Communism was antithetical to everything the United States espoused, but Hall's laudatory stories showed another side. While blacks at home faced economic and employment discrimination, Hall wrote that job opportunities were plentiful in Russia, where no color line existed.[25]

American foreign correspondents traditionally were envoys and interpreters who sought to create an understanding of foreign affairs and awaken in the American public an appreciation for "its global responsibilities."[26] Black international reporting called on the United States to assume its responsibilities toward race members at home, and Hall and others were the envoys and interpreters who conveyed how and why the world's other nations governed the minorities within their borders.

Unlike the mainstream media's, Hall's dispatches focused on race relations, issues of equality, and the status of people of color in Russia. Much as Abbott had done in his reports from South America and Europe, Hall blamed whites or America for the racial injustice and prejudice he observed in Russia. He depicted America negatively. His view of a utopian Russia eventually changed, and his enthusiasm about the "Soviet experiment" became pessimism when he realized that the country was motivated only by self-interest. Many of the blacks who had flocked there in the 1920s and 1930s were gone by the end of the decade. Hall remained and covered the Russian campaign during World War II for the black press and the Associated Press. He was the only African American stationed in Russia. A disillusioned Hall remained in Russia until October 1946, when he left for Ethiopia to work for its press and information office, and he continued to generate foreign correspondence. He remained in Ethiopia until 1962, when he took his wife and two children back to the country he had left three decades earlier.[27]

The Afro-American: Casting a Light on Africa and Haiti

The Afro-American tried to keep pace with the *Chicago Defender.* The Baltimore weekly newspaper had begun covering the West Indies and Liberia in the late 1920s. It was determined to keep up its coverage in the 1930s. Freed black slaves had founded Liberia in 1822; that was a source of pride for *The Afro-American.* According to historian Hayward Farrar, the newspaper endeavored to showcase "a strong, independent black community" that was "competently and honestly administered by blacks."[28] Despite its goal of portraying Liberia in a positive light, the newspaper eventually exposed the country's slave trading, corruption, and mismanagement. An article that ran in June 1929 reported on the "revolting revelations of open slavery and illegal conscription of natives for forced labor."[29] A Liberian tribal chief had provided that information to a commission probing the slave trade. Later in 1929, the newspaper called for the resignation of Liberian President Charles D. B. King, citing his incompetence.[30] A prominently positioned front-page article with a Paris dateline suggested that the newspaper was concerned that Liberia's precarious state would lead to its takeover by the West. The article both condemned human trafficking in Africa and revealed that Europeans were speculating that the United States would use slavery as a pretext for intervening in the country.[31]

The Afro-American's coverage of Liberia increased in 1933 when managing editor William Jones made a three-month goodwill trip to Africa as a guest of the Liberian government. Jones filed several pieces on his voyage home and wrote a twelve-part series after his return. He sought to awaken the consciousness of African Americans at home and to enlist their help in pressuring the United States to support the continued sovereignty of Liberia. A major piece that bore a Monrovia dateline and was filed by cable via France told readers that the Liberian government was rejecting a United Nations plan that would essentially "turn the country over to white foreigners whose authority would be superior to that of the Liberian government."[32] Reporting on an interview with Liberian Secretary of State L. A. Grimes, Jones was clearly displeased with the plan; he suggested that the predominant white advisor in the country was a dictator whose annual salary of twelve thousand dollars was more than the Liberian president's.

In a brief press cable filed from the *Wadai,* Jones stated that the Liberian legislature had placed its future in American hands, hoping the United States would appoint black advisors, allow immigration from America, and assist Liberia with "internal development."[33] But Jones also wrote about West Africa as a tourist Mecca and a mixed-race couple whose business in Sierra Leone was thriving as a result of trade expansion in Liberia. In late December, Jones filed a summary of his three-month tour. He described Liberia as a country in crisis that nonetheless "was united against the U.S. and the League of Nations plan to place a dictator in charge of the republic."[34] Filing from a German steamship, Jones explained why *The Afro-American* had sent him to Africa: the Liberian government had invited him because it hoped African Americans would gain an understanding of the country's plight, and that their support might affect U.S. policy regarding a plan that could undermine the nation's sovereignty.

The Liberian government overestimated the clout of African Americans in the United States; their influence was virtually nonexistent. The black press and African American leaders were vocal protesters against social and political inequities, but they were almost powerless to change the status quo. Also, the Great Depression had an especially negative impact on blacks, who were already struggling with economic and social discrimination. According to historian John Hope Franklin, 38 percent of blacks did not have the means to support themselves in 1934, compared to 17 percent of whites, and 65 percent of blacks in the South were on the relief rolls.[35] Despite these dire circumstances, *The Afro-American* elevated the discourse and contributed to a growing consciousness of what was transpiring in Africa.

Jones's foreign correspondence was similar to that of Marcus Garvey in *Negro World* a decade earlier. He wrote from an economic perspective, arguing that profit making was the cause of Western imperialism and the domination of Africa. His characterization of America was highly unfavorable. The twelve-part series "Liberia Today, Tomorrow" described the customs and beliefs of native Liberians, but it did not gloss over the problem of slavery. Jones decried the practice of "pawning," using human beings to pay a debt.[36] "There is also no question that in this enlightened day there should be no place in this world whereby one person is forcibly, or even made without his own free consent, to work for another person," he wrote.[37] *The Afro-American* appeared to be presenting all sides of the story, even when a side was not favorable.

Jones's findings and the state of affairs in Liberia prompted *The Afro-American* to launch a nationwide drive to aid the struggling country, and to place the situation on President Franklin D. Roosevelt's agenda. The newspaper promoted its aid campaign, even suggesting that the effort could become a worldwide movement. The names of blacks and whites who supported it ran in the paper and enhanced the perception of the campaign's success. But this effort to influence both national and global politics was largely unsuccessful. Some blacks were indifferent, while the Depression had zapped the resources of those who might be willing to assist. African Americans' lack of political clout with the federal government also was a contributory factor.[38]

Jones was part of the international story he reported, fulfilling *The Afro-American*'s role of advocacy and action. While Jones was a guest of the Liberian government and treated almost like royalty, he was also the voice that presented information and a perspective blacks believed were missing in the mainstream media. *The Afro-American* held the United States to a higher standard than what it was practicing and promoting in Liberia and called on it to change its policies and actions.

The Afro-American also reported from Haiti during the 1930s. Carl Murphy, who had sent letters from Germany to his father's newspaper before World War I, was now the publisher. In that capacity, he went to Haiti as part of the (Robert R.) Moton Commission that President Herbert Hoover had set up to explore conditions on the island and its ability to sustain itself.[39] Percival Prattis, who had joined the ANP news agency in 1923 and was now its assistant editor, was also on that trip. Both Murphy and Prattis were against the American occupation of Haiti.[40] The Moton Commission arrived on June 17, 1930, and Murphy's front-page dispatches began running on June 21. As many as three of the publisher's dispatches ran weekly during the six weeks the six-member commission was in Haiti.

Murphy presented a holistic view of the locales from which he reported. His dispatches described developments in Haiti, its terrain, and its government. He also wrote about the Haitians' distrust of America.[41] His first pieces stated that Haitians had greeted the commission members warmly. He described a long, rugged trip on dirt roads over a three thousand-foot mountain in a long article that revealed the reasons for strained relations between Haiti and the United States. Haitians, according to Murphy, believed that improvements to the country's education system and infrastructure had been "rammed" down their throats instead of being developed cooperatively. The islanders also despised U.S. marines and blamed them for the establishment of brothels where none had existed before. Finally, Haitians disliked the American press because they believed that the marines who were correspondents for the Associated Press and United Press news agencies were biased and did not tell the real story.[42]

Other articles provided a complimentary view of the commission by outlining its activities. Murphy implied that the commission was hard-working and that Moton had succeeded in averting a strike at a U.S.-run university where the enrollment had shrunk from more than two hundred to fewer than thirty-eight students under white administration.[43] His dispatches provided context for what fifteen years of U.S. rule in Haiti had meant to the nation. Murphy clearly supported the Haitians' desire for the United States to leave the country, although the people were grateful for improvements to roads and the education system, and for freeing the country from revolution.

"Get Out of Haiti" was the headline of an editorial that ran after Murphy's return. The piece discussed the economic, social, and political ramifications of the occupation; while the United States had done good works in Haiti, it had also injected "white supremacy in liberal doses" and created an environment in which blacks had no rights that whites "were bound to respect."[44] The editorial also charged that American marines, teachers, and businessmen were exploiting Haitians and destroying their culture while preparing for a permanent occupation. This same system of oppression flourished in the United States, the piece opined. One of Murphy's especially hard-hitting pieces compared racial policies and practices in Haiti to the dynamic in the United States. "In places similar to the ones they filled in Dixie, there stand today the hard, cold Americans in Haitian schools, talking to the Frenchmen in English, despising their scholars' race and their scholars' culture, one eye on the clock and the other on the payroll. . . . To us there seems to be one decent and proper thing to do; namely, to get out of Haiti in 1936, and then stay out. . . . Nothing else can save the United States from its own greed, restore its self-respect, and clear its own conscience."[45]

Murphy's militant reporting reflected his independence; although he was in Haiti as a representative of the U.S. government, he did not hesitate to reveal inequities and criticize his own country. He wrote from the perspective of a black American, not just an American. He acknowledged the positive aspects of the U.S. occupation, but believed Haiti deserved its independence and its people their basic rights.

After Murphy's return from Haiti, *The Afro-American* continued its commitment to foreign reporting. In 1932 and 1934, it commissioned educator and historian Rayford Logan to cover the Cuban revolution. William Jones reported on communism from the Soviet Union. Meanwhile, other black newspapers also provided a steady stream of international news. Adolf Hitler's march to war soon became a primary theme.

Prelude to The Great War: Chronicling Hitler's Aggression

Black newspapers initially appeared to support Germany, which editors viewed as oppressed by the Allies after the ratification of the Treaty of Paris, which had stripped it of its territories. But a few years would make a tremendous difference in their views. In 1932, the *Chicago Defender* appeared to express pride in Hitler when it quoted an American student who received the newspaper in Berlin as saying that it "was regarded as a Hitler paper."[46] The student said that the postal worker who delivered his newspaper had pointed to the swastika in the headline on page 1 and expressed surprise "that Hitler was getting co-operation from our Race in America."[47] The *Defender* did not disavow Hitler in that piece.

An editorial in the *Pittsburgh Courier* pointed out that Germany's action was a lesson for African Americans. Germany had become a "down and out" minority after the Treaty of Versailles, the *Courier* said, but the country had taken matters into its own hands—unlike U.S. blacks who passively accepted the status quo. Germany became "militantly organized" to remove "the military boot of the allies firmly on her neck."[48] Equating Germany with a weak and oppressed group, the *Courier* stressed that, for African Americans to get what they really wanted, they should be less timid and put up an unapologetic "solid, united front," as Germany had. Failure to demand liberty or death—as

Patrick Henry did—was one reason blacks had never reached a higher social and economic status; Germany may not have the world's sympathy, but it was getting its "place in the sun."[49]

As Hitler advanced toward war, the black press ran many articles about the Nazis, German aggression, and the plight of the Jewish community in Germany.[50] The *Chicago Defender* reported that the International Olympic Committee was reconsidering its decision to award the 1936 games to Berlin. When the city was chosen, no one really knew who Hitler was, the newspaper maintained. Now the *Defender* called him a "blustering imitation for Mussolini" who was "storming around Germany trying to put on a Ku Klux Klan act of its own."[51] *The Afro-American* reported that Hitler was on a quest to make Germany "a pure Aryan race" and that the country had placed some three hundred "mixed and colored families in a precarious situation."[52]

While Jim Crow dominated national news in the black press, Hitler dominated foreign correspondence. "How Jews Fare under Hitler Regime; Noted English Correspondent Reveals Inside Facts of Horrors Perpetrated by Germans on Defenseless Minority Groups; Nazis Stop at Nothing in Their Campaign of Barbarous Cruelties; A New Reign of Terror," read the headline on a *Defender* story in June 1934.[53] The *Defender*'s foreign news service alone provided coverage from Paris, London, and Switzerland. The *Atlanta Daily World* ran ANP stories, and its Scott News Syndicate joined the group of black publications receiving news directly from overseas. "Figures in the Grim Drama of Germany's 'Second Revolution,'" the *Daily World* announced on July 6, 1934, and the following week, "Hitler Worried over Many Problems of Germany's Future." Hitler's racism was the topic of a piece about the dictator's banning jazz in Germany.

Although the Olympic Committee reconsidered the location of the games, it allowed Germany to keep the event. By 1935, the *Pittsburgh Courier*—and the rest of the black press—wanted to know how the German chancellor would treat black and Jewish athletes. The *Courier* took the bold step of sending a cable to Hitler on July 15. Surprisingly, the newspaper received a response. On September 7, 1935, a banner headline announced, "*Courier* 'Scooped' Nation on Inquiry about Germany's Attitude toward Negroes in Olympics." The story revealed that the "German Reich Athletic Committee" had replied that the athletes would not face discrimination. It also pointed out that the *Courier* "was on the job" well in advance of other newspapers and was aware "of the subtle efforts to make Negro athletes the 'goat' in a fight in which they had no direct interest."[54] When the games finally began, *Courier* editor Robert Vann was on the scene.

The historic event became even more significant for blacks because sprinter/jumper Jesse Owens and other talented black athletes were competing in racist and fascist Germany. Vann realized that covering this momentous event was not a job for correspondents, stringers, or travelers. As owner and publisher of the *Courier*, he had the desire and the means to travel to Berlin to be an eyewitness to history. His August 8 dispatch indicated that Hitler had saluted Owens,[55] and gave an account of the track star's triumphant performance at the Olympics. More important, the dispatch stated that Hitler had to eat his words. A member of the race that Hitler considered subhuman won gold in the 100- and 200-meter races, defeated Germany's Luz Long in the broad jump for another gold medal, and ran on the 4 x 100 relay that also won gold. Owen set or tied world records in all four events; he had "stamped himself the greatest athlete in modern Olympic history," the newspaper boasted.[56]

Vann quoted Owens following his victory over Long: "I am proud that I am an American. I see the sun breaking through the clouds when I realize that all Americans will recognize now that what I and the boys of my race are trying to do is attempted for the glory of our country and our countrymen. Maybe more people will now realize that the Negro is trying to do his full part as an American citizen."[57]

The 1936 Olympics gave the black press the opportunity to expose the fallacy of Hitler's ideology and to convey racial pride by chronicling black achievement of monumental proportions. Following the defeat of Ethiopia, blacks in the United States had been dejected and disappointed but they now had something to uplift them. News of Owens's memorable performance came not only via the *Pittsburgh Courier*, but also from the *Chicago Defender* and other African American publications as well as the mainstream press, which covered Owens's wins in detail.

Although the *Defender* provided coverage primarily via its foreign news service, the first piece about Owens's arrival in Germany was written by Joe Jefferson. Owens and the two other black members of the U.S. track team had received a cordial reception, Jefferson reported. Although Hitler personified racial hatred, he could not openly slight, segregate, or discriminate against any member of an Olympic team because, as Jefferson noted, the Third Reich was host to the games and any such action "would be a blot on the international sports horizon."[58]

The *Defender* relished the fact that Owens had "demonstrated his superiority" by equaling the world record in the 100-meter final. That win disproved Hitler's claim of black inferiority. Owens was the "god of the sports fans" in Germany, the *Defender* proclaimed, pointing out that thousands in the stadium had given the Olympian a standing ovation when he edged into the lead after breaking from fourth position. The spectators stood up to honor a "brown-skinned boy, to one whose race [was] winning battle after battle in his homeland against tremendous odds."[59] Here, and in other pieces, the *Defender* reinforced the theme of black achievement as a route to racial elevation. The newspaper pointed out that other black athletes, including high jump gold medalist Cornelius Johnson of California, also had stellar performances despite clearly discriminatory treatment.[60] Johnson's fighting spirit and coolness under pressure were evident in a story that said some Olympic officials had refused to accept his Olympic record jump of six feet, eight inches, while others had tried to unnerve the athlete. The officials measured the bar several times while Johnson waited. One could almost sense the anxiety of his coaches, who feared the wait might cause Johnson to lose his focus. He did not. "He walked back, carefully measured his stride, moved in slowly with his head on one side as though he had a stiff neck and in one of the most perfect leaps ever witnessed, cleared the bar perfectly."[61]

During the next two years, the black press wrote about Germany's view of communism and Hitler's demands of Great Britain. "Four-Power Lineup in Europe Sought to Solve Problem; France, Britain, Germany and Italy Seen as 'Guardian Quartet'; Nazis Ask Colony" was the headline for a dispatch in the *Chicago Defender* on July 25, 1936. A month later, the *Atlanta Daily World* proclaimed "Success of Spanish Rebels Stirs Alarm in Europe." The *New York Amsterdam News* followed with "Hitler Ideas on Race Are Bunk, Savant Says, Hitting 'Aryans.'" Acrimony toward Hitler was so great that in August the *Pittsburgh Courier* opined that he was "Just Poor White Trash," adding, "You can drag a man out of the gutter but you cannot drag the gutter out of a man."[62]

Black foreign correspondents filed dispatches calling attention to international policies and practices and contrasting them with America's exclusion of blacks from the social, political, and economic mainstream. The *Chicago Defender* editorialized in November 1937 that forces in the United States were in the same category as fascist-led Germany, Italy, and Japan as they sought to control and suppress the masses worldwide. The first camp included the dominant political parties in the United States, the Ku Klux Klan, the Liberty

League, the Black League—all fascists, according to the *Defender*—who were "preparing with all energy, ruthlessness, and demagogy to seize control of government."[63] Neither camp was acceptable, the editorial argued, stressing that fascism could not be allowed to take hold in the United States because it would erase all the advances blacks had made. Blacks should join liberals in America to secure their future.

The role blacks would play in a world war was addressed by the *Pittsburgh Courier* in "an exclusive 'inside story'" about why the British and the French had capitulated to Hitler's demands. The piece stated that "detached" and "dispassionate observers" from the two nations believed "a million black men" in their African colonies would have been "pounding" on Germany's back door, no longer willing to fight for their exploiters.[64] The article found the British and French empires "decadent" and charged that Western powers derived "their comfort and position in the world of affairs from the backs of black and brown men, millions in Africa and Asia."[65] These same men who lived in grinding poverty could no longer be counted on to protect the empires. The *Courier* then reminded readers that Emperor Haile Selassie had warned the League of Nations that if it sacrificed Ethiopia, other nations might soon fall. These newspapers were no longer detached, and they had long since stopped viewing Germany as oppressed. Once they realized that Hitler's worldview was as detrimental to the world's darker people as the United States' color-line problem, black publications ran foreign correspondence that not only placed the troubling developments on the public agenda, but also molded public opinion regarding the impact of this global event.

Covering a Coronation: A Respite from War

Ralph Matthews was walking down a street in Harlem one night when he noticed that the African and West Indian people he passed were talking about the upcoming coronation of King George VI in England, Hitler's rise in Germany, and the exile of Ethiopian emperor Haile Selassie. Matthews sent his boss, *The Afro-American* publisher Carl Murphy, a wire that read: "Have you noticed that when he becomes King of the British Empire he becomes ruler of three-fourths of the black people of the world [sic], the *AFRO* can't ignore that." Murphy's quick one-line response was "Get the next boat."[66] An expense account accompanied the directive.

Matthews related that exchange in a tribute to Carl Murphy when the publisher died in 1967. Matthews, who had worked for the newspaper for forty years, explained the rationale not only for *The Afro-American*'s decision to cover the coronation but for its whole approach to foreign correspondence: "Either [Murphy] was pitching me forward passes or I was pitching them to him, and they carried me around the world. He could always see the news possibilities of a news scoop without drawing a map. I always felt we were building a new image of the colored press getting away from the crime and humdrum trivialities of the ghetto, getting out into the mainstream. Before many months had passed he had assigned other correspondents to every theatre of World War II in Europe, Asia and Africa, and got a kick out of keeping his men spotted on the map with pins so he could contact them on a moment's notice."[67]

Matthews headed for Great Britain in April. He and Fay Jackson of the ANP were the only African American correspondents on the scene. This coronation was more than the anointing of a ruler; it was an event that would have an impact on people of color throughout the world.

The Afro-American had been unable to field correspondents during the Italian-Ethiopian War, but now Murphy could boast that his newspaper would provide firsthand, eyewitness coverage. *The Afro-American* devoted an entire page of the May 8, 1937, issue to articles that Matthews and the ANP had filed from England and Africa. Matthews reported on how African leaders felt about home rule and on "England's betrayal of Ethiopia." Jackson was probably the source of the British coverage, although she did not have a byline.

Both Matthews and Jackson reported through the lens of race. The two dozen stories Matthews filed highlighted racial achievement and discussed opportunities for blacks in England. Soon after he arrived, he filed a story about discrimination at the festivities. He wrote that India's Mahatma Gandhi and the "oppressed masses he represented were almost forgotten" during the coronation, while India's princes received a royal welcome. "There is no time or place for the forgotten man as pomp and circumstances of many nations, races and people crowd all else out of the picture," he observed.[68] He explained that under British colonialism brown-skinned princes did not consider themselves subservient to the British but saw themselves as allies, and the British treated them as such. Nevertheless, those who wanted independence for India were brewing dissent.

Matthews's eyewitness accounts illuminated Great Britain's role in the developing global conflict. England, he wrote, was recruiting troops and rearming in the event of war. British shipyards were bustling with activity; one of the country's largest carriers had "suddenly been recalled from condemnation" and was being outfitted to carry troops.[69]

Like Matthews, Fay Jackson reported on the treatment of darker populations. Dispatches headlined "Only Twenty Native Troops at Coronation" and "Colored Subjects Given Back Seats at the Coronation" described the invisibility of black citizens of the British Empire. Jackson went beyond coverage of the festivities and provided social and political commentary. One dispatch, for instance, quoted a South African defense minister who said that the country allowed "the colored man every opportunity for development under European guardianship, but under no circumstances social or political equality."[70] The official maintained that non-Europeans in Asia were weary of white supremacy, and that black South Africans would probably soon become allies of the East. To make her stories more believable, Jackson cited stories in the mainstream press in the same fashion as previous black foreign correspondents.

The lone ANP correspondent revealed that although the British Empire had four hundred million black people under its rule, only two African chiefs were official representatives at the coronation. "In this gigantic procession, where will the black peoples stand?" she asked. "What place in the panoramic sweep of the human family do they occupy?"[71] She wrote that Africans and African Americans had both been enslaved and exploited. "The American black man has given labor and love; song and science; blood and art to his country. What does he get in return? The African has given these—gilt-edged when civilization was young—plus the wealth from above and beneath the ground of his native land. What has he got in return? The British African as well as the American of color stands sadly alone, neglected and weak among the human family of the world today. Nobody cares. Ethiopia's case showed that; the coronation will prove it."[72]

Such stories contradicted previous foreign correspondence, which had touted amicable race relations in Europe. Jackson had even alluded to an absence of overt prejudice in a letter to Claude Barnett in April, but less than a month later she unveiled overt racial discrimination in England and at the coronation. She wrote that "people talked about and admitted racial bias existed below the surface. . . . When it comes to jobs, a Jig just doesn't have a chance and that goes for all darkies: Indian, Africans, Malayans, etc."[73]

In the 1930s, when blacks were almost invisible in the mainstream media, the black press placed people of color on its front pages and provided a unique perspective on foreign affairs. Black correspondents provided not just straightforward accounts of events but also an interpretation of what it meant to be black. Their reporting enlightened readers about the impact of world events on African Americans and kindred people worldwide, especially the interactions of the United States and Western countries with weaker nations. They depicted the class struggle and exploitation that preserved the status quo. They educated, informed, and shaped public opinion. At the end of the decade, African American international journalism was poised to become even more aggressive in reporting on the forces that would shape the world in the years to come.

[7]
Getting the Inside Information
The Italian-Ethiopian War

The 1930s had barely begun when Tafari Makonnen was crowned Haile Selassie, emperor of Ethiopia. The country had a rich history that dated back more than two thousand years, and Selassie claimed direct descent from King Solomon and the Queen of Sheba. His ascent in the independent black state was a source of pride for blacks' psyche. Black editors viewed coverage of Ethiopia as their duty and often ran front-page stories on it, as well as letters from people who supported the African nation. A *Chicago Defender* story with an Addis Ababa dateline blared on October 25, 1930, "Abyssinia Ready for Coronation."[1] The *Pittsburgh Courier* also had its own "inside story" on the coronation, thanks to correspondent Joel Augustus Rogers, who had been freelancing from abroad since 1923.[2]

Five years after the historic coronation, Ethiopia struggled to maintain its sovereignty. In October 1935, the fascist government of Italy's Benito Mussolini invaded Ethiopia. That event took African American foreign correspondence to a new level as the Associated Negro Press (ANP) news service, the *Chicago Defender,* and the *Pittsburgh Courier* brought firsthand coverage of the war to their readers. In fact, the *Courier* became the first African American newspaper to send a foreign correspondent. "I am in this historic, ancient city [Cairo] tonight . . . and I'm getting inside information direct from the war zone, which gives a different slant to this Ethiopian-Italian war," Rogers reported in November 1935.[3]

As Italian troops advanced on Addis Ababa on October 3, Western powers refused to impose more than the mildest economic sanctions against Italy. France and Great Britain were far more concerned with the burgeoning threat posed by Hitler's Germany than with the Italian invasion of Ethiopia. European powers feared that a harsh admonition of Italian aggression might alienate Mussolini and prevent his signing of the collective security pact upon which they depended to counter the German threat.

Haile Selassie petitioned the League of Nations for support but was met with a tepid response. Because Selassie was suspicious of the European powers whose colonies surrounded Ethiopia, he sought the intervention of a disinterested power, the United States. But America's policy of isolationism and nonintervention precluded its involvement. President Franklin D. Roosevelt ignored the National Association for the Advancement of Colored People's (NAACP's) appeal that he and the State Department condemn Italy's aggression, cease issuing loans to Italy, and stop selling Italian war bonds.[4] Assured of free rein in Ethiopia, Mussolini embarked upon a campaign of indiscriminate violence to subdue the African state. Italian troops employed all the weaponry of modern warfare, including poison gases.

African Americans roundly condemned Italian aggression in Ethiopia and rallied around the Ethiopian issue. Black newspapers universally supported Ethiopia and "dismissed Italian claims as fascist fabrications."[5] Thanks to growing subscriptions and advertising, the black press, which had long depended on subsidies from political parties, could speak more freely.

Before the war began, *The Afro-American* had sent William Jones, editor of its Philadelphia edition, to cover the proceedings at the League of Nations. A story on September 14, 1935, reported Ethiopia's resolve to protect its sovereignty if the League of Nations failed to act on its behalf. Two weeks later, Jones filed a story stating that Ethiopia's foreign minister had told the league the country would not bow to Italy's ultimatum that it be colonized. The National Urban League and the NAACP published pro-Ethiopian articles in their magazines, and Ethiopian relief organizations raised funds to support the country. Two black American aviators, Col. John C. "Johnny" Robinson and Hubert Julian, went to Ethiopia to defend the African state. Ultimately, however, blacks' impact on the war proved almost negligible. The Great Depression limited African American support. The Justice Department's threat to revoke the citizenship of any American who enlisted in Selassie's army further curbed black involvement with Ethiopia.

The ANP Tries to Get a Head Start

The ANP tried to obtain coverage from Africa, but lacked the means to send reporters there. Col. Robinson sent stories that ran under the byline Wilson James. Nancy Cunard, the British socialite whose parents had disinherited her because she associated with blacks, also filed stories about the conflict. In February 1935, Claude Barnett asked Malaka Bayen to translate news of interest from newspapers he was receiving from Africa, and to recommend individuals who could report from the continent. Seven months later, Barnett expressed disappointment because he had not heard from Bayen. "Just what is the difficulty? . . . The Negro papers are full of Ethiopian affairs."[6] Bayen eventually responded that he was not getting much from African newspapers he received.

The ANP and major black publications were fighting to survive. P. L. Prattis of the *New York Amsterdam News* told Claude Barnett in July 1935 that he was "feeling around to discover a method for paying cable tolls from Ethiopia" that cost one hundred dollars for five hundred words.[7] In November 1935, Barnett wrote to Prattis, C. A. Scott of the *Atlanta Daily World*, and P. B. Young of the *Norfolk Journal and Guide* to suggest that two or three newspapers pool their resources to pay for "two or three hundred words once or twice a week from Addis Ababa."[8] Barnett told them he had not heard from Robinson in three weeks and proposed that the editors join him in using Robinson's dispatches along with material from the news services. Prattis turned him down, saying that the *Amsterdam News* was forty-three thousand dollars in debt and insolvent. Moreover, it was having trouble paying its ANP bills.[9] The other publishers said they would consider the proposition, but they never contributed. The ANP had no choice but to rely on Robinson.

Their arrangement was fraught with pitfalls. Robinson was not a writer. His primary role was volunteer pilot and leader of the Imperial Ethiopian Air Force. He had gone to Ethiopia at Selassie's behest, acquiring a visa by telling U.S. authorities he was going there on business. He arrived in May 1935, took charge of one of the better aircraft, and began flying reconnaissance missions, transporting supplies, and even piloting the emperor. The dashing fighter pilot, dubbed the Brown Condor, wanted to oblige the ANP, but his first duty was waging war.

Robinson had difficulty obtaining information from Ethiopian sources who sometimes stonewalled him. His letters often reached the ANP late and contained outdated information. One communication was especially embarrassing to the ANP. Barnett wrote to Robinson in mid-October, "We received your letter in which you said there would not be a war in your opinion, and as soon as the paper hit the streets with the story, the Italians started shooting. We got razzed a bit on that one."[10]

Several stories based on Robinson's reports ran in *The Afro-American* in October 1935. One account quoted Robinson as saying the Ethiopian air force was hopelessly outmatched, while another revealed that nearly two thousand Ethiopians had been killed in a bombing raid.[11] In December 1935, Barnett informed Robinson that two of his letters had finally arrived. He had not heard from Robinson in weeks, and he feared the lines of communication had been damaged.[12] Four months later, Barnett told Robinson that his letter of February 28 had not reached the ANP until April 1. Robinson was preparing to leave Ethiopia and return to the United States. Things were going poorly for Ethiopia, Barnett later wrote, but the United States was pulling for the African country. "These white nations must feel pretty cheap, letting an armed nation like Italy triumph over an unarmed people in that fashion."[13]

The ANP's arrangement with Robinson indicated the precarious nature of the news service's war coverage. Barnett, for instance, based several stories on the aviator's letters but protected his identity.[14] The quasi correspondent did not try to paint a glowing picture of a triumphant Ethiopia. Things were not what Robinson expected—they were "in some cases much better and in other cases 100 percent worst [sic]." Robinson reported to Barnett that blacks would only succeed if they possessed "A Strong Stomach—A Silent Tongue—A Kind Heart—An Iron Hand—The Patience of Jobe [sic], and above all things, Know His Line of Work."[15]

Because the black press gave primacy to the interconnectedness of Africa and African Americas, Robinson's letter had major racial and social implications. He revealed that Ethiopians did not have a good opinion of American blacks, primarily because strong white influence had turned the Abyssinians against them. This observation was especially sobering because blacks at home took pride in the oneness of Africans and their descendants. Robinson also addressed the economic status of Ethiopians, explaining that whites, Indians, and Greeks—not blacks—controlled Ethiopia's commercial businesses.[16]

The ANP also ran dispatches from Nancy Cunard, the white British activist turned correspondent who first reported from Moscow and London. Cunard's major focus was communism, which she embraced, and fascism, which she detested. Her first dispatch, in the *Pittsburgh Courier*, expressed her concern about the lack of coverage of the Italian-Ethiopian War in European newspapers.

Cunard's stay in Moscow was brief; by December, she was back home and reporting on the war from London. One article reassured blacks that other race members were on the side of the Ethiopians. As proof, Cunard stated that black writers and intellectuals had gathered in France in a symbolic protest against Italy's attack on Ethiopia. She argued that governments and missionaries promoted French colonialism. "Yet out of this what kind of race equality has come?" she asked. "None."[17]

As the battles in Ethiopia continued, Cunard moved to Paris and wrote even more about the conflict. She argued that most citizens of Europe were not guided by fascist principles. She summarized letters from Italian citizens who denounced the war against Ethiopia, quoting Italian officers who said that the war was "not of the Italian people's making but of Mussolini's."[18]

The *Pittsburgh Courier* Brings the War Home

The *Pittsburgh Courier* did not want to rely on the ANP, so it sent Joel Augustus Rogers to Africa. A respected historian and gifted lecturer, Rogers had periodically written for the paper; as the first black foreign correspondent that the black press fielded, he had earned the *Courier* a place in black and media history. He left for Ethiopia in late October 1935. The *Courier*'s editor wrote that he had sent Rogers to the war zone because "white sources about the Italo-Ethiopian War were unreliable and unsatisfactory, [and] that the real news of what was going on must be secured by Negro journalists whose color and known Ethiopian sympathies would enable them to get the truth."[19] The newspaper's decision to field its own correspondent reflected its concern that a great nation was in jeopardy. If Ethiopia were defeated, what would be the impact on other nations populated by blacks? The sovereignty and preservation of Africa was the same concern *The Afro-American* had had regarding Liberia in the 1920s and that George Washington Williams had had about the continent in the late 1800s.[20]

The *Courier* announced in a page 1 story that Rogers was going overseas to get the inside story and the exclusives. It charged that censorship prevented the previous correspondent (whom the newspaper did not name) from getting out accurate stories.[21] Columns in the newspaper detailed the positive responses readers had to Rogers's reports from East Africa and offered quotes from individuals who said they were glad to have someone whose reporting they could trust covering this important event.[22]

The War through Rogers's Eyes

In his earliest writings on the war, Rogers eschewed the Eurocentric coverage in the mainstream media. While the *New York Times* called it the Italo-Ethiopian conflict, Rogers recast the crisis as the Ethiopian-Italian War,[23] thus asserting the centrality of the African state in the conflict. He saw the Italian invasion of Ethiopia as significant in its own right rather than as a collateral concern in Great Power politics. The *New York Times* emphasized the international context and focused on the potential for the conflict to precipitate a larger European crisis if French and British officials could not find a way to mollify Mussolini.

Other mainstream papers also gave Ethiopia second-tier status and largely ignored the rest of Africa. In October 1935, the *Chicago Daily Tribune* focused on the Italian military and the impact the war would have on other European countries,[24] with scant mention of its effect on Ethiopia and other African countries. The *Tribune* reported on October 8 that three areas in Ethiopia were in Italian hands and that a League of Nations council had called Italy's invasion of Ethiopia an "act of war against all other members of the league."[25]

To counter such coverage, Rogers pointed out inaccuracies in its war reports. His stories emphasized the brutality, inhumanity, and illegality of the Italian invasion and its indiscriminate bombing campaign; he also wrote about the pluck of the Ethiopian defenders.[26] The *Courier* made no attempt at journalistic objectivity and instead gave Rogers the oxymoronic order to report "the unbiased news from Ethiopia's point of view."[27] Rogers functioned as an advocate for Selassie and the Ethiopian cause. His reports attempted to counter inaccurate information, based on Italian propaganda, which was perpetrated by the media in Europe and the United States. This partisan reporting reflects the advocacy and activism that historically characterized African American newspapers, which saw themselves as vehicles for social change and racial solidarity.[28]

Rogers's dispatches—sometimes two or three per issue—appeared in the *Courier* between October 1935 and April 1936. The paper also ran articles by an unnamed correspondent who portrayed Ethiopian fighters as gallant and Italians as barbarous. "Bravely advancing into the barrels of the Italians' death-dealing machine guns," ran one report, "the fierce Danakila tribesmen courageously charged upon the Italian advance parties."[29] The *Courier* subtly acknowledged that the Ethiopians were losing but couched the defeat as a source of pride for African Americans. Rogers's coverage, while sympathetic to the Ethiopian cause, reflected a more professional journalistic standard; his stories were less vitriolic and more factual. But he often assumed a triumphant tone in accounts of Ethiopian counterattacks on Italian bombers. On one occasion, he described the Africans as "among the greatest sharpshooters in the world" and hailed Selassie as a "master-diplomat" who was "ruthless when the need arises, but generally soft-spoken and tactful."[30] Rogers cited examples of "Italian propaganda" that went unchallenged by the mainstream press. Of the Italian version of the capture of Makale following fierce fighting, Rogers declared, "This is all a lie. The town was ordered evacuated by Emperor Haile Selassie, and very few, if any, lives were lost."[31] Mainstream journals attempted to divide Ethiopians and African Americans by claiming that Haile Selassie identified himself as a white man. This, too, was a lie, Rogers told readers. "Don't Be Fooled," he cautioned them, and he urged them to send assistance to Ethiopia.[32] The reporter scored an exclusive interview with a defiant Selassie, who vowed to fight until the last Italian had left Ethiopia and who solicited support from African Americans.[33]

Rogers acknowledged that he relied on official communiqués from the Ethiopian army but justified this with the argument that no foreign reporter was telling the Ethiopian side of the story. The Ethiopian government did not allow reporters within hundreds of miles of the fighting, ostensibly to ensure their safety. The *Courier* reminded its readers that every other American newspaper was covering the Italian side of the war and that Rogers was the only correspondent reporting from the Ethiopian side.

After five months in Ethiopia, Rogers left the country, still asserting that Italy had not subdued Ethiopia.[34] He concluded that Italian successes had been overstated and predicted that poor morale and exorbitant costs would precipitate Italy's withdrawal from Ethiopia. History tells us that was not the case. Such assertions deviate from standard journalistic practices and reflect the mythical status assigned to Ethiopia by many African Americans. On April 25, Rogers noted the impending fall of the Ethiopian capital and blamed the League of Nations' impotence and the Italians' indiscriminate bombing campaigns.[35] While Rogers's coverage of the conflict was polemical and uncritical, his presence provided a much-needed balance to the dominant portrayals of the crisis. His work was not embraced by all blacks, however. W. E. B. Du Bois commented that "no man has revealed so many important facts about the Negro race as has Rogers. [But] his mistakes are many and his background narrow."[36]

Not to Be Outdone: The *Chicago Defender* Covers the Conflict

Rogers's coverage of the Italian-Ethiopian War catapulted the *Pittsburgh Courier* to national fame as a pioneer and leader in the black press.[37] The *Chicago*

Defender also ambitiously reported on the conflict. The newspaper had shown its commitment well before the war started. Not long after Selassie assumed the throne, the *Defender*'s foreign news service reported on the emperor's plan to end slavery. Three days into 1931, foreshadowing the Italian-Ethiopian War, the news service reported that an Italian raid had killed more than two hundred Ethiopians. The war began four years later, but the seeds of conflict had been planted in 1931.

In January 1934, the *Chicago Defender* presented Ethiopia's side of the story in a piece from its bureau in Geneva. The article said that the League of Nations' foreign minister in Addis Ababa had telegraphed that the Ethiopians and Italians had recently clashed on the border of Somaliland.[38] When war seemed inevitable, the *Defender*'s headlines painted an optimistic picture of Ethiopia's preparation for war. "Doom and Destruction Await Italy in Ethiopia, Says Expert; Mussolini's Troops Can Never Conquer African Warriors," read one. A *Defender* story on March 9, 1935, offered this rosy assessment: "Day after day new troops headed by their chieftains ride down from the mountains that almost completely hide this town from the world, and stack their arms in view of the Emperor's castle."[39] The writer described Selassie conferring with his advisors on the best way "of keeping the troops from far-off Italy from grabbing up his kingdom as white soldiers have gobbled up the rest of Africa."[40] A June 1935 article predicted that war would begin by September and charged that European diplomats were tying Ethiopia's hands so Italy could steal the country's mineral resources.[41] By August, an unnamed *Defender* correspondent in Lima, Kenya, charged that Arab nations were profiting at Ethiopia's expense.[42]

The *Defender* boasted the following year that it "had scooped all newspapers by nearly two months" in predicting the start of the war.[43] Credit for such a scoop belonged to the newspaper's correspondents, its "intelligent grasp of the situation," and its ability to unveil the Italian plot to invade Ethiopia, the newspaper boasted.[44] A July 1935 editorial advised African Americans who wanted to go to Ethiopia to fight not to do it because they did not have independence at home.

The *Defender* relied on two correspondents in Ethiopia, Martin Dwyer and "Operative No. 22," a pseudonym for foreign editor Metz Lochard.[45] The identity of Dwyer is unknown; he may have been a real correspondent using a pseudonym or a reporter at home rewriting stories from mainstream dailies. The *Defender* said that he had been in Ethiopia for several years before the war and had also reported from Paris and Cork, Ireland. Eighteen stories under

Dwyer's byline ran between June and December 1935, when he was purportedly in Ethiopia. The July 20 issue of the *Defender* ran three large photos of military maneuvers under the headline, "Ethiopia's Artillery Readies for Mussolini—Volunteers Pour in for War."[46] This dispatch reported Selassie's resolve not to accept France and Great Britain's proposal to give Italy "certain territorial privileges."[47] A laudatory piece on August 24 depicted Selassie as a man with the weight of the world on his shoulders but up to the task. "Being a man of destiny, he carries his cross as did another Man of Destiny at Golgotha, 1935 years ago in Palestine across the Red Sea."[48]

In an earlier posting, Dwyer had optimistically reported that a "super-efficient secret service system," which provided Selassie with information about the remotest parts of Ethiopia, would thwart Mussolini. "Without benefit of telephones, radio, or telegraphs as developed in Western countries," Dwyer wrote, "the Emperor's scouts, runners, and spies have so supplied their government with information that the Ethiopian campaign has practically been mapped out before the conflict begins."[49] Such coverage was skewed and misleading, but it contributed to racial pride in America.

On May 2, 1936, Selassie fled Addis Ababa to begin a five-year exile in England. Despite the refusal of the United States and the Soviet Union to recognize Italy's conquest and annexation of Ethiopia, Mussolini proclaimed himself king of Italy and emperor of Ethiopia. Guerrilla fighting persisted over the next five years, and Selassie returned to power in 1941. The Italian-Ethiopian War had significant international political implications. The inability of the League of Nations to mediate the crisis made the organization irrelevant and precipitated its demise. France's and Great Britain's acquiescence to Italian aggression did not preclude a German-Italian alliance. Antagonized by French and British condemnation of the invasion of Ethiopia, and emboldened by the Western powers' failure to curb his imperial aspirations, Mussolini entered into a Rome-Berlin Axis pact in October 1936. He withdrew from the League of Nations a year later. World War II was in the making.

Despite its sometimes biased and misleading characterization of the war, the black press lifted Ethiopia from its marginalized status and provided a view of the Italian-Ethiopian War that the mainstream media did not. The *Chicago Defender* explained a year after the war's end that it could have done no less. It "had kept its fingers on the pulse of Ethiopian developments" because Haile Selassie's coronation was "an event that roused the world to the knowledge that such an empire as Ethiopia, free and independent, existed."[50]

Historian Brenda Plummer notes that the Italian-Ethiopian War "opened national frontiers to the race question in unprecedented fashion and linked domestic reform to vast changes in the world at large."[51] Black foreign correspondence played a crucial role in opening those frontiers. As the war ended, the ANP and the African American media were reporting that the league had set a dangerous precedent that could have severe consequences for blacks around the world.[52] The consequences would come to fruition through the actions of an Austrian paperhanger turned chancellor, Adolf Hitler.

[8]
A Racialized View of the Spanish Civil War

And well have the American Negro volunteers realized that the first stage of the world fight for racial justice lies right here and now in Spain. Negroes in the states have to be rightly proud of Salaria Kee and of the colored volunteers over here. They are an honor to the race—as indeed, they are to internationalism.

—NANCY CUNARD

With these words, Nancy Cunard offered one reason the black press covered the Spanish Civil War from 1936 to 1938.[1] The Associated Negro Press (ANP) and black editors focused on how the conflict would impact Africans who lived under colonial rule in Germany, Italy, and other European nations, as well as ramifications for people of African descent throughout the world. The story of black troops fighting for the Popular Front in Spain's Second Republic was one the black press wanted to tell, for it wanted to provide its view of the truth.

The black press also wanted to draw parallels between fascism abroad and racism in America and show the harsh impact of both on nonwhite people. Cunard told part of the story. Langston Hughes, the Harlem Renaissance author, poet, and playwright, told another part—the conflict as seen through the eyes of a black man. Black editors and publishers lacked the resources to send correspondents abroad, but some secured the services of persons who were already overseas. Thyra Edwards, a Chicago social worker who went to Spain to study the war's impact on the Spanish people, became an ANP contributor.

One Person's View of the War

Nancy Cunard filed from Europe and Africa as early as 1935, despite receiving only sporadic compensation from the ANP's Claude Barnett. With a world war almost on Europe's doorstep as Francisco Franco and his fascist army threatened civil war in Spain, Cunard remained focused on the African Diaspora.

In August 1936, reporting from Paris, she placed the unsettling developments in Spain on the black community's agenda. She framed events negatively and argued that fascist rebels in Spain, who wanted to overthrow the Spanish government, were using black North Africans as cannon fodder. She returned to that theme often over the next two years, writing that the war was further exploiting oppressed people. Poor Africans, she charged, were used to massacre poor Spanish workers who opposed the fascists; similarly, the French used Senegalese soldiers to murder French organizers. She wrote that imperialists had turned two seemingly similar parties against one another for economic gain. Cunard predicted that Europe was on the brink of another major war—a war she feared would turn out badly for blacks in Europe and have negative ramifications for blacks worldwide.[2]

The leftist Cunard wrote that fascists in France would not be able to win a civil war without the assistance of Germany and Italy, two powers that were waiting for the opportunity. Moreover, she believed, hundreds of thousands of African troops from Senegal, the Ivory Coast, and other French colonies would play a major role in the conflict. The writer also charged that the "betrayal" of Ethiopia was "one of the first stages in the next world war."[3]

The ANP distributed Cunard's dispatches from Loyalist-controlled Valencia from October to December 1936. A piece in the *Atlanta Daily World* introduced the element of class into her reporting. Cunard transmitted almost verbatim a flyer that appealed for all Africans to help fight the fascists and Gen. Franco. Muslims and Africans should not be misled into fighting the Spanish workers who opposed the fascists, she wrote, because the workers were "struggling not only for their own liberty but for that of all those who are exploited in the whole world."[4] Indeed, fascism in Spain would mean the beginning of the end for Morocco.

After three months in Spain, Cunard went to Paris, where she wrote that Moroccan troops hated their role in the war. Her dispatches revealed compassion for the desperate North Africans who were in an untenable position. Cunard explained that none of the Spanish Loyalist soldiers held ill will toward the Moroccans because they knew the horrible position these "wretched natives" were in. Cunard expressed her optimistic belief that the fascists would fail to take Madrid.[5] Of course, the fascists did.

War moved to a larger, international scale when the United Kingdom and France declared war on the conquering Nazi-aided Spanish fascists—and, in effect, on Germany and Italy. Cunard traveled to "forgotten" Morocco. She reported that the Spanish Civil War had claimed the lives of many Moors who fought on the front lines for the European powers. In relating the inhumanity visited upon marginalized North Africans, she gave them visibility. She reported conversations with grieving families and black soldiers in Tangier, providing a perspective on colonialism practiced by the ruling classes of Europe.

The black press reported that blacks and Muslims were in an untenable position, either manipulated by fascist officers or forced to fight at gunpoint. To recruit Moorish and black troops, the fascists offered five hundred francs, a massive sum; the ten francs a day that enlisted Moroccans were promised never materialized once they went to Spain.[6] Cunard wrote that black troops suffered immense casualties because the fascists placed them on the front lines in every battle.

In July 1937, Cunard went to Geneva for a front row seat at the League of Nations. She illustrated the link between the crisis in Spain and the lack of international intervention in Ethiopia, explaining that "behind the scenes politicking and favoritism of western nations led the league to its current state of ineptitude."[7] She lambasted the convention and its members. "While the powers pass resolutions, international Fascism kills; and there is not one single non-fascist being who does not admit that the present Spanish tragedy has come out of the Ethiopian one."[8]

After that trip, a frustrated and exhausted Cunard returned to Paris and reported on rumors that Italy was preparing to send more than 30,000 black North African troops into Spain to aid the fascist rebels. The news was deeply unsettling to Cunard, who continued to transmit stories that mingled antifascist messages with firsthand accounts of conversations with soldiers and the poor populations of North Africa. On one occasion, she recited the contents of an especially vitriolic letter she said Italian soldiers had left on the battlefield. The missive was full of bigotry and hatred for blacks.[9]

As the war in Spain intensified, Cunard returned to that country in December 1937 and stayed through March 1938. She reported on black soldiers and nurses whose performance on the battlefield and care for the wounded were instrumental to the survival of Loyalist Spain. From Barcelona she filed a dispatch about the heroism of Capt. Oliver Law, an African American who died while leading troops in battle.

Not long before Cunard ceased her coverage of the war, she again explained her rationale for returning to the battlefront and her passionate opposition to fascism. "No, I have not come to Spain only to write of people of color, but because I simply cannot stay away too long at a time from that terrible struggle. I feel I must know how it is going and must see for myself the people of the republican Spain in any way I can. Must pay tribute to their whole outlook on life which is that all men are equal and deserve the same chance of happiness. There is NO prejudice of any kind in the government of Spain."[10] Exhaustion and a weakened immune system prevented Cunard from filing regular dispatches between May 1938 and May 1939. Her first reports following her illness charged that Hitler's ambition was to retake Cameroon as an African colony. Again, she was in an awkward position of opposing fascist colonialism while supporting France and its occupation of African territories.[11] Cunard's view of imperialism was one-sided. During a time when the very existence of people of color was threatened, she saw the colonial exploits of France and Britain as the lesser of two evils. She rationalized her view by asserting that French colonials and native French people were "united as never before, beyond all ideology of political party" in their fight against Hitler, for he was the cause of the war.[12]

One can argue that Cunard viewed colonialism through an aristocratic lens, yet she provided African Americans in the United States an understanding of the rationalizations with which Europeans justified colonialism. She had genuine concern for people of color, and she put herself in financial and physical danger to support their cause, but her perspective on race and colonialism was somewhat naïve and reflected her position in society.

Langston Hughes, like Cunard, also saw the war through the lens of race and class. Unlike Cunard, he provided coverage from the battlefield. He also highlighted the accomplishments of race men and women engaged in the war.

Hughes in Spain: Six Months with the Loyalists

In the fall of 1937, Langston Hughes went to Spain to report from the warfront on a three-month assignment for *The Afro-American*. His specific charge was to report on blacks from the United States and other countries who had gone to Spain to fight for the Loyalists in the International Brigade. He stayed with Loyalist troops for six months before being injured and returning home.

Hughes's reportage gave *The Afro-American* an advantage it did not have before. Cunard focused primarily on Africa, but Hughes was an eyewitness to the battles. The *Chicago Defender* and the *Pittsburgh Courier* had led the field in foreign war correspondence and promoted their exclusives during the

Italian-Ethiopian conflict. *The Afro-American* could do the same after Hughes accepted its offer to go to Spain. The *newspaper* boasted that its correspondent would "bring exclusively to *Afro-American* readers a vivid and accurate picture of the bitter struggle that is now going on."[13]

Hughes welcomed the assignment because the Great Depression had had a negative impact on the Harlem Renaissance and he had earned virtually no money from his writing that spring.[14] He relished the assignment as a chance to write about a different type of black living in Europe—not the entertainer, but the fighter. He wrote in his autobiography, "Among the things I wanted to find out was what effect, if any, the bringing by Franco of dark troops to Spain from North Africa, had had on the people in regard to their racial attitudes. Had color prejudice been created in a land that had not known it before? What has been the treatment of the Moorish prisoners by the Loyalists? Were wounded Moors segregated in prison hospitals? Were there any Moors at all on the government side? How were American Negroes received in the cities of Spain when they came on furlough from the Brigades?"[15]

Hughes had always wanted to return to Spain since making a brief stop there when he was a merchant seaman. He sailed from New York to Paris in June and remained there for several weeks, renewing relationships with black expatriates who had found a haven there. He went to Barcelona on the very day newspapers announced the "worst bombing" the port city had seen thus far.[16] He next spent a week in Valencia, and then went to Madrid, the battlefront.

Hughes's articles from Spain began running on October 23. From the beginning, he likened fascism abroad to racism at home. He used words that directly addressed the ethnicity of the people he encountered: "colored" Cubans, Portuguese, and Haitians; "a brown-skinned Canary Islander"; "a dark Puerto Rican." He pointed out that these men were fighting for freedom in Spain, a freedom they did not have in their own countries. Yet they were willing to put their lives on the line for a place that lacked a color line. He explained that Italy was fascist and France was democratic, while Spain was torn between the ideologies. He pointed out that Spain was once a possession of the Moors, "a colored people ranging from light dark to dark white." Now the Moors were again in Spain and the "fascist armies" were using them "as cannon fodder for Franco." Blacks of "various nationalities" were also fighting for the Loyalists as members of the International Brigades.

> Naturally, I am interested in the Moors, too, and what I can find out about them. As usually happens with colored troops in the service of white imperialists, the Moors have been put in the front lines of the Franco offensives in Spain—and shot down like flies. They have been brought by the thousands from Spanish Morocco where the fascists took over power in the early days of their uprising.
>
> First, the regular Moorish cavalry and guard units came to Spain; then civilian conscripts forced into the army, or deceived by false promises of loot and high pay. When they got to Spain, as reputable newspaper correspondents have already written, they were often paid off in worthless German marks which they were told would be good to spend when they got back to Africa.
>
> But most of the Moors never live to get back to Africa. Now, in the second year of the war, they are no longer a potent force in Franco's army. Too many of them have been killed![17]

Hughes also wrote about people of color who had achieved fame and status in Spain, including the same Capt. Oliver and Salaria Kee whom Cunard had introduced to readers. Hughes's journalism placed readers of *The Afro-American* right in the middle of the fight, with vivid descriptions of war's devastation and the tenacity of Madrid's citizens, who went about their daily lives in the midst of carnage.[18]

In the fourteen articles Hughes wrote for *The Afro-American* while on assignment and after his return in December 1937, he framed fascism as evil and presented positive portraits of more than one hundred soldiers he had talked to or observed on the battlefield. He wrote about the irony of the Moors returning to an area they had once ruled, Spanish Morocco. Now these "shock troops" were meeting their demise.[19] His readers learned that fascism was as bad as, or worse than, racism and discrimination at home.

The war correspondence of both Cunard and Hughes sent racialized messages to black publications. Their readers gained an understanding not only of the threat of fascism but of the plight of the oppressed in what Cunard called the "forgotten" African countries. They helped their readers see the world in a new way.

[9]

World War II

The Fight for the Right

On July 18, 1942, the front page of the *Pittsburgh Courier* promoted its first black foreign correspondent of World War II, Edgar Rouzeau. On his way back to the Egyptian front, Rouzeau was "assembling stories on what America's black fighters [were] doing for Democracy abroad and at home."[1] He had set the tone for his correspondence in an article on the causes of the war and its impact on the black community. "Disasters are like gigantic rolling pins. Ever [sic] so often, Mother Nature employs them in the leveling process to which she subjects mankind in order that civilization may continue its onward surge. This leveling process kneads out prejudice, humbles the arrogant and uplifts the meek to a plane of universal equality. . . . The white man has used them to devaluate the Black man. And the Black man, no less a guilty party, has used them to devaluate his Black fellow being."[2]

Rouzeau's mission was to illuminate black contributions to the war effort. His first dispatches drew attention to black soldiers' presence in the conflict.

> Some phases of this far-flung and titanic combat I have already seen in the course of a five thousand miles air tour of active and inactive fronts. . . . Then Cairo has something more—something strangely comforting to the tormented minds of those who are seeking an answer to the slaughter and destruction now raging less than two hours flight from here. . . . Close your eyes, flick a cigarette, and you will hear this soldier's throaty oath. . . . Name your state—anyone from Florida to California and from Maine to Texas—and a Black American will speak up.[3]

Rouzeau focused on men who willingly sacrificed themselves for a nation that continued to deny them civil rights. Black troops were assigned to go overseas in March 1942. One contingent landed in New Caledonia in late April and another in Northern Ireland in June. Rouzeau arrived in July.

In August, *The Afro-American*'s Ollie Stewart flew by clipper to London on his way to North Africa. The newspaper had applied for Stewart's accreditation in March, but the War Department had stated that black soldiers on the European front had their quota of correspondents—it probably meant Rouzeau. Because Stewart's approval was delayed for four months, *The Afro-American* had paid six hundred fifty-six dollars for him to fly rather than take the longer voyage by boat. Stewart arrived in North Africa with the rank of officer and a uniform. He had the same privileges as correspondents for the mainstream media, including such renowned white correspondents as Ernie Pyle of the Scripps Howard newspaper chain.

Unity was a key factor in the black press's ability to champion the cause of African Americans and assign correspondents abroad. In April 1942, in an effort to keep down costs, the Associated Negro Press (ANP) appealed to editors to pool their resources to send a correspondent to the front. Several editors said they could not afford the cost. *The Afro-American*'s Carl Murphy said he would not release Stewart from his staff, but he would join the ANP in sending someone else. A year later, the *Pittsburgh Courier*, the *Norfolk Journal and Guide*, and *The Afro-American* agreed to pool for publication news releases filed from different areas of combat by Rouzeau, Stewart, and Thomas Young of the *Journal and Guide*.[4] The ANP eventually secured the services of Rudolph Dunbar, a composer and conductor who had long been a stringer for the service; Homer Smith, who wrote under the name Chatwood Hall; and George Padmore. All were already living abroad.

While Rouzeau and Stewart were the first two accredited black correspondents, they were not the first blacks reporting on World War II from overseas. Smith, who had lived in Russia since 1932 and had written for several major black newspapers and the ANP, had been accredited by the Russian government in 1939. He wrote in his autobiography: "I was the only Negro journalist ever stationed in Russia. I was the only Negro correspondent on the Russian-German front, and . . . I was the first Negro to be accredited a war correspondent."[5] Padmore wrote about the political implications of the war from London for the ANP, the *Chicago Defender*, and the *Pittsburgh Courier*. A native of Trinidad, he had lived briefly in New York before moving to Russia and eventually to London. Both Smith and Padmore had gone to Russia to escape racism in America. Both men, disillusioned with communism, eventually left the Soviet Union.

All told, thirty black correspondents covered the war for the black press.[6] Some were already practicing journalists, while others became war reporters out of necessity. Art Carter was *The Afro-American*'s sports editor when the newspaper sent him to replace Stewart in Italy. Enoch Waters had been on the staff of the *Defender* for ten years and had been made executive editor before Pearl Harbor. John "Rover" Jordan and Lem Graves were reporters and columnists for the *Norfolk Journal and Guide*. Edward Toles was the attorney for the *Defender*. Thomas Young was the business manager for the *Journal and Guide* and also the son of its publisher. Deton Brooks volunteered to be a *Defender* correspondent after an injury kept him from serving in combat. No blacks were accredited as photographers, but Jordan, Charley Loeb, and Billy Rowe functioned as photographers in an unofficial capacity. Ollie Harrington filed illustrations from the battlefield in southern Europe.[7]

Let Us Serve, Let Us Fight

The black press was always on a quest to ensure future rights for African Americans by being their eyes, ears, and voices during times of peace. The effort it sustained during World War II surpassed any previous initiative and has not been matched since. The battle to have blacks represented as soldiers and reporters was waged long before they were allowed to serve. Three million blacks registered for the armed forces under the Selective Service Act of 1940, but fewer than 800,000 served. Approximately a half million men were shipped overseas. Their rate of rejection was 18 percent compared to 8.5 percent for whites. Discrimination by draft boards, and the belief that blacks lacked intelligence or had social diseases, were among the reasons they were turned down for military service.[8] Few blacks saw combat, and those who did fought in the later stages of the war. Most were assigned to supporting roles. In 1943 and 1944, the army converted many black combat units to support and labor units. The navy assigned black sailors to menial roles such as mess men.

Segregation was the order of the day; lynching and racial violence were common. Enoch Waters wrote that he felt safer covering the war in combat zones than during the eighteen months he had spent reporting in the South.[9] World War II gave African Americans the opportunity to focus world attention on America's color-line problem.[10] An increasingly educated and engaged black public had greater race pride and was ready for collective action.

Black publications led the way in fighting discrimination in the military and championing the right of blacks to serve. In October 1939, the ANP demanded that Secretary of War Harry H. Woodring explain via the black press why bias predominated in the military. Why weren't black reserve officers allowed to qualify for commissions in the army? Why did the military have only two black line officers and two black chaplains? Following the traditional expectation of the black press that evidence of patriotism would end racial subjugation, the letter also suggested that civilian organizations would open their doors if the federal government cleared the way by using black troops in all fields.[11]

Front-page articles, editorials, letters to the editor, and photographs documented and condemned segregation and demanded change. In April 1940, for example, the *Norfolk Journal and Guide* reported that black men were not yet being trained as pilots and mechanics for the Army Air Corps. The following month, the newspaper urged blacks to register their discontent with the War Department for adding the word "colored" to the name of the 369th Infantry Regiment in New York, the first time in history that such an appellation had been attached to a military unit. Similar stories ran in other black newspapers.

Black editors and leaders continued their verbal assault on injustice through ongoing contact with the government via letters and even meetings. In May 1940, a group met with President Franklin D. Roosevelt and asked him to guarantee a representative proportion of blacks in the military.[12] In February 1941, the ANP's Claude Barnett met with Col. P. A. Allen of the War Department's public relations branch. Barnett followed up by pledging to use the ANP's sixty-eight newspapers to educate readers about black units in the service. In a meeting in June 1941, black press representatives called on the president to end segregation in the federal government and the defense industry. Roosevelt acquiesced and created the Fair Employment Opportunity Commission, but he did not order the integration of the military.

When the Japanese attacked Pearl Harbor on December 7, 1941, major black publications agreed that they would not be silent about the race problem, even as they expressed their support for the Allies. The *Chicago Defender* chastised the government after the War Department initiated yet another meeting, on the day after the attack, with twenty black journalists in an attempt to shore up support. In spite of their vocal protest, the journalists were told that segregation in the military would not only continue but would be extended. The *Defender* responded in a page 1 editorial.

> White America must learn now—especially those who inhabit the South—that a Negro in the armed service of his country; in the uniform of his government, must be respected as a defender of democracy; a soldier, regardless of color, who is willing to lay down his life in defense of his homeland, its principles, it institutions. . . . White America must first "bomb the color line"; blast discriminatory practices, both in the North and the South, and grant civil liberties, absolute freedom and justice and full citizen rights to the black soldier, his kith and kin, with a solid, united front that will bring democracy a victory worth fighting for.[13]

In January 1942, the National Association for the Advancement of Colored People's (NAACP's) Walter White solicited signatures on a letter to the president asking why he had failed to appoint any blacks to the War Labor Board; that failure kept blacks from helping make and execute plans for a successful war. White charged that black soldiers had endured "unbelievable brutalities" and insults approved by army officers "who slavishly submit and subscribe to racial attitudes indigenous to the most backward states of our country."[14] While acknowledging that conditions for blacks would be worse under Hitler, the letter stated that the government's negative approach could create passive loyalty on the part of blacks. In October 1942, *The Afro-American* demanded, "Speak Out, Mr. President: Tell the Minority Groups What They Are Fighting For; Define Democracy as It Applies to Them."[15]

Opposition to the black press was great during the war, and the loyalty of its journalists was questioned. In December 1942, Roosevelt notified Walter White of an impending Justice Department indictment of several black editors for sedition.[16] Despite the fact that the Federal Bureau of Investigation (FBI), the U.S. Post Office, and other federal agencies had investigated black publications, the editors continued to advocate for the race and to question the motives of the United States abroad.[17] The FBI especially considered the objections to undemocratic practices unacceptable. Director J. Edgar Hoover even wrote to Claude Barnett to deny ANP reports of rumors that postal authorities were opening, examining, and copying letters sent to the news service from the South. The ANP's statement about the rumors was made "either maliciously or without any thought given to its content," Hoover wrote. He added, "In these times of national stress when the one objective of this great country is to win this war, I think it is agreed that spreading rumors and making unsubstantiated allegations merely serves to impede our efforts."[18]

Such suspicion of the black press made support from the black community even more important. On a CBS program in 1942, the *Pittsburgh Courier*'s executive editor Percival Prattis stated that the black press and the government could work together to win the war and better society. A properly functioning black press, Prattis said, "becomes an arm or agent of the government whose inescapable duty it is to provide for the complete employment and use of every citizen and every minority in everything to win the war."[19] Tuskegee Institute president Frederick Patterson vowed that black patriotism could be "counted on in full measure." Mary McLeod Bethune stated, "No blood more red, more loyal penetrates the vein of mankind than that which flows through the body of the Negro American. America can depend on us."[20] Blacks supported the war by purchasing war bonds and holding rallies. In February 1942, the *Pittsburgh Courier* launched the Double V campaign after receiving a letter from James Thompson, a cafeteria worker who said victory abroad over Nazism and fascism should be accompanied by victory at home over the enemies of the race.[21] This rallying slogan and a symbol of interlocking Vs acknowledged blacks' dual existence as Americans first and black Americans second. Back in 1903, W. E. B. Du Bois had called this "the struggle to be both a Negro and an American without being cursed and spat upon by his fellows, without having the door of opportunity closed roughly in his face."[22]

Soon after the launching of the Double V campaign, Barnett, the director of the ANP, reinforced the concept during a CBS radio program. Other than the black church, Barnett said, the black newspaper was "the most powerful influence operating" among blacks who thought of themselves "first as Americans and then as a black Americans." Black people who read the daily paper, he said, found no information about the "doings of Negroes other than that which is criminal or comical." As a result, blacks turned to the 250 newspapers and periodicals that addressed their "separate life."[23]

The black press had some success. Its demand for a combat role for blacks is credited with the establishment of the Ninety-ninth Fighter Squadron that went to Africa in the spring of 1943 and flew its first mission that summer. Another victory was the deployment of the Ninety-second Division, the major black combat unit that arrived in the Mediterranean Theater in the fall of 1944 and was operational by November 1. Equally important, the black press assigned correspondents to cover their own race soldiers from the battlefield—a point the editors continually promoted.

With the deployment of black troops a reality, editors and publishers began to strategize about how they could send their correspondents overseas. They filed accreditation applications, met with government officials, and sent follow-up letters to speed the process. When the *Chicago Defender*'s Enoch Waters applied to the Department of Defense to become an accredited war correspondent, he found that the government considered black reporters communists. Decades later, in his history of the black press, he wrote, "Every Negro newspaper writer, speaker or attorney who called for observation of the Bill of Rights or opposed racial discrimination was a suspected communist agent."[24] In a letter to John H. Sengstacke, editor and publisher of the *Defender*, Truman K. Gibson Jr., assistant civilian aide to the secretary of war, stated that the publisher's applications for Al Monroe and David Orro would take five weeks to process. He added, "My personal advice to you is not to submit the name of Enoch P. Waters. I recall that just a short while ago, he was rather seriously ill and as I recall it, he showed symptoms of Tuberculosis."[25] Waters believed that the government delayed his accreditation in an attempt to intimidate the *Defender*. The delays coincided with the time when "the newspaper was accusing the government of condoning discrimination in the armed forces and defense industries."[26]

Sengstacke suspected that the retaliation stemmed from a letter Waters had written to Roosevelt in January 1941 demanding that FDR personally answer why he had approved the formation of an all-black squadron in the army air corps, why the Jim Crow squadron had been set up, and whether the policy represented the president's attitude.[27] The publisher wrote to Secretary of War Henry L. Stimson in early February to apologize for Waters's letter, calling his city editor's action "an infraction of administrative policy" and promising that it would not happen again. Stimson replied almost immediately that he was gratified that Waters's letter did not "represent the thoughts of your organization."[28] During 1942, Sengstacke was meeting with government officials and sending follow-up letters; he walked a fine line between aggressively pushing for black rights and alienating the government. In April 1942, Sengstacke wrote to Secretary of the Navy Frank Knox asking similar questions, but he adopted a conciliatory tone, pledging the *Defender*'s "cooperation in providing participation and recognition to the Negro in our American life."[29] Sengstacke wrote other letters pledging that the newspaper would do all it could to improve African American morale; asking Steve Early, secretary to the president, to allow the black press to attend the president's press conferences; and reminding Byron Price, director of the Office of Censorship, of the offer to have the black press actively participate in developing a voluntary censorship plan.[30] In May 1942, Sengstacke received accreditation applications from the War Department, as well as assurances that his concerns were being addressed.

Monroe did not go overseas, but Orro arrived in England in 1943. Waters was notified of his clearance on March 22, 1943, and directed to report to Fort Mason in California on May 4. He arrived in Australia in June to cover the Pacific Theater. Years later he recalled that being a war correspondent was the toughest assignment he had ever had. He was, he wrote, totally unprepared for the "arduous physical demands required to perform what was expected" of him.[31]

Although delays in accreditation applications were an ongoing problem, the *Chicago Defender*, the *Norfolk Journal and Guide*, *The Afro-American*, the ANP, and the National Negro Press Association (NNPA) eventually joined the *Courier* in sending correspondents or hiring blacks already living abroad. Once overseas, the reporters did not have the flexibility to move from one theater of the war to another—a situation the NNPA called to the attention of the government in July 1943. News representatives pressed the government to address escalating racial tensions in the military, and they pushed for increased mobility for black correspondents and more coverage of black troop activities by army public relations and signal corps.[32] The War Department responded that it would investigate reported cases of unfair treatment of soldiers, but it would not place black writers on the Washington Bureau of Public Relations staff, and it would leave decisions on correspondents' mobility up to the commanders of the theaters of war. The government stated that "facilities were not always available in the desired theatre for the acceptance of additional correspondents."[33]

Once they were allowed in various theaters, black correspondents were generally treated like their white counterparts. Ollie Stewart related one incident of discrimination—a white colonel would not allow him to stay in the same hotel as white correspondents, causing him to be away from the action. But Stewart was one of several correspondents selected to interview President Roosevelt, and he was one of three invited to review the troops when the president and Prime Minister Winston Churchill made a surprise visit to Casablanca in January 1943. Stewart was also among the journalists who accompanied the president to battle scenes, attended his press conferences, and even shook the president's hand. Black reporters also were selected as pool reporters whose stories could be carried in any media, as was the case with Jordan and Harrington, who covered the Normandy Invasion in August.

Following Our Boys and Telling Their Story

Ollie Stewart was the first of ten black war correspondents who covered the tan yanks—as the black troops were called—in the Mediterranean Theater. In September he arrived in London on the first leg of his assignment in North Africa, and he immediately began writing about his impressions of the war-torn city. He filed stories on soldiers and discrimination. He spent two days interviewing men from Baltimore, Philadelphia, and New York, and reported that they were in good spirits and were not homesick—although they wanted letters from home.

Following an Afrocentric agenda, Stewart addressed racial discrimination in one of his first dispatches, a story about black soldiers who were barred from certain London nightclubs and dance halls at the request of U.S. military officials. American headquarters refused Stewart's requests for comments. The average British subject was puzzled about such actions; Stewart quoted a storeowner who observed, "Black men are in England today to fight for freedom, their own as well as the freedom of mankind. To erect bars against them savours of what Hitler is doing."[34]

Stewart sailed to North Africa in a well-protected convoy of British and American ships. He was the only black person on the vessel; the five white correspondents included Ernie Pyle of Scripps Howard newspapers; Bill Land of *Time* and *Life:* Red Mueller of *Newsweek;* A. J. "Joe" Liebling of the *New Yorker;* and Bob Neville of *Yank* and *Stars and Stripes.* Stewart spent sixteen months with the campaign that routed Field Marshal Rommel out of North Africa, and he covered the invasion of Sicily. After some time at home, during which he made a lecture tour of colleges, he returned to Europe to write about the Normandy Invasion and the liberation of Paris. Although the Normandy Invasion was a major initiative of the war, black correspondents were unable to cover it as per Gen. Dwight D. Eisenhower's order. The twelve thousand black soldiers who fought in the June 6, 1944, invasion represented one-tenth of the troops involved. Toles, Dixon, and Stewart followed within a month. Toles wrote that the first black troops had "landed and fought gallantly to drive a wedge into the continent."[35] Although he was not on the scene, he provided the eyewitness account of troops he interviewed. A white lieutenant with the Supreme Headquarters Allied Expeditionary Force (AEF), who had just returned from the front, assured Toles that black troops had been in the first assault group. "I know because I was there. All over the beach, I saw them with grim determination to get that beach organized, to get those all-important supplies and reinforcement moving. . . . I saw fighting units also, and it was no easy job to work with snipers and dead bodies sprawling over the shore."[36] Toles wrote several other stories based on interviews with eyewitnesses—troops who were "trained to perfection" and excited because they were finally going to see action. He reported one story in the words of the tan yanks who had withstood "twenty-four bloody hours" of mortar fire and guns pounding but "kept going out to ships transporting their loads."[37] Other stories related that "our yanks" were routing the Nazis in France and keeping the Germans on the run. Stewart and Rudolph Dunbar were together most of time they were in Normandy. The NNPA was concerned that so few black correspondents were with the troops at Normandy. Harry McAlpin wrote that, based on past indicators, the 450 white correspondents would ignore the blacks who were "represented by servicemen risking their lives daily for their home and their country—whether repairing airfields, loading and unloading ships, carrying back the wounded, manning guns on naval or coast guard vessels, building roads or storming beaches."[38] Two black correspondents could not cover the entire front, wrote McAlpin, so the War Department was obligated to inform the public.

The situation was a bit different during the invasion of southern France in August 1944, when John Jordan and Ollie Harrington were pool correspondents with the combined U.S. press. Six other black correspondents—Dixon, Toles, Stewart, Dunbar, Morrison, and Ottley—joined them. The performance of black pilots was described in countless stories of heroism. On September 22, Jordan reported that black fighter pilots had downed twenty-six Germans. A week later, he reported that twenty-two planes had been destroyed on the ground and the pilots had routed German interceptors. An early September dispatch reported that the Ninety-second Division had broken the German line in Italy, taken prisoners, and contributed to the fall of Pisa.[39] But the reporting was balanced; stories that reflected negatively on the troops also ran.

Padmore, who wrote more than six hundred articles for the *Chicago Defender* and the *Pittsburgh Courier* during the war, was one of only two black correspondents who reported on black soldiers for the entire period the United States was involved in the war. Padmore, who was never on the front lines but reported from London, praised black soldiers' contributions and reported on how their heroic deeds affected race relations.[40] An article titled "Nazi Bombs Blást Racial Prejudice in Big Convoy" chronicled how a major assault on a convoy had changed the views of white sailors.

> It took a heavy shower of Hitler depth bombs and torpedoes to smash Jim Crow on a recent convoy taking munitions from America to the Soviet Union. . . . The Nazi Luftwaffe blasted apart the artificially-erected race barrier set up by some of the Dixie white seamen who refused to mix with the Negro crewmen. . . . Up to that time the color bar had been rigidly observed. But the heroic courage displayed by the colored seamen changed the outlook of the white sailors. As the Nazis launched their fierce barrage, two Negroes on duty at the wheel stuck to their posts without flinching.[41]

That violent encounter, in which black soldiers proved their ability as death rained from the skies, forever changed race relations among the men on that boat. Padmore quoted John Venaccia, an "American-born Italian member of the crew," who said, "There was a good deal of color prejudice among our crew when we set out but by the time we reached Archangel, there wasn't a trace of it left."[42]

While Padmore reported from London, many black correspondents followed the troops through all of the theaters to tell what they called "our story" and chronicle the war from the black perspective. Headlines often included the reporters' names. The *Chicago Defender* ran a February 13, 1943, story with the headline, "Orro Sees 14 Soldiers Commissioned in London." A month later, *The Afro-American* ran the headline "Ollie Stewart Tells What It's Like in the African Big Push: Boys Ride with Angels under German Bombing and Artillery Fire for Three Months." (The censored story was sent via cable and appeared in the March 27, 1943, issue of *The Afro-American.*) "Toles Sees Chicagoans Blast Nazis in Brittany" and "Toles See Gunners Take St. Malo's 'Mad Colonel'" headlined articles in the September 2, 1944, issue of the newspaper.

Like mainstream media correspondents, black war reporters infused their stories with their own experiences. Jordan described the terror he felt when a plane crashed almost at his feet, and recounted his escape when he was caught in the crossfire at Toulon in August 1944. Carter wrote of traveling by plane, train, ship, jeep, truck, oxcart, and borrowed bicycle during fourteen months covering the Italian campaign. As a member of the North Atlantic convoy to Africa, he left the United States in October 1943 and spent twenty-five days on a ten thousand-ton liberty ship, wondering, watching, and waiting for what might happen. "Seconds seemed like minutes, minutes like hours, and hours like days," he wrote. During the voyage, he shared a space about thirty by thirty feet with two newsreel cameramen and four other correspondents.[43] Stewart wrote in *The Afro-American* that he had helped to win a battle in the Sicilian campaign by carrying a truckload of hay to the front.[44]

The correspondents sometimes were intermediaries between the soldiers and the military, noting concerns and sometimes getting redress about bias and issues that concerned black troops. One of Waters's major goals was to let the tan yanks speak for themselves, to forge a "psychological link between the individual soldiers and friends and relatives back home."[45]

Even before blacks landed in North Africa, Rouzeau filed a story in which he called the first black soldier to set foot in the Middle East an unsung hero. Of black troops stationed in Northern Ireland, he wrote that *Collier's* magazine correspondent Quentin Reynolds had told him that black soldiers were "well disciplined, have tremendous respect for white officers, and rumors that their landing in the country provoked resentment among natives is all bunk."[46]

Because black soldiers did not engage in combat until the later stages of the war, human-interest stories dominated coverage. The human touch is common in foreign correspondence because such stories "offer a way to make distant events intelligible to at-home audiences" and "in the case of war reporting, feed the public's interest in the fate of its servicemen."[47] Ernie Pyle achieved fame—and a Pulitzer Prize—for such reporting.

Fletcher Martin's reporting for the NNPA pool consisted nearly exclusively of descriptions of the gallant accomplishments of black soldiers in the Pacific Theater. From Bougainville Island near New Guinea, he covered the successful mission of the "first Negro line officer to lead troops into combat in the South Pacific area."[48] Capt. Frederick Douglas Jenkins, of Alexandria, Louisiana, a "quiet and studious" officer, led the Ninety-third Division into battle and "ripped to shreds an enemy force."[49]

In July 1943, Stewart reported that the Ninety-ninth Division had lost two planes over Sicily, but one of the missing pilots was assumed safe after flying escort missions. Pride seeped into the dispatch as Stewart stated that the squadron was credited with the "first positive destruction of a German plane" and that all members had "received the personal congratulation and handshakes of General Eisenhower" and other top military brass.[50] When the Ninety-ninth Pursuit Squadron and the Ninety-second Division joined the conflagration, black correspondents were as eager to report on the fighters as the men were to fight. Stewart wrote on July 24, 1943, about the Tuskegee fighter pilots, "I have, and have had for weeks, a ring-side seat for one of the most history-making dreams the world has ever seen—the assault on Naziland from the south. I have watched from my Mediterranean peep-hole, the developments for invasion step by step, and can now report that every possible precaution against failure was taken before one man's life was risked. . . . Colored fighter pilots were in the vanguard of devastation by air which paved the way for Allied landings in Sicily, just as they were before and during the capture of Pantelleria."[51]

Correspondents for the *Pittsburgh Courier*, the *Norfolk Journal and Guide*, and the *Chicago Defender* filed similar stories. The *Journal and Guide*'s Thomas Young, Jordan, and Graves illuminated the accomplishments of the Ninety-ninth Pursuit Squadron. Readers learned that pilots shot down German planes, that engineers and communications officers ensured maintenance of vital contact, and that the squadron played a crucial support role in driving the Germans and Italians out of Sicily. Carter also covered the day-to-day activities of the Ninety-ninth and the Ninety-second. Articles from the Italian front zeroed in on individual pilots, the jobs they were doing, the missions they flew, and the planes they shot down. Stories about promotions, the awarding of silver and bronze stars, good-conduct medals, and letters of commendation reinforced the perception of the race troops' performance.

Stewart reported in August that race relations were amicable in Sicily; he acknowledged that attitudes about race might change when the troops returned home, but overseas, "the common danger, the common foe and hardships of battle are bringing American troops together."[52] A month later, he stated that black soldiers had reacted negatively to race riots in Detroit and Beaumont, Texas, and that the troops were concerned that race relations would not be better when they returned home.[53]

Stories sent via cable, Mackay radio, or mail verified that black soldiers were battling for democracy. As guns pummeled Rommel in April 1943, Stewart was with black artillerymen as they captured the enemy position.

> This is a story I have wanted to write since I left America in August—the story of colored troops in actual combat, exchanging lead with the enemy. I covered many miles to be on the spot when they began writing a glorious page in the history of the North African campaign. But now that I have seen our lads in action, I am both proud and humble. I am proud because they covered themselves with glory as well as with mud—humble because I cannot tell the story as it should be told. A correspondent can have only a bird's-eye-view of a battle front such as this one, and when I found a field artillery unit blasting the Germans out of the mountains just before we took Gabes, I took a front-row seat for an hour without actually knowing the full importance of the action.[54]

Black troops were not engaged in direct combat, but Stewart emphasized that *all* of the units at the front were combat units. Quartermasters, engineers, and truck drivers who encountered the enemy were "prepared to fight their way out of a crack."[55] He gave a vivid description of the men. "Unshaven and looking like bearded Arabs, living in caves, dirty and tough as leather, our boys are helping every time the Allies gain mileage in the push, which we all hope will be the last in this theatre of operations."[56]

As the conflict wore on, the number of stories increased. In November 1944, readers learned from Carter that the Ninety-second had killed 15 Nazis in a day, that the Fifth Army had annihilated 2 enemy divisions and captured 250 prisoners from 5 villages it Italy, and that the 332nd had destroyed enemy equipment, including locomotives, railroad cars, tank cars, and gun positions.

On January 15, 1944, Carter wrote about Lt. James Thomas Wiley of the Ninety-ninth Pursuit Squadron, who became the first black pilot to have fifty sorties to his credit. Lem Graves, who was also attached to the Ninety-ninth, wrote another story in February, when Wiley completed his eightieth sortie. These journalists reported on the all-black divisions that included the Ninety-ninth Pursuit Squadron, fighter pilots under the command of Lt. Col. Benjamin O. Davis Jr.; the Ninety-second Infantry Division; and the different units that made up the larger 332nd Fighter Group, into which the Ninety-ninth was eventually absorbed.

Graves filed a piece that focused on the fact that black and white soldiers could fight together as a unit. The men of the Ninety-ninth, he wrote, "were the pioneers—those people who can win acclaim because they are 'firsts' if they are successful but who have the cards stacked against them and who can so easily fall." Graves added that the "quiet but effective assimilation of the Ninety-Ninth with the Seventy-Ninth Fighter Group" was the "most significant event in the first year of the Ninety-Ninth and indeed one of the most significant in the history of the Negro's progress." To drive home the point, Graves wrote that the men "mix together, work together, and fight together."[57]

Although they reported on the success of black individuals and all-black divisions, the correspondents had difficulty finding tan yanks in combat. On January 1, 1944, Rouzeau described his quest to find blacks manning a gun on the front lines. Jack Thompson, a reporter for the *Chicago Tribune*, told Rouzeau he had seen a "Negro artillery outfit" engaged in combat in Algiers in the Battle of Tunisia.[58] But, Rouzeau wrote, "[T]he nearest thing I could find to a colored artillery outfit was a colored ordnance outfit which was temporarily attached to a white gun battery."[59] Rouzeau questioned the commander of the battery unit, who had served in several artillery units in the war. "The officer shook his head. 'Never heard of any.' He turned to a sergeant: 'Have you, Frank?' Whereupon Frank burst into a guffaw: 'Colored men on guns?' He said this as if he could not believe he had heard correctly. 'I think they gave you a bum steer, Mister. The only thing we use colored troops for is to unload ships and do hauling, except for a few like these ordnance boys who pass ammunition.'"[60]

Martin expressed similar sentiments in the Pacific: "There are no Negro combat units, including anti-aircraft, in the area."[61] Tubbs, *The Afro-American* copyeditor turned war correspondent, arrived in Australia in June 1943. Two months later, he reported that thousands of black troops were still waiting for the "long-overdue visit" of Japanese bombers to New Guinea, but a visit was unlikely. Tubbs, like his colleagues, wrote about the day-to-day activities and achievements of black soldiers, identifying them by name and hometown—just as white correspondents often did. Writing from "Somewhere in England," Edward Toles lauded the industriousness of two black battalions that had been commended for building a large airbase in Britain. "'What did you do?' I asked one smiling chap, who was heavily built and was very quiet, when approached. 'Work like hell' was his laconic reply."[62]

Invisibility

The black community and the black press were critical of the lack of acknowledgment of race members during the war and at its end. Soldiers were bitter about their invisibility. In April 1944, Carter wrote about soldiers who told him that no one had mentioned their battalion, although it was extremely active during the early bombing in Italy. "What we are doing now is dangerous but routine," one soldier said, adding that the men had been "subject to bombing every hour during the day and three times at night."[63] The *Journal and Guide* reported in October 1944, that the War Department had finally lifted its prohibition against newspapers identifying the Mustang Fighter Group by its official designation as the 332nd. NAACP administrator Roy Wilkins wrote to Andrew Heiskell of *Life* magazine to criticize its omission of blacks from its pictorial history of the war. Wilkins called it "a serious editorial blunder" and added that *Life* had "done a great injustice to 15,000 Americans who are struggling against great odds to identify themselves as citizens measuring up the finest traditions of the Nation." Heiskell responded that *Life* chose pictures on the "grounds of vividness of action" and used no other criteria. Wilkins responded that it was not true that black soldiers had never taken part in any "vivid action."[64]

Mainstream media weighed in on the issue of invisibility, and blamed part of the problem on the black press. Two *New York Post* columnists covered a meeting between the executive committee of the NNPA and President Roosevelt about how to get more news of black war activities into the mainstream press. The columnists noted that during the meeting the president had praised a three-page statement by Percival Prattis of the *Pittsburgh Courier.* Roosevelt had directed his secretary Steve Early to allow the publishers to make the statement public. But when representatives of mainstream dailies requested copies of the document, John Sengstacke of the *Chicago Defender* had refused to release the statement because he wanted to write the story himself. Later he said that he would hold the story until black weeklies had looked at it first. This was a wasted opportunity, the columnists noted. "And that's the ironic story of how the Negro publishers—anxious though most of them were for recognition of their race by the white press—missed out on one of the best chances they'd ever had for a really big, sympathetic, dignified news break in last Sunday's editions of white dailies all over the country."[65]

The mainstream media did sometimes provide positive coverage of black troops. In an article reprinted by the *Chicago Defender,* Seymour Korman of the *Chicago Tribune* noted the good record of the black fighting group. Korman pointed out that the army had been reluctant to train blacks as pilots and had been even less enthusiastic about sending them into combat. But "these young men have made good, as everyone who was not blinded by prejudice knew they would. Their record is another reminder—if any were needed—of the heavy price which this country pays for handicapping the Negro."[66]

As embedded journalists, the war correspondents made the black press one of the most effective forces in American society during World War II. Crusading on the home front against discrimination and reporting from abroad on the accomplishments and sacrifices of the soldiers, the journalists provided the missing pieces of the story. So substantive was their coverage that media historian Armistead Pride notes, "Readers might well have gained the impression that . . . [black troops] were making the greatest sacrifices."[67]

Their reporting emboldened African Americans to press even more aggressively for social justice. Black troops returned from the war determined to gain their rights at home. The seeds had been planted for the civil rights movement that would forever change American society and the lives of both African Americans and whites.

[10]
Spotlight on Africa

When *Ebony* was founded half a century ago, Africa was still viewed in White America as the Dark Continent occupied largely by savage tribes and ferocious jungle beasts. Little, if anything, was written in the U.S. press about the ravages and exploitation visited on Africa and its people by greedy European colonialists and even less about the valiant struggle waged by Africans to free themselves. *Ebony*, although only an infant at the time, helped change all that. From the outset it paid almost as much attention to the Black freedom struggle of our African brothers and sisters in Africa and the West Indies as it did to the one waged at home.

—LINDA JOHNSON RICE

CEO Linda Johnson Rice explained on *Ebony*'s fiftieth anniversary in 1995 why the magazine ran so many articles about Africa.[1] In the decade after World War II, African countries were trying to end years of colonial rule. Other countries under colonialism were doing the same. In the United States, blacks who had fought for freedom abroad demanded justice at home. Their desire for a better America led to the civil rights movement. *Ebony*, which was based in Chicago, was determined "to project a dimension of the Black personality in a world saturated with stereotypes" and to give African Americans "a new sense of somebodiness, a new sense of self-respect . . . to tell them who they were and what they could do."[2]

The first issue of the slick publication sold out its press run of 25,000 copies within one hour after it hit the newsstands in November 1945. Publisher John H. Johnson immediately printed an additional 25,000 copies that were snapped up by blacks starved for information. They embraced stories and images that portrayed them as individuals who got married, held jobs, and were successful. *Ebony*'s circulation grew to more than 400,000 in less than a year. Stories about "the *Ebony* miracle" ran in the mainstream press.[3] *Newsweek* magazine praised the publication and even reprinted one of its stories. "We were a legend after only six months of publication," Johnson wrote in his 1989 autobiography.[4] *Ebony* became the first African American publication assessed by the Audit Bureau of Circulations.[5] The magazine quickly surpassed individual black newspapers that had reached their zenith during World War II with a collective circulation of two million weekly; readership slowly declined and revenues dwindled after the war. *Ebony* became an influential voice in the black world community, helping define events that materially affected it. In January 1946, the magazine began reporting on the African Diaspora and deconstructing the myths and stereotypes perpetuated by the mainstream media.[6] *Ebony*'s agenda was to extend intellectual and political boundaries, to provide a different perspective, and to negate the "truths" that predominated in the establishment press. Like African American newspapers, *Ebony* tailored its global journalism to black interests, provided a broader perspective, and created a consciousness that legitimized an entire continent. Correspondents who reported from Africa sought no input from U.S. government sources or representatives of the dominant society.

Ebony initially focused on domestic affairs, but it always recognized the importance of the African Diaspora to the black community at home. The publication recognized that the struggle of African nations for liberty mirrored those of African Americans. In the early 1950s, *Ebony* ran numerous stories on race relations and civil rights in the United States. At the same time, it dispatched correspondents to African, European, and Caribbean countries. Johnson and other *Ebony* editors assumed roles as special ambassadors to African countries and frequently traveled to them.[7] (Johnson's publishing company even launched a magazine devoted entirely to the people of South Africa after the end of apartheid in 1996, but *Ebony South Africa* ceased publication in July 2000 because of poor sales.)

Ebony embraced the familiar themes of economic exploitation and discrimination. An April 1946 article explored the impact of Jim Crow in South Africa, where economic conditions were dictated by skin color; black miners held some of the lowest-paying jobs. *Ebony* compared the plight of South Africans with racial discrimination domestically, showing the widespread impact of such policies. A year later, *Ebony* ran an article about trained doctors in new laboratories using scientific approaches, who were replacing witch doctors. The tone was grimmer in November 1947, when *Ebony* told its readers that "700,000 homeless squatters [were] dying in the world's worst slums" in cities constructed "out of rubbish and trash."[8] The magazine reported on the progress African countries were making in their quest for independence despite impediments imposed by their former colonizers. The magazine ran profiles of leaders and ordinary people doing extraordinary things.

A Pioneering Woman Chronicles the Progress of a People

Ebony stepped up its foreign correspondence in the 1950s when it hired Era Bell Thompson. She wanted to go back to the land of her ancestors to see for herself whether it was "as dark and hopeless as it has been painted and to find out how it would receive a prodigal daughter who had not been there for three hundred years."[9] In 1953, she visited eighteen African countries.

From the time Thompson was born on August 10, 1905, in Des Moines, Iowa, until she moved to Chicago decades later, she had lived in a white world. She was the only daughter of Steward "Tony" Thompson and Mary Logan Thompson, both children of former slaves. In 1914, the Thompsons moved their daughter and three sons to the small community of Driscoll, North Dakota, where they were the only black family.

After graduating from Bismarck High School in 1925, Thompson enrolled at the University of North Dakota in Grand Forks, where she excelled in track and field. An extended bout of pleurisy in her sophomore year left her too debilitated to run track and forced her to leave school, but she is still recognized as one of the state's greatest athletes. She moved to Chicago and worked in a variety of short-lived clerical jobs before finding work at a magazine. She earned ten dollars a week and "learned how to run a magazine on hope, patience, and a very worn shoe string; to proofread and write advertising copy—and keep warm by burning magazines in an old fireplace."[10] In her free time, Thompson went to the library, where she discovered the works of Langston Hughes, Claude McKay, and other Harlem Renaissance writers.

Fate intervened, and Thompson returned to North Dakota in time to say good-bye to her dying father and close his secondhand furniture store. After working briefly for one of her uncles, she moved to St. Paul, Minnesota, where she worked as a typist for the *Bugle*, a black weekly. After only a few months in St. Paul, she moved to Grand Forks, North Dakota. She went at the invitation of a white minister, Rev. Richard Riley, and his wife; Thompson lived with them and attended college in exchange for doing chores. When Riley became president of Morningside College in Sioux City, Iowa, Thompson moved there with the family. Two years later, with a degree in journalism, she headed back to Chicago.

The country was in the midst of the Great Depression and, despite her optimism, Thompson did not become a writer for almost a decade. She made the rounds of African American businesses and newspapers but was unable to find work as a journalist. She managed to secure an interview with Robert Abbott, the founder and publisher of the *Chicago Defender.* A frail Abbott, long past the glory days when he had changed the face of African American journalism, gave Thompson a note to take to his office. But she did not hear from the newspaper. She later wrote that Abbott "knew in his heart that his recommendation no longer carried weight."[11] More clerical work followed before Thompson landed a job as an interviewer with the Illinois State Employment Service. She put her journalism skills to use by writing and distributing a one-page publication, the *Giggle Sheet.*

Thompson first came to the attention of John Johnson in 1947, when he read her autobiography *American Daughter.* He was impressed with her account of her life as an African American girl growing up in the Midwest, but he was even more impressed with her prose. He went to her Chicago apartment and asked her to join the staff of his new magazine. A petite woman about five feet tall, Thompson was not afraid to speak up. She had been looking for work as a journalist for years, and now, standing before her, was the publisher of a successful magazine. Instead of grabbing the job, she hesitated, telling Johnson that she "knew nothing about Negroes." Undeterred, he replied, "That's all right. We'll teach you."[12]

Thompson was a quick study; within two years she was promoted from staff writer to associate editor. Four years later, Johnson sent her to the land of her ancestors, intent on telling stories that would change the perception of Africa. Thompson guided *Ebony*'s coverage for forty years, serving as associate, managing, and international editor. The magazine did not remove her name from its masthead until 1985, the year before she died. She never married. *Ebony* was Thompson's life.

Ebony sent Thompson on a journey to debunk myths about Africa. She wrote in her autobiography that the continent had "moved into the headlines" after World War II as attention was focused on its rich natural resources. "Big-time newspapers and magazine correspondents . . . soon outnumbered anthropologists and men of God, for there was a sudden urgency to shed new light on the Dark Continent. . . . Europe was looking to the gold, diamonds and uranium in 'them thar' Africa hills. . . . America was looking toward Africa for new land, air bases, and strategic raw materials. The African himself was demanding to be heard, and the same wave of nationalism that set brown Asia free was knocking on black Africa's door."[13]

Thompson broke new ground when she reported for three months for *Ebony* and a book to be published by Doubleday, a major source of funding for her trip. Working in an arena where women and blacks were not often found, Thompson ascended to the elite ranks of foreign correspondents. Only 6 percent of foreign correspondents were women before 1970. In 1975, a year after Thompson ended her tenure as a correspondent, 10 percent of American foreign correspondents were women.[14] Black female foreign correspondents were even rarer. Although black journalists had gone abroad to cover wars, and some had continued reporting from overseas, no black woman had worked as a foreign correspondent on a sustained basis before Thompson.

Her stories about and photographs of the history, culture, and geography of various locales contributed a new perspective on Africa. Soon after arriving, she headed for the town of Ife, the ancient Yoruba city in southwestern Nigeria, which legend says is the site of the Garden of Eden. At its zenith, Ife had been an artistic center. Thompson reveled in its treasures, writing, "Here, indeed, was proof of the African cultural past, priceless art fashioned by black hands, many centuries ago. If these were my ancestors, I had reason to be proud."[15]

The Road to Independence

The first stop on Thompson's first trip was Liberia. Founded by free blacks and former slaves, the country occupied a special place in the black consciousness. Readers learned that its president, William V. S. Tubman, abhorred inequities based on race. Tubman wanted independence for his country, but he did not subscribe to the theory that Africa should be solely for Africans, as some leaders advocated. Independence was on the agenda of many countries. Thompson reported on the leaders and the liberation struggle.

She wrote about the economic condition of Africans in Liberia and other countries. She was surprised at the lack of black involvement in businesses. Asians were the traders, while Europeans were either business owners or managers. Lest the reader draw an unflattering conclusion about Africans' attitude toward work, Thompson explained that colonialism's repression of Africans accounted for their lack of skill and business acumen. The problem would plague the continent and other colonies as one country after another gained independence but was unable to sustain viable governance.

Ebony also published articles about Africa by other writers. The November 1962 issue ran a feature by John Bowles, who went to Nigeria to see for himself whether "unbelievable stories of business opportunities" were true.[16] Bowles reported that the country's economic market was equal to or better than the market in America. He had expected to find "a backward country, a backward people, hopeless political entanglement."[17] Instead, he found a nation using progressive business models and engaging in robust trade. Bowles also reported that the United States was withholding economic aid that Nigeria would use as investment capital to create employment opportunities. Bowles cast America in an unfavorable light but assured readers that the African nation would survive and thrive without the country's help.

In May 1964, Thompson reported that Ghana was proving wrong those who had predicted that Africa would "revert to the jungle" when "left to its own people's rule."[18] The West African nation had achieved independence in 1957, led by its American-educated prime minister Kwame Nkrumah, who had waged a successful campaign against British domination. With the change in the world order after World War II, Africans wanted a voice in guiding their continent. They wanted to benefit from its vast resources that were under the control of colonials from England, France, and Belgium. Nkrumah returned from Guinea after the war and became a leader in the independence movement, which resulted in a schism with more conservative Africans.[19] Thompson's article and photographs showed that Ghana was not "wasting time" disputing the "prophecy." Instead, it was using its resources, together with technical and financial aid from the United States and other nations, to build "an industrial economy unlike any colonial Africa had ever seen."[20]

Several months later, Thompson reported on another African leader, Moise Tshombe, whom she saw as shrewd, deliberate, and presidential. Tshombe had been elected president of the secessionist Katanga Province in 1960, the same year the Congo obtained its freedom from Belgium. After losing the election for president of the United Congo to Patrice Lumumba, Tshombe declared Katanga a separate country. Three years later, with the intervention of the United Nations, Tshombe was deposed; he eventually landed in exile in Madrid, Spain.

Thompson noted that the former Belgian colony had been unnoticed in international politics in 1963, but it had "exploded once more into the headlines" after Tshombe's return.[21] She described long days at his office in Madrid, where he reviewed reports from home, met with journalists and supporters from around the world, and waited for his chance to return to Africa. She expressed caution about the future of African independence, pointing out the hardships and economic challenges the continent faced as its nations fought for independence and then wrestled with governing after achieving self-rule.

During Thompson's tenure as international editor, infighting, corruption, and economic woes plagued the newly freed countries. In Ghana, a nation that Thompson had reported was making great strides, Nkrumah moved toward socialism and saw the economy fail and the tax base dwindle. He had successfully led Ghana to independence in 1957, but less than ten years later, he was deposed.

That was reason enough for *Ebony* to send one of its former editors to Ghana. When Charles Sanders arrived in September 1966, Nkrumah had already escaped the country in fear for his life; the National Liberation Council had led the revolt against his government. Sanders's straightforward, highly unfavorable article dissected Nkrumah's political career and his reign over Ghana in the 1950s and 1960s. His reporting on the deposed leader was based on interviews; he portrayed Nkrumah as a corrupt man who had squandered the opportunity to make Ghana a better country while amassing a fortune of one hundred million dollars, which he deposited in banks in Egypt, Holland, Germany, England, Switzerland, and France.

> If one believes the testimony of men who were once his economic advisors and closest ministerial cronies, Nkrumah not only was the most corrupt man in Ghana, but was at once an economic gambler who brought his country almost to bankruptcy while salting away a personal fortune in foreign banks, a Marxist-minded ideological shark who all but made Ghana an appendage of Eastern Communism, a great lover of light-colored women, and a megalomaniac so intent on ruling all of Africa that he bled his own country's treasury to finance revolutionists in neighboring states and probably set up one or two African presidents for assassination.[22]

Ebony's frank coverage of Nkrumah illustrates that it did not sacrifice journalistic objectivity and focus *only* on good news. The story revealed how a nation, a continent, and a people were affected politically, economically, and socially by the actions of one man. A powerful person of color had not lived up to the expectations of darker people. Some would argue that he fit the negative stereotype so often found in mainstream media in the West.

Beyond Independence

A decade after Thompson first reported from Africa, she went abroad to write about race relations. The civil rights movement in the United States dominated the news. Thompson juxtaposed other countries' treatment of blacks or Africans with the treatment of African Americans at home. In May 1964, she asserted that in South Africa, "apartheid out-Jim Crows segregation—its U. S. counterpart."[23]

Thompson revisited the African Diaspora fifteen years after she had first asked African leaders if they would accept African Americans. In 1968, several heads of state and a tribe of former African American Hebrews told Thompson they doubted that African Americans would be happy in a land with no cinema, no electricity, and a different perception of what it meant to be black. The leaders viewed African Americans as privileged, and although they condemned the United States for its racist attitudes and actions, they also criticized blacks in America who would give up a life Africans could only dream of simply because it was too hard.[24] Possibly African leaders had adopted this viewpoint because of exposure to the negative, stereotypical portrayal of African Americans in the media. This was not the positive story that *Ebony* preferred to publish.

Thompson profiled Ellen A. Sandimore, the first female mayor of Monrovia, Liberia. The story not only highlighted black achievement and progress, but commented on the women's liberation movement at home. In addition to running the city, Sandimore was a Presbyterian minister, mother of ten, and publisher of the *City Hall Journal*.

Of the 211 pieces about Africa that *Ebony* ran between 1946 and 2006, 9 ran between 1945 and 1950 and 31 ran between 1945 and 1959. Sixty-six features ran between 1960 and 1969, representing an increase in coverage of anticolonial fervor and independence movements in Africa and the parallel civil rights movement in the United States. In the 1960s, 32 African nations gained independence from colonial powers—11 between 1962 and 1966 alone. There was sparse coverage of Africa early on, but independence and nation-building dominated coverage in the 1960s.

A decline in *Ebony*'s coverage in the 1970s and 1980s coincided with turbulence in Africa. News from Africa in the mainstream media was rarely positive. Idi Amin was infamous for his brutal regime in Uganda. Both Haile Selassie of Ethiopia, whom the black press had championed in the 1930s, and Jean-Bedel

Bokassa, the self-styled emperor of Central Africa, fell from power. Apartheid continued in South Africa, and nonviolent antiapartheid activist Steve Biko died under mysterious circumstances. *Ebony* did not cover these events.

The sharp decline in coverage fit *Ebony*'s goal of telling "happy" stories since other media focused almost exclusively on negative ones. The black community in the United States had little in common with African nations, many of which were headed by corrupt leaders. In contrast, African Americans made more significant gains than ever.

In the 1990s *Ebony* made up for its lack of coverage in the two preceding decades. The magazine revisited Nigeria and published a special supplement to the February 1990 issue. "Modern Nigeria is the fascinating story of a people's determined and sustained hunt for an enduring democratic system," one article stated.[25] The story portrayed Nigeria as a modern country that was moving in a positive direction. A follow-up piece the following month called Nigeria the "African Giant" and a nation in transition. It ignored the economic instability and political turmoil in the country and created an unrealistic picture for readers.

Soon after the new decade began, *Ebony*'s attention turned to Nelson Mandela and South Africa. The magazine ran thirty-one stories about that nation alone. The black community had long identified with the struggles of South Africans. Numerous articles on the country appeared between 1990 and 1994, focused on the freeing of Mandela and the first open elections in the country's history. The magazine covered Mandela's winning the Nobel Peace Prize, the dismantling of the apartheid regime in South Africa, the country's first democratic elections, and Mandela's election as president. The May 1994 issue featured an exclusive interview with the new president, who shared his dream for a "free, democratic and non-racial South Africa," and drew parallels between the African American struggle for civil rights in America and his people's fight for self-determination.[26] Coverage continued the following month with excerpts from Mandela's letters from prison. In the same issue, correspondent Hans Massaquoi wrote about Namibia's freedom from South Africa. "So when independence finally came to Namibia after 106 years under colonial rule, it sent ripples of euphoria throughout Africa and the African Diaspora while raising demands for a free South Africa to a new pitch," he wrote.

One should not underestimate the importance of *Ebony*'s giving a voice to the marginalized and disfranchised. Johnson sent Era Bell Thompson to the scene throughout the African liberation movement. She had virtually unlimited access to leaders and ordinary people, and she illuminated their views, expectations, setbacks, and accomplishments. One could argue that by primarily presenting the positive side of Africa, *Ebony* was not telling the complete story. But that was not the magazine's goal. Its mission was to present African nations and black people in foreign countries in a favorable context, focusing on their triumph over adversity. Only seven negative or unflattering stories on Africa made it into the magazine. *Ebony* consistently avoided calling attention to crises and conflicts, devastating wars, genocide, famine, and government coups.

During the latter half of the 1990s and the 2000s, *Ebony* was a leader among black publications in both circulation and advertising revenue.[27] Paid circulation was approximately one and one-half million and readership was between nine and twelve million monthly. Today, the magazine is more entertainment oriented; it rarely runs stories about a continent that continues to struggle. Johnson wrote in the magazine's first editorial that not enough was "said about all the swell things we Negroes can do and will accomplish. *Ebony* will try to mirror the happier side of Negro life—the positive, everyday achievements."[28] As nations moved from colonialism toward freedom, *Ebony* overwhelmingly accentuated the positive.

The Associated Negro Press (ANP) Sets the Pace

Around the time that *Ebony* began to cover Africa, Claude Barnett, founder of the ANP, tried to provide coverage from the continent for the more than one hundred black publications the news agency serviced. On June 18, 1946, Barnett asked C. A. Scott of the *Atlanta Daily World,* C. C. Dejoie of the *Louisiana Weekly,* Leon H. Washington Jr. of the *Los Angeles Sentinel,* and more than twenty other publishers to join forces to pay a correspondent to report regularly from West Africa. Barnett argued that the particular slant given African news by the Reuters and Havas agencies meant that "the news exchange between Africa and American Negroes should be direct."[29] The proposed arrangement fell through because most of the publishers could not afford to pay a correspondent.

The ANP had some success. It sent out an article dated January 12, 1946, about a strike of Liberian dock workers against an American company building a naval base in Monrovia. African workers objected to earning only forty cents a day—approximately one hundred ten dollars a month—while imported Brazilian workers earned three hundred dollars a month. Strikers also objected to being forced to work long hours and on Sundays and being arrested for vagrancy if they refused.[30]

While this dispatch did not accuse the Americans of racial discrimination and exploitation of Africa's resources, the facts left no doubt that that was the situation in Liberia. The article charged that a New York firm was forcing mining concessions on Liberia and would hold more than a half million shares of the country's territory. This assertion was similar to one made by Marcus Garvey's black nationalist movement in the 1920s, after the collapse of his organization's efforts to engage in business in Liberia. Amy Jacques Garvey, the *Negro World*'s managing editor from 1924 to 1927, called for an end to colonialism. She also criticized the agreement between American rubber manufacturers and the Liberian government, which gave more than a million acres of land to the companies for the exploitation of rubber.

As it had done in the past, the ANP relied on travelers or businessmen to provide stories. Correspondence among Barnett and several reporters reveals both the inner workings of the ANP and the type of foreign correspondence it wanted. In March 1948, Barnett engaged Milton Macaulay to provide photographs from South Africa. But an undated letter from the publisher's secretary told Macaulay not to spend time or money taking and mailing photos of the unveiling of the Franklin Roosevelt monument because the photographs were of no value to black publications. "If in some way a Negro was involved in the unveiling," I. Roland wrote, "then that would be of interest to Negro newspapers and might justify your sending photos."[31]

Barnett also arranged to obtain news from Clifton Hardy, an advisor to the Liberian government. Hardy already had ANP credentials that enabled him to gather news for the service while he was in Paris. On January 1, 1955, Barnett wrote to Hardy that he was well positioned to give black tourists a favorable view of France. When Hardy moved to Liberia, the ANP accepted his offer to continue to provide information at no cost. "It is quite possible that the A.N.P. can use some material on Liberia, in view of this nation's tremendous strides in becoming a first class country. If so, I shall be only [too] happy to serve," Hardy wrote in February 1958.[32] Three months later, Barnett responded that the ANP would welcome stories about developments in the African state and that Hardy's post would enable him to present facts that would benefit Liberia.[33]

There was no doubt about what kind of coverage the ANP wanted and why.

In 1961, Hardy relocated to Paris because of ill health, but he promised to send the ANP "worthwhile stories."[34] ANP stationery listed him as Paris bureau chief, but it is not clear whether his stories ever made it into print; the ANP disseminated the dispatches, but its member newspapers decided whether to run them.

By the late 1950s, the ANP had also established a service that provided news and feature packets in French and English; one hundred African newspapers subscribed to it. Barnett was so proud of this service that he tried unsuccessfully to market it to black colleges and schools as a resource for teaching journalism and French.[35] The ANP maintained detailed lists of its subscriber newspapers and of payments to its correspondents in Africa, India, England, Jamaica, and Panama.

The ANP was more aggressive in its news gathering in the 1960s, with at least five correspondents in Africa. A February 20, 1960, memorandum outlined its African operations and reiterated its goal. The ANP wanted to avoid articles about "internal quarrels or bitter philosophical clashes"; when that could not be avoided, the correspondents were to "make a special effort at impartiality by reporting both sides as fairly as possible" and by avoiding personal bias or prejudice.[36] Like *Ebony* the ANP steered clear of negative stories.

David Talbot was an advisor to English publications in Ethiopia and later advisor to the minister of press and information in Addis Ababa. Barnett asked him to file periodic updates on African Americans working in Ethiopia.[37] Talbot filed seventeen dispatches before Barnett informed him that the ANP could no longer pay him seventeen dollars and fifty cents per month. The agency was suspending its world news service because of insufficient subscribers.[38]

The Good and the Not So Good: Enoch Waters's Postcolonial Coverage

The ANP made a major investment in 1960 when it decided that its executive editor and a seasoned foreign correspondent would report on postcolonial Africa from the continent. Correspondent Enoch Waters wrote about the hurdles they had to overcome: "Little is now or has been written about the experiences, attitudes, and observations of those who did the legwork for black newspapers. It was, and is, they who faced racial barriers, ridicule, insults, and even violence in the efforts to carry out their assignments. They had to devise techniques and stratagems to overcome and circumvent obstacles meant to prevent and discourage them from obtaining information needed to carry out the mission of the black press."[39]

As a correspondent for the ANP, Waters reported from postcolonial Africa in the early 1960s. Just as *Ebony*'s Era Bell Thompson had done, Waters interviewed leaders of African states and prominent figures in the independence movements. He also laid the groundwork for the ANP's news service on the continent, to facilitate a news exchange between the black press in the United States and the press in Africa.

Waters had had a distinguished career as a foreign correspondent who covered World War II from the Pacific Theater for the *Chicago Defender*. He was editor of the *Defender* when it became a daily in 1956. By 1960, he was executive editor of the ANP. In October 1960, he went to Nigeria to cover its independence celebrations. Over the next eighteen months, he filed one hundred reports from fifteen countries. He wanted to be on "African soil" to share "the exuberance and hope of the people in 1960–61 when twenty-one of the present thirty-two countries in black Africa became independent."[40]

Waters filed a favorable assessment of western Nigeria, the first stop on his itinerary in 1960. The headline "Royal Titles Abundant in Democratic Nigeria" topped a story from Sokoto about the country's many people of noble blood. Not only were Africans experiencing great success, so were African Americans who had moved to Nigeria after World War II.[41] From Ibadan, Waters wrote that black men ruled the country, made deals with foreigners, and owned corporations. Here was the land that Marcus Garvey had envisioned four decades earlier.[42]

Waters's reports were not always favorable. Alhaji Sir Ahmadu Bello, the premier of Nigeria's northern region, told Waters that "Negroes in America made no gestures of friendship during his visit" in 1960.[43] Africans in the country's western region also believed blacks were "unconcerned about their African brothers," but they hoped African Americans would come to live on the continent and share their talents.

A Great Celebration

Waters reported on Nigerian independence celebrations. He was joined in the country by ANP editor Claude Barnett and his wife, who were touring Africa. The fact that Barnett visited Africa three times in one year demonstrates how important the continent was to black leaders and the black press. "How often does one have the opportunity of being in the delivery room at the moment of the birth of a nation," Waters wrote, adding that he "and thousands of others were fortunate and privileged" to be on the scene.[44]

Waters was more than a bystander or observer; he was a participant in the celebration. He met "lords and ladies, chiefs and ministers, bishops, including the Archbishop of Canterbury, and many other titled" and "top drawer people, the VIPs from all over Nigeria, most of Africa and the rest of the world."[45] His stories exuded pride in Nigeria. "This city [Lagos] conducted itself like any big American city fortunate enough to be the stage for a historic event of worldwide significance."[46] Such a favorable appraisal challenged past assumptions about Africa.

Waters also wrote about problems brewing in Nigeria. Many public officials believed the country was making progress, but others thought it was sliding backward. The writer cited as evidence of growth the expenditure of more than one hundred million dollars in construction, including fifteen million dollars for a wharf extension and ninety million for an iron and steel plant. Social and educational services were expanding as teachers and health workers arrived from America, Canada, and Great Britain. "The inventory of progress in all fields could continue for pages, but it would only document the rapid strides that have been taken during the past year," Waters stated.[47] He then quoted Chief Obafemi Awolowo, an opposition leader, who said that this type of progress was meaningless because it led to moral collapse.

Waters acknowledged that the "shocking and bitter charges" were indeed valid and cited as evidence the practice of young Nigerians who wrote "begging letters" to people in other countries.[48] Waters's manuscript elaborated on growing problems between the northern region of the country, which had a large Muslim population, and the southern region, which was Christian and Westernized. He suggested that the problems were akin to growing pains that other nations had successfully navigated. "The future of Nigeria is yet to be determined, though is favorable," Waters wrote.[49]

The stories Waters filed from Ghana were full of hope and excitement. "Mann on the Job" was about "a big, tractor-strong, gray eyed American engineer from Newbern, N. C.," who was using the knowledge and expertise he had acquired at the all-black Hampton Institute, Drexel University, the University of Mexico, and Tuskegee's army air base to help the nation "build itself in a very literal sense."[50] Another dispatch reported that Ghana had once imported

144,000,000 expensive eggs yearly from South Africa; now Ghanaians were producing their own eggs, thanks to a young native student who had studied at the Tuskegee Institute, returned home, and started a poultry farm with 600 chicks. He now had 22,000 chickens and produced 7,000 eggs daily. This was a story not only of progress but also of a link with African Americans.

In a dispatch from Liberia, Waters wrote that the nation had struggled against threats from native tribes, British and French exploitation, and American indifference. The African republic was still "embarrassingly primitive" and a source of shame for blacks in America, but it was a living refutation of colonialist charges that blacks were incapable of self-governance and an "inspiration to the Africans longing for their freedom and independence."[51] Waters also wrote that the United States and the Soviet Union were seeking control in Guinea. In one dispatch, Waters introduced a topic that is still timely, the United States' dependence on foreign oil. "It has been characteristic of white Americans to underrate those of different races, religion and nationality," he wrote. "We have been led to believe that we have achieved our status as the wealthiest and most powerful nation in the world on our own and that we are invincible."[52] He suggested that the United States look at Rome and Greece, former world powers whose arrogance had led to their demise.

From Dakar, Senegal, Waters wrote that an aerial view gave "the impression of a clean and immaculate city." But on the ground he found slums "worse than any in Chicago, Philadelphia or New York . . . carefully concealed behind high walls, shrubbery and hidden away in courts. Here one finds the miserable families that exist on 50 cents a day or less."[53]

Waters wrote about a different Africa from the one *Ebony* depicted. Early on, he filed positive dispatches about countries full of hope, but he did not ignore the realities of the situation. His coverage of Africa was vastly different from that provided by the ANP during the Italian-Ethiopian War, the Spanish Civil War, and World War II, when colonialism, imperialism, fascism, and Nazism were blamed for the problems of the continent. By the time Waters ended his reports from Africa, some nations had been free for more than twenty years. He reported on events in much the same way as the mainstream media did.

With Waters's departure from the ANP, and with the demise of the news service in 1967, blacks in America had to rely on other sources to give them the black side of the story, or what the black press called the true story. *Ebony* wanted to primarily show a progressive Africa, but much of the story was overwhelmingly negative and tragic. The *Chicago Daily Defender* stepped up to provide coverage of conflicts on the continent. The newspaper became a daily in 1956.

Beyond Independence: The *Chicago Daily Defender* Fills the Gap

Ethel Payne arrived in Nigeria in the middle of a civil war that pitted rebels from the eastern region against the military government. Since 1966, the *Chicago Daily Defender* had relied on United Press International (UPI) for reports on the escalating crisis in Nigeria. Those articles reported on failed coup attempts, the assassination of a Nigerian military official, and the outbreak of civil war. The war had been raging for almost two years when Sengstacke Publications, which owned the *Defender* and fifteen other black newspapers, dispatched Payne, its Washington correspondent, to Africa in February 1969. She was to report "exclusive stories dealing with the 'true' story behind the war."[54] A year later, Payne traveled to ten African nations with Secretary of State William Rogers on a fact-finding mission.

Payne's career as a reporter had an unusual start. While working as a hostess at the army's Special Services Club in Tokyo in 1948, she had written an article about relationships between black servicemen and Japanese women and instances of racism and discrimination on the army base. The *Defender* published it, and publisher John Sengstacke offered Payne a job. "Hell, if you can write like that, why don't you come home?" he asked.[55] She did.

Payne covered the Bandung Conference in 1955. She was one of only three African Americans and the only black woman who covered the Vietnam War for the black press. Her assignment to Africa in 1969 was her first trip there. Although Nigeria had been free since 1960, its vast land mass and multiple ethnicities contributed to disunity and distrust. In May 1967, the central government had divided the four regions of the country into twelve states; the eastern region rebelled against this action in which it had had no input. The eastern sector declared itself the separate and independent state of Biafra. Failing to reunite the country civilly, the Nigerian government employed force. War broke out on July 6, and within a month, Biafran rebels had expanded the war into the midwestern region.

Payne's articles framed the war in terms of global politics driven by the quest for economic gain. She wrote that the country was not in charge of its affairs or its destiny, and she examined the roles of Great Britain, the United States, Portugal, France, and the Soviet Union in the civil war. Biafran rebels wanted control of the eastern region, where rich oil deposits were located. The former colonial powers were jockeying for access to those resources. Payne noted that the Nigerian government distrusted the British because their media slanted coverage, distorted the facts, and spread pro-Biafra propaganda.

Payne asserted that relations between the United States and Nigeria were strained because the United States had supplied cargo planes to carry relief supplies to Biafra. "Nigeria considers it an unfriendly act and unfortunately, it has been interpreted as further evidence of playing a concealed hand in the game of high stakes for economic imperialism," she wrote.[56] Her next dispatch stated that relations were almost at the breaking point because the Nigerian government distrusted Richard Nixon's administration.[57] The distrust had begun when Nixon made pro-Biafra statements while campaigning for the presidency; Massachusetts Senator Edward Kennedy also supported the rebel cause. Payne wrote that the Nigerians accused Kennedy of consorting with southern senators. That part of the story resonated with blacks at home and reinforced the message that the United States stepped on darker people in pursuit of economic gain, both abroad and at home.

Payne's stories sought to educate readers about how policies and practices of nations ruled by whites had a detrimental, even deadly, impact on darker people. This was different from the narrative in the mainstream media in which such economic exploitation was not a frame. When Payne accompanied Rogers on his 1970 trip to discuss aid to African nations, she filed a story about unrest brewing in Ethiopia. According to Payne, Rogers told Ethiopian emperor Haile Selassie that U.S. aid was dependent on Congress and the administration had no control over Congress.[58] The message was that Africa could not count on the U.S. aid.

Through Payne's reports, the *Chicago Daily Defender* and its sister publications filled a gap by providing episodic coverage from Africa during the 1970s. The ANP had gone out of business in 1967; most black publications relied on national news services, primarily UPI, for news from abroad. Gone were the days when the black press fielded thirty foreign correspondents during World War II. Sengstacke Publications was in a different situation. The *Defender* was a daily with a national circulation, and to some extent it was a national news service. It sent Payne to Africa periodically to cover significant events. She reported from Liberia in 1971 on the funeral of President Tubman; from Nairobi, Kenya, in 1975; and from six sub-Saharan nations in 1976, covering Secretary of State Henry Kissinger's visits with the goal of increasing economic development.

African American foreign correspondence set out in the late 1940s to report from Africa and to fashion an image of the continent. Over the next three decades, African American journalists presented an overwhelmingly favorable impression of developments and people on the continent and often highlighted the common bonds between blacks in America and the people from whom they descended. Black foreign reporting continually lessened during the ensuing decades. Individual enterprise would once again characterize the genre.

[11]

Tan Yanks in an Integrated Military

James Hicks and Albert Hinton boarded an airplane in the United States on their way to cover the Korean conflict in 1950, but only one of them made it. Hinton, the managing editor of the *Norfolk Journal and Guide* in Virginia, was to report for that weekly and other black publications that relied heavily on the Negro Newspaper Publishers Association (NNPA) news service. Hicks was on assignment for *The Afro-American* and its chain of weekly newspapers. They flew the first leg of the six thousand-mile flight to Tokyo together, but took separate planes for the last 116-mile leg of the trip because Hicks wanted to pick up additional clothing. Hinton died when the C-47 transport plane carrying him disappeared into the sea between Tokyo and Korea. Hicks covered the undeclared war, but he was not the only black correspondent.

Some newspapers ran accounts generated by mainstream media organizations. The *Atlanta Daily World* ran forty-seven dispatches generated by the International News Service's Howard Handleman in 1950 alone. The number and nature of stories in the mainstream media, however, did not satisfy the black community. Between July and December 1950, when each black war correspondent was generating dozens of in-depth stories, the influential *New York Times* ran ten stories that mentioned the all-black Twenty-fourth Division, integration, or "colored soldiers." The race perspective was missing, as the 1952 *Negro Year Book* stated. "The Negro inevitably reads about the war, but the war becomes the more real and the source of more pride to him when he knows the American Negro is contributing his share. Occasionally, a few lines, such as the capture of Yechon by the Negro elements of the 24th Infantry Division, July 21, 1950, crops into the daily news dispatches, but there are no names there and there is no story of individual heroism. That coverage becomes the obligation of the colored press of the country."[1]

The Afro-American, the *Chicago Defender*, and the *Pittsburgh Courier* filled the void, sending five correspondents to the front. The ten-year-old NNPA provided stories to subscriber periodicals before Hicks and his colleagues arrived in the war zone and after they went home. While the NNPA also used stories from some of the newspapers' correspondents, most of its stories were provided by Milton Smith, Theodore Stanford, and Bradford Laws, a GI in the United Nations forces who was listed as the Far East correspondent.

The *Chicago Defender* wanted to be a leader in national and international reporting. On July 15, 1950, it ran a picture of a dapper-looking Alexander Wilson holding a telephone to his ear. The newspaper's "ace" reporter would provide exclusive coverage of the Second and the Twenty-fourth Infantry Regiments.[2] Wilson had experienced combat as a marine during World War II, and the newspaper considered him an expert on the Far East. The Florida native had graduated from historically black Florida A&M University and taken graduate courses in journalism at the University of Wisconsin. He had worked as a teacher, assistant principal, and principal in Florida while freelancing for the black press. He had eventually joined the staff of the *Defender.*[3]

The Afro-American made a larger commitment by dispatching more correspondents for longer periods to the front line. By the time the *Defender* made its announcement about Wilson, Hicks was already reporting from the strategic location of Yechon, Korea, where black troops were holding back the enemy. Before getting the assignment as a pool correspondent for *The Afro-American,* the Akron, Ohio, native had covered civil rights for the newspaper. He began his journalism career as a reporter in 1935 for the *Cleveland Call and Post* after studying at Howard University in Washington, D.C., and at the University of Akron. Hicks had risen to the rank of captain during World War II, where he commanded a quartermaster troop in the Pacific before going overseas to represent *The Afro-American* and several other newspapers. He was battle tested, an advantage in his new assignment. The knowledge and experience he had gained covering integration gave him insight into that issue in Korea.

Frank Whisonant, a World War II veteran who had risen to the rank of first lieutenant with the Ninety-second in Italy, reported for the *Pittsburgh Courier.* Ralph Matthews, one of the newspaper's star correspondents, reported for *The Afro-American* after Hicks and remained until December 1951. Matthews had covered the coronation of King George VI in 1937 and reported during World War II. William Worthy Jr., who later reported from abroad in defiance of U.S. travel bans from the 1950s through the 1990s, went to Korea for *The Afro-*

American in August 1953 to write about black and white prisoners of war at the end of the conflict.

The correspondents enabled the black press to continue its role as advocate, crusader, chronicler, truth-teller, and defender of the race. With black soldiers again heading to the battlefield, black newspapers wanted to ensure that accurate accounts of their role in the war would reach home. In his comprehensive book on the Twenty-fourth, William T. Bowers points out that the valor of the all-black regiment in wars dating back to the colonial period, including the Spanish-American War and World War II, was minimized or denied because official army versions highlighted its failures and portrayed it as innately inferior.[4] Black editors were determined not to allow that misrepresentation to continue during this conflict.

The ability to send their own reporters to Korea was a big deal for the three newspapers. When Wilson arrived in Asia, a *Defender* promotional piece included a large map of Korea with the star reporter's photo squarely in the center. The former combat veteran was "bringing to *Defender* readers the facts . . . first."[5] The newspaper stated, "Wilson left the United States fully equipped to give us the complete picture of this conflict in far off Korea. His camera records on film the daring of our boys. His typewriter describes the fighting in terse, sharp, down-to-earth language. His background on far eastern affairs helps him piece together the mysteries of the land."[6]

Although Hicks reached Japan in the last week of July, his stories from different places in Korea and Japan began to appear in the newspaper in the first week of August and continued through November 1950. Dozens of dispatches flowed from the typewriters and arrived via cable as the intrepid reporters covered tan yanks and mixed units wherever they were fighting. As many as four stories ran on page 1 of each newspaper every week. Hicks's reports appeared under "War News from Korea," while Wilson's appeared under "Along the Korean War Front" and Whisonant's under "Reports from the Front Lines." Human interest items ran in Wilson's "Front Line Grapevine" and Hicks's "Up Front with Hicks" columns. There was no indication that the war reporters faced any obstacles as they accompanied units that included the Twenty-fourth Infantry Regiment, the Twenty-fifth Infantry Regiment, the 159th Field Artillery, and the Seventy-seventh Combat Engineering Regiment.

When President Harry S. Truman ordered ground forces into South Korea in June 1950, the Twenty-fourth was closest to Korea. The *Chicago Defender* reported on July 15 that African American air force, navy, and army personnel were "thrown into the conflict" as the North Koreans forced American fighters to retreat.[7] The military strategy was to have the Twenty-fourth meet the initial attack and slow its advancement until the arrival of additional U.S. forces.

As soon as he reached Korea, Hicks began to report on the tan yanks; he was a vital link between the fighting men and their kin at home. Parents and wives asked *The Afro-American* publisher Carl Murphy to forward letters to their sons and husbands. Murphy obliged. In a letter to one mother, he wrote that he was sending her letter to Hicks: "I trust he will be able to help you as he is helping other parents come upon their children. So many of our boys forget to write when they get overseas. They don't know the anxiety of the fathers and mothers back home. Don't you stop writing him because he is not writing you. So you keep your chin up and keep on writing your boy. We will do our best to help you find him."[8]

Hicks's dispatches stressed the importance of letters from home. To facilitate communication, he included the names and addresses of soldiers who wanted letters, and he suggested that folks at home send writing paper and stamped envelopes to make it easier for the troops to reply.[9] In one dispatch, he cautioned, "Don't try to tell him that he shouldn't be fighting. . . . Don't tell him that you are in love with him. These guys are not that dumb. . . . Don't keep him waiting. Write him—right now."[10] *The Afro-American*'s initiative was successful. Hicks reported in one column that mail for one battalion had increased by 50 percent because girls and wives sent letters with photographs.

Hicks had a close-up view because he was with the marines on their first major offensive and obtained information from official sources—in this case, the public information officer of the First Cavalry in Japan. "The 24th is doing surprisingly well and I say this without bias," he wrote in the August 12 issue of the newspaper. "With each communiqué we get word of attacks and withdrawals on many fronts but very few of them state that the 24th withdrew, though all say they were attacked. The correspondents [mainstream newspaper correspondents at the front] are taking judicial notice of this."[11]

Hicks and his contemporaries filed objective and straightforward stories, but they also were advocates. Their reporting followed the same pattern and themes their counterparts addressed during World War II. Then, war reporters highlighted discrimination at home and abroad while chronicling the experiences of the soldiers.[12] The black press still hoped that accurate information about troop performance and loyalty, as well as the progress of integration, might lead to equality at home.

The Conflict through Our Eyes

Although Hicks's dispatches did not state that the tan yanks were attempting to prove themselves, they certainly suggested it. The headline "24th Soldiers Do Impossible" ran above one of his first pieces. He wrote that the men were doing a great job in "unbelievable conditions" despite the fact that they were in a situation he described as a "point of no return."[13] Months later, Hicks shared news about a tan yank whom authorities called one of the best pilots on an aircraft carrier.

Other publications followed suit. "Tan GI Mans Guns Alone; Halts Attack," read one headline on the *Defender*'s front page; another banner headline blared, "Tells Feat of Negro Marine Hero." Another piece reported that the tall, thin reporter Alexander Wilson had come under fire with the troops. Wilson wrote that the tan yanks were carrying "the fight to North Korea over the red-clay hills, mountains and through the valleys of this country from Yechon to the southwest coast."[14] A white commanding officer confirmed the troops' grit, telling the *Defender* that black soldiers at Battle Mountain were "out for victory."[15]

Whisonant reported that GIs fighting in muddy gullies were responsible for two hundred Korean deaths. "With their machine guns, automatic weapons and rifles stitching a line of death up and down the mountainous terrain . . . accompanied by the thundering crescendo of heavy artillery and the searing orange explosions of bursting rocket shells . . . men of the gallant Twenty-Fourth Infantry Regiment last week in some of the fiercest fighting of the Korean war killed more than two hundred of the enemy . . . halted and drove back North Korean troops, after they had overrun one company of the regiment . . . and otherwise continued to distinguish themselves as first-class fighting men."[16]

Some news was disquieting, especially accounts in *The Afro-American* and the *Courier*. Whisonant had not yet made it to the battlefield when he ran into a white correspondent who said the Twenty-fourth had suffered heavy casualties, and that he saw "rows of seriously injured tan yanks" as he left the battlefield.[17] More dreadful news followed on August 19 as Hicks reported that the infantry continued to fight even though the men's clothes were tattered and they lacked equipment. Not only had the army miscalculated, Hicks asserted, but the military brass had not replenished the depleted ranks.[18] Again, the correspondent portrayed the race troops favorably and the United States negatively. September and October brought more graphic accounts of the impact of war on the Twenty-fourth.

Both *The Afro-American* and the *Courier* highlighted massive casualties, including the accidental bombing by U.S. Navy planes that killed ten and wounded twenty-three men of the Twenty-fourth. Another story reported that the unit had sustained more than 1,400 casualties. As if that news was not bad enough, Hicks and Whisonant provided more. Both wrote that the problems went beyond mere miscalculations and blunders. An effort to undermine the black troops was an underlying cause. The black correspondents were offended by personal comments, published reports, and official statements that misrepresented the tan yanks—even while acknowledging that at times the actions of some of Twenty-fourth tended to hurt all of them. The words "prejudice," "bias," and "discredit" appeared in the headlines above *Courier* and *Afro-American* stories that highlighted troop valor. One series of stories received such play in the *Pittsburgh Courier* that the National Association for the Advancement of Colored People (NAACP) called for an investigation, especially after reports that the Pentagon had refused to comment on the veracity of whether the unit would be dismantled or reconfigured into noncombat units, but "intimated that the crack outfit may be removed from the front line in Korea because of 'battle fatigue.'"[19] Weekly accounts presented evidence that race troops were treated unjustly but kept fighting.

A *Pittsburgh Courier* headline asked if the Twenty-fourth was being made a scapegoat for the enemy's breakthrough on September 1. An "accusing finger" had been pointed at the unit, and now the "combat efficiency of the once crack" unit had been reduced by about fifty "due to the questionable tactics" of the division's leaders—who were white. "These troops, once the pride of the Eighth Army, are now less than a shadow of their old selves," Whisonant reported.[20] An *Afro-American* dispatch titled "Army Passes Buck" left no doubt as to the paper's position.

> The green young, courageous . . . boys of the 24th Infantry Regiment are battling in South Korea with more responsibilities on their shoulders than any soldiers have carried since Leonidas and his Spartans stood off the Greeks at Thermopylae Pass. . . . The reputation and in-

> tegrity of the colored people as fighting Americans is on the wings of every bullet, every bazooka shell.[21]

As the war continued, the steady drip of negative news about the toll on the tan yanks continued in *The Afro-American* and the *Courier*. These stories were meant to inform readers of what was happening to their fellow blacks on the battlefield and to pressure the military brass to be accountable. Meanwhile, the *Defender* stuck primarily to reporting success stories. One story that the other two papers ran in 1950, but the *Defender* ignored, was about a black officer who was sentenced to death.

The Case of Lt. Leon Gilbert

In the fall of 1950, Frank Whisonant of the *Pittsburgh Courier* reported on the case of Lt. Leon Gilbert, a twice-wounded member of the Twenty-fourth. A court-martial board had sentenced Gilbert to death for refusing to obey orders that would have sent him on a virtual suicide mission. The soldier had had a similar experience when he followed orders and led most of his men to their deaths while pushing back the enemy. This time, he suffered the consequences of making a decision in the best interest of his men. Whisonant asked Gilbert whether he had refused to take his company back to the hill around Sangju as ordered. Gilbert explained his actions.

> Yes, but not in the way Col. Horton V. White accused me of refusing. I had been holding an outpost position with twelve men when the enemy overran my position and was surrounding us. As I withdrew with my men to keep them from being killed needlessly, I met Lieut. Col. Paul Roberts, regimental executive officer, who told me to take the men to the main line of resistance which was to the rear. I started out, but was stopped by Colonel White who had no idea of the situation to the front. The colonel ordered me to take my men back to the position which the enemy now held. When I told him it would be possible suicide, he ordered me again.
>
> On the second order I told him I would go around a route which I knew where the enemy's guns were located, but he ordered that I go directly into the enemy lines. When I said that route was nothing but suicide and meant certain death to the men, I was placed under arrest.

I don't deny that I was scared that night, but so was everybody else.

When my trial came up on September 6, all men and officers of my company wanted to testify for me, but the court-martial board said they could not be released from frontlines.

I think the decision was cut and dried before the trial.[22]

The *New York Times* had also reported on Gilbert's case in September and October. A storm of protest erupted; veterans groups, national groups, and civil rights organizations demanded that Gilbert be cleared and released. The black press also reported that black soldiers were being court-martialed in far greater numbers than white soldiers, although there were fewer black soldiers overseas. Black soldiers were also receiving harsher penalties. The *Courier* appealed directly to President Truman to spare the life of Gilbert, a husband and father of two young children with a third on the way. NNPA reports stated that the army would review the case to avoid criticism. *Courier* readers had learned of the case on September 30; the newspaper reported that Whisonant had had the story on September 17, but army officials had ordered the correspondent to hold it.[23] The censorship worked for a while, but Whisonant used the time to dig up more information and to score an exclusive interview with Gilbert.

Hicks was unable to interview Gilbert until November, shortly before the correspondent left for the states. *The Afro-American* published the interview as a front-page "exclusive" and proclaimed "Lt. Gilbert Will Not Die!"[24] The soldier told Hicks that he was being treated well and that he believed the death sentence would not be carried out. Milton Smith confirmed this on December 2, when he reported that the sentence had been commuted to twenty years. The sentence was subsequently commuted to five years.

Integration: Is It Working?

Integration was on the black agenda even before the tan yanks went to the front lines in Korea. Stories about discrimination, prejudice, and human rights violations were prominent in black publications, which advocated against the racism that was condoned on the home front. Despite Truman's executive order integrating the military in 1948, the armed forces were not completely desegregated. Aggressive challenges to America's undemocratic status quo appeared in virtually every issue of the weekly newspapers, but the appeals often fell on deaf ears. In July 1950, after tan yanks had moved to the front lines, the *Chicago Defender* began a campaign to have army brass appoint an African American general in Korea. The newspaper argued that the communist North Koreans were using propaganda to divide and demoralize black troops. The newspaper's campaign went on for two months, but the military did not act. In a July 29 column the *Defender* again called for integration.

> Give Us Eyes to See
>
> In the wee sma' [sic] of many a sleepless night, we try to figure what's substituting for a soul and a conscience in the prejudice-racked bodies of lotta [sic] Southern bigots we know. We wonder how human rights atheists like Mississippi's Jim Eastland and Georgia's Dick Russell can keep a straight face before the Almighty and stay eternally poised to launch depraved attacks against Negro Americans at the dropping of a color bar. Now Negroes have helped to bail out American democracy in every armed conflict this country has ever faced. Like in this present Korean set-to. It was Negro doughboys who drove North Korean Communists out of Yechon to occupy the important rail and highway city. For 16 hours, black soldiers whom Eastland publicly ridiculed as cowards forged ahead under a barrage of artillery and mortar fire to win the first sizeable American ground victory in the Korean War. These also are the boys who Georgia's top fascists claim will contaminate white military units in a racially integrated U.S. Army. These boys, and many more, will whip back the Communist onslaught with their blood—some with their lives, only to return home to find it's still open warfare on the extension of American rights to all citizens regardless of race.[25]

Black journalists wrote about the success of the racial experiment. The *Defender* especially focused on the democratizing impact of race mixing in the military[26] as it sought to influence the dominant power structure in America. Wilson wrote that integration overseas gave black troops opportunities that were out of reach in the United States. This war meant the end of Jim Crow in the military, even though blacks still lived under that repressive system at home.[27] The war was "the purgative of race hate among comrades on the front lines" and showed that tan yanks and white soldiers could "pray together, eat and sleep together, work together and fight shoulder to shoulder—and like it, if left alone."[28] Another dispatch stated that the desegregation of the Ninth

Infantry Regiment was necessary because of high black casualty rates and the need for replacements. Integration would enable the United States to continue to successfully wage the war and destroy the enemy.[29] "If racial integration will work on a volunteer basis," Wilson wrote, "it can and will work by decree."[30]

Wilson continued to push for integration when he returned home, writing a series that touted the success of the racial experiment. He argued that the "tragic Korean conflict" was "another milestone in the forward march of the Negro and other minorities toward complete integration in the democratic way of life."[31] He quoted white officers who believed that integration was making the war more winnable.

The *Courier* and *The Afro-American* also supported integration of the military, but their coverage was more balanced than the *Defender*'s. Whisonant wrote about a heated exchange he had with a white army colonel who said that the United States would be defeated if the Twenty-fourth continued to lose guns to the Koreans. Whisonant explained that the tan yanks had first abandoned and then recaptured the one gun in question. The enemy had never possessed the gun.

> I then turned to the Colonel (who was the chaplain) and asked him if he knew how much equipment the Thirty-Fifth Infantry Regiment had lost to the enemy on the same morning and during the same attack. When he said he didn't know, then I informed him that the enemy had taken *all* the mortars from one [white] company.
>
> From that minute on he began explaining how it was all right for one outfit to lose its guns while another one could not afford to lose even one gun. When he had finished he sounded more ridiculous than he had when he came in.
>
> Realizing he sounded ridiculous, the Colonel then spoke up and said he was definitely prejudiced being from Houston, Texas.
>
> When asked if his feelings were in accordance with the Bible, the Colonel admitted they were not, but stated they were his own and that he intended to keep them.[32]

The *Courier* vociferously demanded equal treatment, especially when blacks learned that South Korean troops, instead of black soldiers, were being used as replacements in all-white units. "The only thing a South Korean has in common with a white American is their common struggle against the

Communist-directed and supplied North Koreans, whereas white and colored American lads have everything in common except color," an editorial charged.[33] "For any officer to contend now that likewise integrating American Negroes into 'white' units 'would not work' becomes not only ridiculous but criminally stupid if not downright disloyal. . . . The present Administration, which has talked more than any previous one about abolishing prejudice, segregation and discrimination based on color, can make this change NOW, and colored America will hold it accountable if this is not done."[34]

Whisonant blamed white racism and jealousy for rumors that the Twenty-fourth might be disbanded. He reported that white troops had said that the Twenty-fourth's soldiers were cowards, afraid to fight. The tan yanks had replied that "if they had done any running at all then they did 'a damn good job of holding the ground' assigned to them" while retreating.[35] White soldiers, in turn, called their black comrades liars. The unrest and discontent of the Twenty-fourth led to low morale in a unit that had been called "the best fighting regiment in the Korean War."[36] African American reporters were telling a different story from those in the mainstream media and those circulated by the military.

In *The Afro-American*, Hicks advocated for integration on the battlefront, citing the successful performance of mixed units. When the Twenty-fourth finally became an integrated unit, Hicks took note.[37] Mixed units were successful, he wrote; one mixed squad had killed two hundred enemy soldiers. Before heading home, Hicks also noted that the successful air corps was "synonymous with racial integration in South Korea."[38]

Veteran Newsman Off to War

The Afro-American sent Ralph Matthews to Korea in late July 1951. With his stylish hat, smart suit, and white shirt, carrying a camera in one hand and a briefcase in the other, Matthews looked every inch the veteran newsman and world traveler.[39] Months had passed since the other three correspondents had returned home, where they continued to push for integration. Matthews was now the only accredited black war correspondent in Korea and the only reporter the black community trusted when the Twenty-fourth was disbanded. An NNPA story in *The Afro-American* confirmed that the famed regiment was being abolished and its personnel reassigned as replacements in other units. There were no banner headlines. This was a fait accompli, and it was generally well received. Integration of the military was happening.[40]

Peace talks were bogged down when Matthews arrived. He advocated for Dr. Ralph Bunche to be sent to move the talks along. The black diplomat had recently received the Nobel Peace Prize for mediating the armistice during the Arab-Israeli conflict of 1949. Stories about that honor had run on the front pages of black newspapers and in the mainstream press as well.

One of Matthews's first stories revealed that Gen. Matthew Ridgway, MacArthur's replacement as the Supreme Commander of United Nations forces, opposed segregation and had asked the Department of Defense to end segregation in the military units he commanded. Earlier stories in *The Afro-American* had criticized MacArthur for failing to end segregation.[41] Black editors agreed that Ridgway was a superior choice; Matthews quoted him as saying that Korea illustrated that wars could not be won with segregated units.[42]

Reporting from Tokyo, Matthews wrote that integration had progressed "to such a point in Japan that trying to locate colored personnel is like looking for needles in the proverbial haystack."[43] The name of a unit no longer indicated the race of its members. Matthews reported that the signing of the treaty ended Jim Crow in Japan, and he asked, "If it is done in Japan, why not in the States where our heroes are still Jim Crowed?"[44] Matthews also filed photographs he took of black and white soldiers working together. He reported that a white soldier had acknowledged that blacks at home were discriminated against, and another had said, "The trouble was with me so I began to make friends and now I consider some of the fellows here my best pals. The company has a lot of good men and I am proud to be associated with them."[45] Matthews returned home in December.

Their Propaganda Did Not Work

Coverage of Korea in the black press faded as the war wound down. The *Chicago Defender* practically ignored the conflict once the army had been desegregated. The paper's ultimate goal, after all, was integration and equal rights, and both had been accomplished in some measure in Korea. *The Afro-American* shifted its foreign coverage to Africa, where independence movements were germinating. But Carl Murphy believed Korea was still newsworthy. He sent William Worthy Jr. to report on the truce that was signed on July 27, 1953, and on troops being held as prisoners of war.

Tall, slim, serious, and sophisticated, Worthy was a Massachusetts native who had studied journalism and politics at Bates College in Maine. *The Afro-*

American gave him his first job as a foreign correspondent. Worthy filed two articles that ran on August 8, which gave both a black and a white perspective on communism. He did not talk only to black soldiers, as most black correspondents had until then. He also interviewed white prisoners of war and included their take on their situation, reporting what both black and white prisoners of war thought and said. These men, after all, had just spent two years together fighting the communist-led North Koreans. Both groups of soldiers were battle fatigued and apathetic toward news of the peace, Worthy wrote. One private-first-class who had been in Korea for more than five months had "fewer than 30 words of comment."[46]

Worthy was critical of stories in the white media about black soldiers' good humor and "own version of the English language."[47] He pointed out that soldiers of all races were limited in their ability to articulate and were not "gifted with the power of fluent speech."[48] The men he interviewed told Worthy that the Koreans had tried to divide them by using propaganda, telling black soldiers that it was absurd to fight abroad when they were treated as second-class citizens at home. Some black soldiers wondered if a better life awaited them under communism. Worthy's reporting was echoed in Whisonant's reports on Seoul City Sue's broadcasts intended to influence black troops and the Korean government's attempt to get them to desert. Worthy reported that white prisoners of war said the Koreans meted out harsher punishment to white soldiers because of their skin color and because the Koreans presumed they had "biases against their fellow man based on race alone" and "had oppressed all the people of the world."[49]

When the Korean conflict ended in 1953, black war correspondents had ensured that the contributions of tan yanks did not go unnoticed. Black reporters gave black soldiers a human face while reporting information their families and friends craved.

Although some African Americans believed black soldiers were invisible in the mainstream media, that was not entirely the case. Black war correspondents acknowledged several times that white dailies ran stories about black soldiers. An early dispatch by Hicks, for example, pointed out that the Twenty-fourth's victory at Yechon—the first major victory of the war—was being hailed across America. That would not have been possible if only black newspapers had reported it. Stories in the mainstream dailies, however, did not feature the human side of the conflict. Black reporters got that story by interviewing and interacting with the soldiers. A number of large dailies reported as facts the negative comments that elected officials, white soldiers, and official military sources made about black soldiers. The *Courier*, *The Afro-American*, and the *Defender* countered that story by reporting that most black military personnel excelled on the battlefield, often without support, and remained fiercely loyal to their country.

Unfortunately, foreign coverage in the black press had little effect on life in the black community. The Korean War had been seen as yet another opportunity for change. The correspondents had been advocates, defenders, and cheerleaders who told the story of the African American soldier. Their stories made it difficult for blacks to rationalize the insidious and overt discrimination that persisted against them, both in the newly integrated military and at home. Blacks were no longer willing to try to show America that they deserved civil liberties. They were poised to take to the streets, to march, and to fight a different kind of battle to win equal rights.

Change was brewing in black foreign correspondence. The black press had sent dozens of correspondents overseas during World War II. For the Korean conflict, it had sent only four. Race problems at home and lack of financial resources meant that the black press would turn its attention to what was happening in America. The Korean War was the last in which more than three newspapers engaged in sustained global reporting. Starting in the mid-1940s, the black press had faced competition from the liberal white press and the radical black press. That situation was exacerbated by the advent of television and by the integration of the mainstream press in the 1960s, when star reporters were hired away from the black press. One reporter, William Worthy Jr., would become the face of black foreign correspondence as he traveled the world in defiance of the U.S. government to report on stories he believed people had a right to know. Two years after the Korean conflict, he headed to Russia to report on the Cold War.

[12]

Defiance in the Name of Press Freedom

On a cold Christmas Eve in 1956, William Worthy Jr. went to his room on the Harvard University campus, where he was a Nieman fellow, and found a visa and a cablegram had been slid under his door. The cable invited Worthy to travel to China as a reporter. He hastened to Boston's Logan Airport before the State Department could get on his trail and flew to Tokyo. From there he traveled by train and slipped into China along its border at Lo Wu. He defied a government travel ban to the communist country.

For forty-one days, Worthy filed stories to *The Afro-American* newspaper chain and CBS News from mainland China. That was not an easy task, given the climate in America and the dramatic changes in the world after World War II. The Cold War was well underway. Communism was taking hold in Europe and Asia. African nations trying to throw off the yoke of colonialism were also looking to the East. McCarthyism had tainted many Americans as communists or communist sympathizers. In 1951, the State Department invoked the McCarran Internal Security Act of 1950 to proscribe foreign travel to communist nations and to deny passports to persons suspected of affiliating with communists or seeking to attend international congresses, or whose presence abroad was deemed not in the "national interest."[1]

Worthy defied the national-interest argument. He believed world power politics and fear of communism were the reasons for the government's suppression of the press. That conviction guided a career that reads like a spy novel—trips to remote prisons in politically and militarily threatening countries, violence, war, covert exits in the dark of night, false identities, challenges to the government, hardship, and redemption. Even the mainstream media took note of this intrepid correspondent, who dared to enter forbidden countries to cover events on the world stage. In a 1970 interview, he explained that he had done it because "I was trying to stretch to the utmost, my long term faith that sufficient information . . . communicated to a sufficient number of people in this country, will eventually result in some change in direction and policy actions."[2]

Worthy never married. Raymond Boone, a lifelong friend who was like a son to him, said that the globetrotting correspondent wanted to give "a balance by not just hearing the official American point of view, but hearing the other side . . . to also have as many ideas on the table as possible with the view that the best idea would persist."[3] Worthy was further driven by the belief that no nation had the right to suppress people or the press; that a free press was obligated to cover all sides of the story; and that the press and ordinary citizens had the right to criticize the government.[4] Boone was familiar with Worthy's views because he was the editor of *The Afro-American* when Worthy embarked on many challenging assignments around the globe. Michael Meyers, another longtime friend, said the "driving force" in Worthy's life and work was his belief that "in order to be free, we have to know."[5]

When the thirty-five-year-old Worthy received the visa and cablegram, he did not hesitate to leave Harvard, where he was studying topics related to journalism as a prestigious Nieman Fellow. His reporting transformed the role of modern foreign correspondence. Unlike other reporters, who abided by the government's restrictions, Worthy acted on his own. Although other black foreign correspondents sometimes did the same—especially in the early years of the genre—black editors primarily worked through government channels to get news from abroad during conflicts. The black press lobbied the government to send a black journalist to report on black soldiers during World War I. African American editors also went through government channels for accreditation for their correspondents during World War II and the Korean conflict. Worthy asked no such permission. Even the mainstream media, although they reported Worthy's defiant actions, acquiesced to the government's travel restrictions.[6] Some of his friends called Worthy a radical—but "not the bomb-throwing kind."[7]

Born in Boston on July 7, 1921, into a politically involved family, William was the youngest of four children and the only boy. His father, William Worthy Sr., was a doctor and one of the founders of Boston's first black hospital. His mother, Mabel Posey Worthy, was a leader in black service clubs that worked to elevate the race through education, political activism, and social services.[8] Both parents were staunch Republicans, but they left the party in 1928 because they believed it was unresponsive to black concerns. They supported underdog presidential candidate Al Smith, a Roman Catholic and a Democrat.

Interviewed in 2008, Worthy's ninety-five-year-old sister Ruth Worthy remembered her brother as a brilliant loner. At age four or five, he often stood with his forehead pressed into the glass of the front door—as if he longed to find out what lay beyond that door. Often the outside world came to the Worthy home.[9] George Baker, known as Father Divine, regularly had Sunday breakfast with the family. Young William, whom his family called Bill, was at the table when the spiritual leader, founder of an international peace movement, discussed the issues of the day. Others who helped shaped Bill Worthy's view of the world were William Monroe Trotter, founder and publisher of the *Boston Guardian;* civil rights leader and labor union organizer A. Philip Randolph, for whom Worthy would work briefly after college; and a host of other activists who promoted black causes.[10]

While studying economics at Bates College in Maine, Worthy pursued his interests in drama and politics and was on the staff of the school newspaper.[11] His early articles provide insight into his developing views on international relations, war, and racial injustice. During his college years in the 1940s, systematic and legal prejudice against blacks continued unabated in the United States while World War II raged abroad.

The opinionated young writer was probably referring to himself when, in one of his first published articles, he described the "humanitarian pacifist" as one who believed that "decency, tolerance, kindliness, democracy, and freedom are the first victims of war," with "hatred poisoning the springs of culture" and murder becoming "the only business of life."[12] He also wrote that economic injustice and human exploitation were the cause of poverty, racial conflicts, labor disputes, class struggles, and warfare. All people wanted national and international peace, he argued, but few men were willing to do the things that made peace.[13] A pacifist and a conscientious objector, Worthy refused to fight in World War II because he felt that he could not kill another human being.[14]

After graduation, Worthy worked as a labor-union organizer and at a succession of other jobs before he "drift[ed] into journalism."[15] As Boone described him, "He was skeptical right from his soul, and believing that history repeated itself, he was skeptical of government's role in history."[16] His work appeared in *The Afro-American* as well as such elite establishment publications as *The Boston Globe*, the *Boston Phoenix*, *Esquire*, and *Harper's*. When the mainstream media showed no interest in his overseas reporting, Worthy went on the lecture circuit, self-published and disseminated his articles as pamphlets, and appeared on television and radio.[17]

A Non-establishment View

Worthy had not yet begun his career as a journalist when he traveled to Norway and Denmark in 1952 to study worker education as part of his labor-union job. Writing for *The Progressive*, he reported on Norwegians' skewed perception of the United States and theorized that U.S. imperialism was the reason lynching was no longer acceptable in the country. He wrote that he had reluctantly defended his country when a Norwegian reporter asked how he, a black man, had managed to travel outside the United States. At the University of Oslo, Norwegian students asked about the last time Worthy had helped to lynch blacks.[18] He wrote that his trip abroad marked the first time in his life he that was treated like everyone else, and he acknowledged that discrimination in his country was "sufficiently degrading and brutalizing." He answered the first question by stating that black students had to simply apply and pay a ten-dollar fee for a passport, just as other citizens did. To the second question, he suggested that three-fourths of southern whites now disapproved of mob violence against blacks, partly because they feared that continued lynching would cause the United States to lose the "needed support of black people abroad" as it engaged in imperialism.[19] He was examining how international politics affected racial politics at home.

Worthy's leftist convictions were manifested in his non-establishment version of world and domestic affairs and the intersection of race and class. He sometimes used a racial lens to illustrate discrepancies between the principles of freedom and democracy that the U.S. government espoused and the regressive policies it enacted to repress people at home and abroad. The government tried to thwart him many times, but Worthy continued to report from abroad. He believed that the First Amendment's guarantee of freedom of speech and freedom of the press gave him the right to travel to allow different voices to be heard. His classic liberal interpretation of the First Amendment conflicted with the government's attempts to stifle travel and discourse about communism, liberation movements, wars, and revolutions across the globe. He criticized the establishment media's complicity with the government in excluding reporting about world events that was vital to an informed public. In Worthy's opinion, the mainstream media's structure dictated a biased perspective. He wanted to tell the other side of the story. Worthy was an advocate for civil liberties and human rights, not just for blacks but for oppressed people everywhere. Boone observed, "Bill, unlike most newspaper men, had a global perspective with conceptual sophistication. He understood the world was not limited to Americans, and he was always trying to awaken Americans to that reality. In his reporting, he tried to encourage America to live up to its promises and to stop practicing a system of hypocrisy."[20] The work of this "twenty-four hour-a-day reporter"[21] continued the trajectory that black foreign reporting had been following since its beginning.

The Lure of Communism: From Korea to Russia, China, and Beyond

Worthy first showed an interest in covering communism when he filed reports from Freedom Village, Korea, in 1953. Writing for *The Afro-American* on the peace agreement and the exchange of prisoners of war, he reported that the Koreans had tried to turn black prisoners of war against their country, while the whites claimed that the Koreans punished them because of their race.[22] He argued that America's peculiar brand of democracy at home and its actions abroad negatively affected both black and white prisoners of war in Korea and caused a loss of standing abroad.

But the story of the Korean conflict and its effects on race troops was not over. When Worthy returned from his brief stint in Korea, *The Afro-American* assigned him to cover black veterans. He embarked on a two thousand-mile journey across the United States in search of interviews. In mid-August 1954, he showed up unannounced at the home of his sister Ruth and asked to borrow her car. Although he offered no explanation, and although the vehicle was new, Ruth agreed. Worthy took off and for months Ruth heard nothing from him. When he finished his assignment, he returned the car and left again.[23] He wrote a series of articles that explained the tug of war that pitted loyalty and patriotism against the possibility of equality under communism. One former prisoner of war told Worthy he was reenlisting because he preferred life in the army to a low-paying job back home. Others related their experiences in the prison camps and said communist propaganda "went in one ear and out the other."[24]

Worthy became increasingly antagonistic toward Western imperialism as he contemplated the benefits of communism. He grew less tolerant of the government's suppression of communist ideology, believing that discussion and debate would open the door to equality. In 1955, he again traveled abroad on assignment for *The Afro-American*. In April, he was one of three Worldover Press correspondents covering the Asian-African Conference in Bandung, Indonesia. The mission of the conference was to foster economic and political cooperation among countries trying to gain independence from Western nations.[25] The host nation Indonesia appealed for international trade support to a number of emerging nations whose only bond "was a shared notion of Communist ideology and mutual excommunication from Western trade offers."[26] Worthy believed that commonalities among poor nations could help them unite and overcome Western oppression. He did not address black and white race relations; instead, he wrote about the injustices contemporary Western thought and practices wrought on an international scale. He believed that a solution to massive disparities could be found by incorporating communist ideology into democratic thought, not in substituting one for the other.

Reporting from India in July 1955, Worthy again wondered whether communism could provide a way for poor nations to unite and overcome Western oppression. After interviewing African American diplomats in India, he wrote that "brown faces" were working in every embassy and even in the U.S. Information Service Office.[27] "With skeptical eyes of Asia upon them [the West] and with the communist press ever ready to exploit any trace of discrimination, this new personnel is treated with every courtesy and every consideration by their white colleagues."[28]

At the Bandung Conference, Worthy continued his quest to tell the alternative story, especially about communism. As a freelance correspondent with State Department approval, he went to Moscow on assignment for the National Association for the Advancement of Colored People (NAACP) magazine *The Crisis* and as a stringer for *The Afro-American* and CBS News. He became the first American journalist to broadcast via Radio Moscow since 1947.[29] Worthy boasted that he was the "first colored reporter to visit the Soviet Republic."[30]

Worthy's dispatch titled "A Window in Moscow" provided context for global events that continued to affect oppressed people. He did not report on Nikita Khrushchev, the thawing of relations between the United States and the Soviet Union, or the life of the Soviet people, as did mainstream correspondents Clifford Daniels of the *New York Times*, Daniel Schorr of CBS, and Irving R. Levine of NBC radio and television, all of whom went to Russia around the same time Worthy did. Establishment media had been in Russia for years, working under difficult circumstances that included censorship, travel restrictions, and even harassment from Russians who believed they were spies. But with the opening of diplomatic relations and Khrushchev's rise to power, journalists from major news agencies developed a pool system for sharing information while also doing individual reporting.[31]

Unlike mainstream journalists, Worthy was interested in the appeal of the communist East to emerging African nations and to Asia. For four months he talked formally and informally with the leaders of those nations. He interviewed communist-leaning South African delegate Moses Kotane, who fought against apartheid rule that, he said, Western nations supported economically and militarily. The growing group of antiapartheid South Africans sought support from any nation, and the Russians initially came to their aid. Worthy cited Walter Lippmann's theories of governance and warned that the United States would make a fatal error if it backed South African white supremacists, thus opening the door for the Soviets to back Kotane and the black South Africans.[32]

He wrote about the U.S. attitude toward weaker nations and examined his country's undemocratic practices at home and abroad. In a direct reference to America's role in colonialism in Africa, he quoted a source who told him that even American "helicopters and guns" would not enable the French to suppress the nationalist fervor for independence.[33] In October 1955, he covered the visit to Moscow by Senator Allen Ellender of Louisiana. Worthy feared that the staunch segregationist's defense of the indefensible would "by default" cause the world's people of color to cling to communism as an avenue to civil liberties.[34]

In 1957, Worthy entered China on assignment for *The Afro-American*. The newspaper noted that Worthy was "first again to give us a series of articles you won't be able to read in any other American newspaper," despite the fact that several reporters from the mainstream press were also there.[35] Worthy reported on conditions in China, explained how communism had gained a foothold there, and illuminated its impact.

One of his first pieces was based on an interview in Shanghai with a Lutheran minister from Baltimore who was working as a missionary. The Chinese government had imprisoned him on charges of espionage. Worthy saw the missionary's role in China as a continuation of colonialist and imperialist exploitation. He also portrayed the Chinese in a favorable light, reporting that the government was accommodating to its prisoners and to him—a black man. But this portrayal overlooked certain facts—Worthy was not allowed to take notes or use a tape recorder, and he was always accompanied by an interpreter and the jail superintendent, who escorted him to the missionary's unheated cell.[36] Worthy underplayed the lack of heat, noting that the missionary was bundled up in warm clothing. Chinese officials assured him that other American prisoners were not disciplined and received "the extraordinary privilege of listening to radio broadcasts from overseas stations."[37] Worthy appeared to accept that version of reality and shared it without elaboration.

In one dispatch, Worthy equated the Chinese struggles for liberation and equality with the plight of blacks in the United States. Despite the civil rights movement and the passage of *Brown v. the Board of Education* in 1954, the pace of racial progress in America was slow. "Racial Arrogance Gave Birth to Red China" was the headline of a February 1957 dispatch in which Worthy described the dilemma of being an African American man in a place where he was simply seen as American and thus as the enemy. He wrote that he detested dictatorships but could appreciate how some African Americans and other minorities of color viewed China and communism in general as a haven of equality. "Were Freedom from color discrimination the only consideration in the pursuit of human happiness, China of 1957, which has deported or jailed the white top-dogs of yesterday, could be a Mecca for half the population of Mississippi and all the residents of Harlem."[38]

Worthy also addressed the Chinese view of race, explaining that it was formed by the attempt of white colonials to carve up the country for exploitation and relegate the people to second-class status. "If we are to understand the harsh changes and propaganda hostility which former missionaries find so bewildering," he asserted, "we must recall the humiliations of the 'Chinese not allowed' signs which one short decade ago the now expelled missionaries failed to raise their voices against."[39] In March 1957, he wrote about an African American athlete and former GI who had remained "behind the bamboo curtain" to seize educational opportunities unavailable to him at home.[40] In a piece datelined Peking, he reported on several black men who were in the communist bloc to work on various projects, ranging from government diplomacy to literary translation to writing a book.[41]

Look magazine's Moscow correspondent Edmund Stevens and photographer Phil Harrington were also in China, but Worthy was given access denied to correspondents for the mainstream media. As an American willing to provide an alternative perspective on communism, he was a valuable conduit of information from the East to the West. He was considered so important that a search party was launched when he was late for an interview with Chou En-Lai. The Chinese premier told Worthy that the release of prisoners would occur when Chinese detainees in the United States were released. Aware that the United States had threatened Worthy, Stevens, and Harrington with fines and imprisonment under the Trading with the Enemies Act, the premier said,

"The fact that the US government revoked the passports of three American journalists in China shows that the US government hasn't taken into account the desire of the American people to improve relations between China and the US and to have contacts with the Chinese people. On China's part, we are willing to meet this desire."[42]

Even after he returned home, Worthy continued to write about China sporadically in 1957. Most of his articles had a decidedly anti-Western tone. Several decades after the China trip, he recalled the U.S. government's attempts to curtail his activities in China. "Washington was especially disconcerted because my CBS broadcasts contradicted the official nonsense about the 'imminent collapse' of Mao's government," he wrote, adding that one State Department official had complained directly to CBS president William Paley.[43]

Worthy's work was significant for the time. He even thumbed his nose at the anticommunist crusade Senator Joseph McCarthy was waging. When filing stories, he made no pretense of trying to obtain reaction from U.S. government officials; such a request would probably have fallen on deaf ears since Worthy was not even supposed to be in China.

The First Amendment Fight

Worthy's violation of travel restrictions gained national attention in such mainstream newspapers as the *New York Times*, and the *Washington Post*. The *New York Post*, to which Worthy had filed stories from China, was among the newspapers that criticized the government. *The Afro-American* duly noted the support its star reporter was receiving in the face of condemnation from the American government. One piece quoted representatives of major news organizations who concurred that travel was a means of getting to the truth. That article also noted that U.S. Senator Hubert Humphrey had called the ban "incredibly shortsighted" and added that "qualified, recognized newsmen should be encouraged, rather than discouraged from going to any part of the world."[44] According to *The Afro-American*, the nation's press wanted to nominate Worthy for the Pulitzer Prize, and the American Newspaper Publishers Association had filed a formal protest.[45]

After his return from China in 1957, Worthy became entangled in a legal battle because the government refused to renew his passport. He had become an iconic figure to *The Afro-American*, which chronicled the battle. He often made the front page as the lead story rather than the lead writer.[46] "Worthy to Face Passport Showdown" was the headline of a bulletin in the February 16 issue. Worthy had arrived in Boston from London "still in possession of his passport" after successfully evading attempts to confiscate it in Budapest and Vienna.[47] He was immediately whisked off to CBS for an interview with Eric Sevareid. He soon returned to Harvard and resumed his Nieman Fellowship.

Worthy's attempt to renew his passport began in earnest on March 30, 1957, when he made his case during a Senate Judiciary Constitutional Rights Subcommittee hearing. Subcommittee chairman Thomas Hennings, a Democrat from Missouri, had appeared to support Worthy a few weeks earlier when he wrote that "the right to travel, not only within the country, but beyond its borders, is one of the natural rights of a free man or woman."[48] Worthy took his seat at the table and resolutely argued that a free press and a transparent government were cornerstones of democracy. Senator Joseph Mahoney, a Democrat from Wyoming, called for the State Department to apologize for running a smear campaign against Worthy to justify its refusal to renew his passport.[49]

Worthy did not remain silent. In May, he told sixty students attending a banquet at Howard University that the government's action was "one of many restrictions on civil liberties." He stated that blacks were not the only minority that refused to remain silent when denied their civil rights.[50]

In October 1959, after a succession of legal battles, Worthy lost his appeal to renew his passport. The ruling read in part, "A blustering inquisitor avowing his own freedom to go and do as he pleases can throw the whole international neighborhood into turmoil."[51] Years later, Worthy commented, "[C]onsidering the hangover from the anti-communist hysteria of the early and mid '50's, it probably was inevitable that the courts would side with the government on that matter."[52] But he continued to travel abroad.

Off to Cuba

Worthy took his First Amendment fight to the U.S. Court of Appeals in 1958, the same year Fidel Castro seized power in Cuba. The reporter's zeal to cover what was happening ninety miles from the United States led him to dodge U.S. customs agents and use crafty alibis to gain entrance to Cuba, for which he would ultimately face legal consequences. The offensive by Castro's revolutionaries in late 1958, the ineffectiveness of the Cuban military, and the subsequent defeat of U.S.-backed dictator Fulgencio Batista sparked retaliation from the federal government. The Cuban revolution, whose land and wealth redistribution policies stemmed directly from socialist and communist ideology, was a direct challenge to Western imperialism. Following a break in diplomatic relations, the State Department declared Cuba off limits for American citizens.[53]

Worthy's goal again was to tell the other side of the story about the United States' communist neighbor. Without a passport, and traveling on ships from various nations, he made four trips to the island between July 1960 and October 1961 to report for *The Afro American,* ABC, and CBS. He later recalled that he had left for Cuba on "short notice"—his usual pattern—after the Fair Play for Cuba Committee invited him to be part of a delegation traveling there to observe Castro's government. Committee members were black and white activists and intellectuals who, like Worthy, were interested in developments in Cuba. Worthy wanted to ascertain "for the *AFRO* readers if U.S. reporters in Cuba were telling the truth." He concluded that "most of them definitely weren't."[54] According to Worthy, the mainstream press had never exposed the extent to which Cuba under Batista enforced the type of racism found in America. Worthy chronicled political and social developments in Cuba and provided context for Castro's regime, the revolution, and the role of the United States. In an article in *The Afro-American* in September 1960, he gave an overview of Cuban history and argued that socialist ideology offered equality. The new Cuba, which the United States and the mainstream media ignored, did not value light skin over dark, he wrote; nor did Castro follow America's and Batista's practice of segregating public facilities. Cubans and African Americans had been unable to obtain lodging in the Hotel Riviera until Castro's revolutionary government slashed the rates that had been beyond the reach of all but the richest Americans and a few Cubans.[55] Worthy also harshly criticized U.S. policies toward Third World nations. He wrote that his country and other Western powers had supported the Batista regime, which had murdered innocents, but turned against a more peaceful and open post-revolution Cuba.[56] U.S. capitalism and greed had fostered discrimination that suppressed the poor, he wrote.

In other articles Worthy accused Western countries of exploiting dark-skinned people in impoverished nations in the name of expansionism. He also wrote that the mainstream press was wrong in not writing about the issue. "If one duty of interpretative journalism is to puncture fraud, hypocrisy, and double talk, then this reporter is morally obligated to say to his government in Washington the following: 'You have everything upside down and topsy-turvy. Not now, in 1960, but rather back during the seven years of President Batista's dictatorship, you should have advised United States citizens in Cuba to send home their wives and children.'"[57]

On a visit to the United States in 1960, Castro spoke at the General Assembly of the United Nations in New York. The Cuban leader reacted to perceived discrimination at the Shelburne Hotel by moving to the Hotel Theresa in Harlem. He met with black leaders, including Malcolm X, spoke at forums in Harlem, and granted interviews to the black media. An in-depth interview in *The Afro-American* was billed as an "exclusive" coup for the newspaper, which stated that Castro's moving his eighty-member delegation to Harlem "was a direct slap in the face of U. S. racial policies."[58] Castro told the newspaper that the Cuban revolution was "a big lesson for those who practice discrimination" and that weaker and oppressed nations would no longer tolerate exploitation.[59] His comments were welcomed by black leaders who protested America's politics.[60]

Castro's stay in Harlem received widespread coverage in the black and the majority media. The *New York Times* ran several accounts of the trip; some addressed the race issue. Castro "expressed the belief that Negroes would be more sympathetic to the Cuban revolutionaries,"[61] the *Times* reported. Castro told the newspaper that African Americans were not as "brainwashed" as whites by official propaganda about Cuba. In fact, blacks had more sympathy for his government, which, Castro said, had wiped out racial discrimination. After all, Cubans and blacks all were in the same boat and shared a "bond" with Africa.[62] The newspaper reported that some viewed Castro's move to Harlem as propaganda or a stunt aimed at gaining African American support.

The *Chicago Daily Defender* ran several United Press International (UPI) wire stories, including one that quoted Congressman Adam Clayton Powell as saying that Castro was a hypocrite using Harlem for propaganda purposes. Blacks in Harlem had sufficient problems he added, "without the added burden of Dr. Castro's confusion."[63]

Worthy made multiple trips to Cuba between July 1960 and October 1961. In 1960 he co-produced the ABC documentary *Yanki, No!* which focused on U.S. relations with Latin America. The film examined the poverty of the region, specifically in Cuba and Venezuela, and suggested that poverty, coupled with U.S. imperialist policies, fostered anti-American sentiment throughout Latin America.

Worthy avoided legal consequences until October 19, 1961, when customs officials at the Miami airport apprehended him for illegal entry into the

United States from Cuba. He was indicted on April 24, 1962, and ordered to go to Miami to face charges. He surrendered on May 5. Although it apparently disagreed with Worthy's actions, the *Chicago Daily Defender* characterized the indictment as unnecessarily severe. "To invoke criminal action against an enterprising, reputable newsman who committed at best an act of indiscretion is stretching the Immigration Act beyond reasonable application."[64]

Worthy defended his travels without a passport and condemned the mainstream media for excluding or misrepresenting marginalized people. He took the government to task for blacking out news from certain locales, and he urged editors to push for more foreign coverage so Americans could know what was going on in the world. Using *The Afro-American* as his soapbox, he wrote:

> Our daily papers, giant weekly news magazines, radio and television networks will not and psychologically cannot report the hard facts and bitter truth from Latin America, Asia, and Africa. They can't. They have too much of a stake in the status quo—emotionally, financially, and socially. They are not going to report the anguish of an Africa struggling to rid itself of American supported colonialism, Portugal's use of US arms and planes in slaughtering women and children in Angola, or our help to the French in Algeria and Indo-China. The colored press must assume this responsibility. Either the colored press will rise to the great historic need and report the struggle perceptively, sympathetically, and courageously, or the American people will go down the drain of history after dwelling a little while longer in ignorance, fictitious bliss, in a cauldron of daily lies and misinterpretation unequaled in the history of the printed word.[65]

In August 1962, Worthy was convicted of illegal reentry and faced a maximum sentence of five years in jail and a fine of five thousand dollars. A month later, he was placed on probation for nine months. In 1964, the U.S. Court of Appeals for the Fifth District unanimously overturned his conviction, ruling that the travel ban was unconstitutional and that citizens should not be barred from returning to their own country.[66] This was a monumental decision in the history of the press because it opened the door for foreign correspondents to report from all countries even if the government tried to prohibit their travel. The case also was noteworthy in another aspect. Famed civil rights attorney William Kuntsler, who represented Worthy pro bono, wrote in his autobiography that the case was the first time he had been involved in invalidating a statute and that it had launched his career as a civil rights lawyer.[67]

Even while battling the government, Worthy traveled throughout Southeast Asia without a passport. He explained years later that "there came an opportunity for me to be the first U.S. newsman to visit North Vietnam."[68] He left in November 1964 on "short notice" and "in the tense midpoint between the Navy's contrived Gulf of Tonkin incident in August and President [Lyndon] Johnson's massive military intervention in February."[69] During the ten months that Worthy was in North Vietnam, the mainstream press showed no interest in his reporting, so he wrote pamphlets to disseminate his foreign correspondence as he lectured throughout the United States on his return.[70]

For the next ten years, Worthy disappeared from the pages of *The Afro-American*. He was a commentator on the NBC and CBS affiliates in Boston in the early 1970s, and he freelanced for other publications, writing about the black power movement in the United States and how it related to the struggles of oppressed people.[71] He returned to the pages of *The Afro-American* in 1976, writing about American imperialism in such places as Iran and Haiti.[72]

As he chastised the West, Worthy also continued to criticize the press. He was aware that the Kerner Commission Report of 1968 had confirmed that the press in the United States was almost entirely white and that the public was not getting a balanced perspective. In a column on the death of China's chairman Mao Tse-tung, Worthy lambasted the "white" media for "playing footsie with the US government" and only reporting what they knew the government wanted to hear.[73] Deference to government demands, he wrote, made work more difficult for reporters like him who traveled to remote corners of the world to get the truth. "For some in high places there will be sleepless nights ahead, they're just faking. It is really up to us to keep them honest. For none of us is safe as long as official killers and torturers are at large whether at home, or anywhere else in the World, from Haiti, to Chile, to Indonesia, to Argentina, to Iran, to Korea, to the Philippines, to Uruguay, via Lenox Avenue."[74]

Off to Iran

In January 1980 another opportunity arose for Worthy to go abroad. He was teaching in the African American journalism program at Boston University when a group of students, many of whom had been educated in the United States, took over the U.S. embassy in Tehran, Iran, and held fifty-two American citizens hostage. In February, Worthy accompanied a grass-roots delegation of forty-nine Americans whom Iranian students had invited to travel to Iran. He was accompanied by photographer Randy Goodman, his twenty-year-old female graduate assistant, who said the goal was "to learn about the historical, cultural, and political relations between the two nations" and to illuminate why America had become a target. The delegation had invited Worthy because its members felt he "had a more representational perspective."[75]

Reporting from Iran for *The Afro-American*, Worthy criticized the United States and the establishment media. He wrote that "outraged Iranians" saw little difference between the Shah of Iran and Hitler, and that they blamed the U.S. government for propping up the autocratic Iranian leader. He charged that the United States had "muscled its way" into Iran and British, French, and Belgian colonies because World War II had "so weakened those empires that they were too enfeebled and too bankrupt to cling to and to police restless overseas holdings."[76] In another piece he characterized U.S. reaction to the embassy takeover as fascism; he noted a "series of attacks on Iranian students" and stated that the media had revealed students' names and addresses.[77] The headline atop the column signaled Worthy's and his newspaper's goal: "Now the Truth Will Come Out If We Insist."[78]

Worthy had accepted Raymond Boone's request that he represent all thirteen newspapers in *The Afro-American* chain. He dictated dispatches by phone to Boone or his secretary. He was "trying to give a balance, not just hearing and presenting the official American point of view," Boone later explained. "American foreign policy was giving us a black eye."[79]

In one piece, Worthy wrote that the hostages believed "the shah was bad" and should change places with them.[80] Another disclosed that the hostage-takers had given the delegation documents that proved the Central Intelligence Agency (CIA) had "extensive operations" at the embassy, including "sensitive dispatches describing espionage techniques."[81] Worthy also reported that President Jimmy Carter had dismissed "accusations about the United States' complicity in the shah's torture and murder" of innocent people and had not apologized to Iran.[82]

Worthy did not seek reactions from government sources because, in his view, the mainstream media had provided that perspective. And since Worthy was again traveling against the wishes of the State Department, it was unlikely anyone would have responded. When they returned to this country after ten days in Iran, Worthy and Goodman published national articles with photos and lectured throughout New England.[83]

In the fall of 1981, the Iranian government banned U.S. journalists on the grounds that their reporting was one-sided and inaccurate. But Iran granted visas to Worthy and Goodman because of their previous reports and because Worthy did not support U.S. policy there. Worthy, Goodman, and student radio reporter Teresa "Terri" Taylor approached CBS News as a freelance team. They received a contract, equipment, and training in television news production. The team set off in early October. Their two-week assignment turned into two months that cost the network one-quarter million dollars, a substantial financial investment at the time.[84]

CBS did not air any of the sixteen hours of coverage the team brought back. "We were just news gatherers," Goodman explained. Worthy had interviewed military, religious, and political leaders, while the other two journalists collected video footage and shot still photographs. They also documented tours of the Iran-Iraq war zone, visits to Iraqi and Iranian refugee camps, and a speech to military and political leaders by Ayatollah Khomeini. "What we had was an exclusive for American TV," Goodman later stated. "I believe at that time they [the media] could have taken risks, but CBS wasn't interested."[85] This reinforced Worthy's belief that the establishment media excluded information unfavorable to the United States. To counter this, Worthy adopted a time-honored technique of black journalists: he and Goodman went on the speakers' circuit.

Within a week of his return to the United States, Worthy and the federal government clashed again. In December 1981, federal agents searched his unaccompanied baggage at Logan Airport and confiscated books he and his colleagues had bought while reporting in Iran. The multivolume set, known in Iran as *Documents from the U.S. Espionage Den*, were reprints of classified CIA and State Department documents that had fallen into Iranian hands after the U.S. embassy takeover, according to Goodman. Worthy and Goodman attempted to publish the information in the books. They were unsuccessful with the *New York Times*, but the *Washington Post* formed an investigative team to check the authenticity of the Iran papers. The newspaper published a five-part series, "Iran Documents Give Rare Glimpse of a CIA Enterprise," beginning on January 20, 1982.[86] For once Worthy had accomplished his goal of getting the elite media to pay attention.

When the story first appeared, Worthy made a significant step in his battles with the federal government. Standing outside the Nieman Foundation in Boston, he and his colleagues announced that, under the auspices of the Civil Liberties Union of Massachusetts, they were filing a civil suit against the federal government for violating their First and Fourth Amendment rights. The suit demanded that the government return the confiscated documents, which could be purchased in any bookstore in Iran.[87] Eleven months later, the correspondents announced an out-of-court victory that included a cash settlement of sixteen thousand dollars and the return of the documents.

Worthy used his share of the settlement money to return to Iran as a freelance journalist, again accompanied by Goodman. They remained in the country for four months but did not file stories. Upon their return, Worthy published a *Boston Globe Magazine* cover story on Iran's Revolutionary Guard Corps, with photos by Goodman. He disseminated the information to a wider audience by appearing on NBC's *Today* show and on CNN. That gave him the "protective cover that allowed him to be viewed legitimately," according to Goodman, who said that her friend "was always strategizing" and sending her letters about where to go next.[88]

Worthy made two more trips abroad, both financed by grants. From June through August 1987 he traveled in Grenada, Barbados, and Trinidad to investigate the assassination of former Grenadian prime minister Maurice Bishop. Seven years later, he spent five days in Cuba covering the visit of a religious delegation. He filed no stories but instead made the information public through interviews with reporters and television producers.

Conclusion: The Right to Know

Those who knew Worthy describe him as a "real trailblazer" without whom American correspondents would not be able to cover stories from abroad as they do now.[89] Essentially retired, and in the early stages of Alzheimer's disease, he made a rare public appearance in February 2008, to accept the Nieman Foundation's Louis M. Lyons Award for contributions to the field of journalism. With a firm voice and an emphatic nod, he said his longevity was a result of his fight "to challenge the status quo."[90] He reiterated that during a subsequent interview.[91]

Because Worthy refused to play by the rules as the dominant media did, he was often alone with little money, gathering information abroad but finding few media outlets for his work. He told one friend that his refusal to relinquish his passport in 1957 had cost him a full-time job with CBS News.[92]

Worthy's later writings passionately urged others to continue his fight. He was more than a black foreign correspondent who focused on issues of interest to blacks; he was a transitional figure who bridged the gaps among the government, the media, and the public during periods of immense change in the world. He followed the news to at least thirty-eight countries. His career spanned the broad expanse of American and global history, and his stories raised the bar for reporting on the role of America in the world.

[13]

Vietnam

A Turning Point

"Our man in Vietnam is a woman,"[1] the *Chicago Daily Defender* announced on December 17, 1966. The newspaper had dispatched Ethel Payne to cover the war in Southeast Asia. Publisher John Sengstacke had called Payne, who was based in Washington. She flew to Chicago to discuss the proposition. "[I]t would be a unique thing to have a woman cover the war,"[2] Sengstacke told her. Payne's assignment was to gather the "facts behind the hardships and dangers Negro GIs are encountering at Christmas time in the Viet Nam jungles and in Saigon."[3]

Payne relished this new assignment for Sengstacke Publications, which owned fourteen newspapers.[4] She landed in Saigon on Christmas Day and soon dashed off a memorandum to Barry Zorthian, the senior officer in the U.S. Foreign Service. In the memo, Payne wrote that she saw "an important need for documenting the Negro soldier, particularly in the light of the civil rights struggle back home and the constant efforts by the detractors to divide the Negro people on the war. . . . We need to have unusual features such as assignments, acts of heroism, overall performance, Negroes in civilian capacities, human interest angles, what the attitude is of the Vietnamese people towards Negro servicemen, any special problems involving discipline, etc. . . . In addition to the Negro angle, my job is to give also, the total war story as much as possible for balance."[5]

As a girl growing up in Chicago, Payne had wanted "to see the world" and to become a lawyer who would "defend the rights of the poor people."[6] When her father died in 1926, fourteen-year-old Ethel knew her mother lacked the funds to send her and her five siblings to college. "The opportunity for continuing education just wasn't there," she later recalled. So Payne did it "piecemeal."[7] She took a job as a clerk at the Chicago Public Library, after applying to the University of Chicago's law school and receiving no response. Finding the work boring, Payne went to work as a hostess with the army's Special Services Club in Tokyo in 1948.

She recorded in her diary observations of relationships between black servicemen and Japanese women; she also documented instances of racism and discrimination on the army base. When *Chicago Defender* reporter Alex Wilson visited her, she showed him the journal and gave him permission to take it back to Chicago. Wilson shared Payne's diary entries with the publisher, and in 1951 her notes became the basis of stories "with big, bold, red headlines"[8] in the *Defender*. "Many of the things I wrote in my diary were not known in the States," she later recalled.[9] Sengstacke admired her flair for writing and her keen insight. "Hell, if you can write like that, why don't you come home?" he asked her. Payne accepted his job offer and began her career in journalism. She adopted Frederick Douglass's mantra, "Agitate, agitate, agitate."[10]

Less than two years after she began writing for the *Defender*, Payne became the newspaper's one-woman Washington bureau, covering legislative and judicial battles on Capitol Hill just as the civil rights movement began. She soon gained a reputation as a tough reporter; in 1953 her fellow black journalists began calling her the "newsman's newsman."[11] She was fearless in pursuing the news, especially when it concerned black people. That was obvious the day she stood up at a White House press conference and asked President Dwight D. Eisenhower when he planned to ban segregation of interstate travel. This challenge made national news. Throughout the late 1950s and early 1960s, Payne covered civil rights, including the Montgomery Bus Boycott and marches in Birmingham and Selma. Her "blunt" style of reporting led members of the White House press corps to say she had moved civil rights onto the national agenda.[12]

By 1955, the *Defender* was ready to send its star reporter overseas to report on the Asian-African Conference in Bandung, Indonesia. That was the first of many international events Payne covered in eleven countries in Africa and Europe. The Southeast Asian assignment made her the first journalist to cover Vietnam for the black press.

Preparing for Vietnam

Before leaving for Vietnam, Payne was briefed on the purpose of the mission, security requirements, and ground rules for reporting from the front lines. "The Pentagon was very anxious" for her to write "favorable stories," she recalled. She realized that the only way for her to travel in Vietnam was via transportation provided by the army or air force.[13] Her situation was similar to that of Ralph Waldo Tyler, the first and only black to cover World War I. But Payne worked for a newspaper, whereas Tyler had worked under the auspices of the government's Committee on Public Information (CPI). His dispatches had to pass inspection by the CPI and Emmett Scott, the black special assistant to the secretary of war, before being cleared for release to the black press. When Payne arrived in December, her initial excitement soon turned somber. "It was such a sad feeling that came over me," she recalled. She asked herself, "Is this what it is like? Is this war? Does it have to be?"[14]

By the time the Vietnam War appeared on the front pages of newspapers and on the television news, the country was in a state of turbulent transformation. The events of the 1960s had dramatic implications for the country, the black community, and the black press. Despite the passage of the Voting Rights Act of 1965, many blacks in the Deep South were barred from voting and were intimidated when they attempted to register. The unemployment rate for blacks was more than 100 percent higher than that of whites, and 80 percent of blacks lucky enough to be working held the lowest-paying jobs. Riots gripped the country in 1965, but the civil rights movement brought together the energy of blacks, the support of sympathetic whites, and the acquiescence of President Lyndon Johnson to effect massive changes in the status quo. Civil rights legislation gradually enabled blacks to make gains politically, educationally, legally, and economically.

Some in the black community embraced Martin Luther King Jr.'s message of nonviolent social change, while others ascribed to the philosophy of radicals such as H. Rap Brown and Huey P. Newton of the Black Panthers. The Panthers joined some in the black press who criticized America's professed goal of bringing freedom and democracy to Vietnam while racial minorities were denied equality at home. Nevertheless, Vietnam marked the first time blacks were fighting in a fully integrated military, and African Americans were making progress in the quest for civil liberties at home.

The media changed as the country changed. Many news organizations began to cover blacks, providing "largely sympathetic accounts of the civil rights movement."[15] Blacks could now turn to mainstream media outlets for news that affected their lives. Unfortunately, some of the most talented black journalists left their jobs to accept positions with the mainstream media. Years after he signed on with the *New York Times*, correspondent Thomas A. Johnson observed that the white media had offered one hundred fifty dollars a week, while black press outlets were sometimes unable to pay their staffs at all. The talent drain added to the financial stress of the black press, making it even more difficult for it to compete in the area of foreign correspondence.

The Vietnam War and Media Coverage

Before U.S. troop involvement, the media ran little coverage of Vietnam. When American soldiers were deployed, the conflict rose to the top of the public agenda, sparking debate at home. Recent scholarship contends that the coverage was balanced, if graphic.[16] The press supported the presence of American advisors in Vietnam in 1966 but later questioned the likelihood of defeating communism. War correspondents took advantage of the immediacy of television to report directly from the scene without the filter of censorship.

Like the mainstream press, the black press initially paid little attention to Vietnam, instead focusing its attention on the battle for equity at home. The *Chicago Daily Defender* ran articles that asserted the war would overshadow the fight for civil rights. In April 1966, Whitney Young, director of the National Urban League, cautioned, "It is of no use to the future of the movement and of the nation if, at this crucial moment, yesterday's demonstrators and pickets swap their civil rights signs for anti-war banners."[17] The *New Pittsburgh Courier*, which was now part of the Sengstacke chain,[18] criticized black militants and even attacked King in a May 1967 editorial, accusing him of mixing politics with civil rights and damaging the race's cause.

Loyalty to the country won out as blacks hoped that their performance in the conflict would positively reflect on the race. Opinion pieces suggested that an American loss would be detrimental to blacks. *Chicago Daily Defender* columnist Gordon Hancock equated communism in Vietnam with slavery and charged that those who embraced communism were "bidding for the mastery of the 20th century world and the world that comes after." He saw antiwar protesters as the "younger pampered flabby generation"; their willingness to surrender to the communists was giving in to slavery.[19]

The *Defender* stated in early 1966 that blacks were interested in the war although the black media had not "been too articulate on the Asian issue" and black leaders had been "too timid" to truthfully address the war.[20] Citing Department of Defense figures that showed proportionately more blacks than whites had died thus far in the conflict, the newspaper maintained that African Americans had a vested interest in the war.[21] Less than a year later, the *Defender* sent Payne to Vietnam. She was the only representative of the race press there in late 1966 and early 1967. Her almost daily dispatches began to run in Sengstacke newspapers in January 1967. She wrote more than fifty stories, many of which ran on page 1, and a column titled "Saigon Diary."

Although Payne could have joined colleagues who left for the white media, she continued working for the *Chicago Daily Defender* in 1966. Mainstream newspapers and television stations added black journalists to their war correspondents in Vietnam and Cambodia. They included *Time* magazine's Wallace Terry, deputy chief of its Saigon bureau; Thomas Johnson of the *New York Times;* and Ed Bradley of CBS. At the same time, foreign correspondence from the black press decreased. Gone were the glory days when the medium fielded nearly thirty correspondents during World War II. The fact that Sengstacke sent Payne to Vietnam testifies to the tenacity of the *Defender* and its commitment to reporting the news on its own terms.

Payne's Perspective

Soon after arriving in Vietnam, Payne wrote about her impressions of the war. "Your first reaction is a sinking feeling at the pit of your stomach [and] for one brief moment you want to chicken out and climb right back in that plane and fly off to the safety of your own turf."[22] She devoted her first dispatches to educating her readers about the country and its people. To understand the relationship between America and Vietnam, she felt, one needed to know Vietnam's history. The Vietnamese people were resilient, she wrote; despite two decades of war, they continued to live much as they always had. Sixteen million people lived in South Vietnam, two million of them in Saigon, the capital. The Vietnamese had a strong sense of family and a strong sense of nationalism. The black press had often advocated on behalf of the marginalized, and Payne urged readers to help villages in Southeast Asia by sending such items as toothbrushes and children's clothing. She showed the human toll of the war on the most vulnerable members of society.[23] This theme resonated with her readers, many of whom lived in poverty themselves.

Payne wrote that black GIs, many of whom were away from home for the first time, were lonely and hoped that people back home would write to them.[24] In one of her first dispatches, she dramatically portrayed the service the soldiers were undertaking for their country: "For three full years Negro servicemen have extended themselves in jungled fiascos overgrown with almost impenetrable defenses, stalking an elusive quarry . . . and they've died too—on scarred hillsides blended to plastic matter by screaming shells, clutching at the bowels of rice paddies for womb-like support from whining death flailing the air a few inches above the shimmering mud."[25]

Proving Ourselves

Payne focused on the fact that black soldiers were trying to prove themselves, recalling later that this was "the most important thing" she reported while in Vietnam.[26] The soldiers had "a great urge to do a better than average job . . . to prove themselves as soldiers, as personnel."[27] Despite the heroism of blacks in previous conflicts, the soldiers in Vietnam were still encumbered by the stigma "that blacks couldn't do certain things because they weren't capable, or else they were cowardly."[28] She sought to dispel that myth and later acknowledged that she was so busy concentrating on how well black soldiers were doing that she did not dwell on the purpose or validity of the war.

In March 1967, Payne profiled Gen. Benjamin Davis, who had enrolled at West Point in 1932 and for four years "endured 'the silent treatment' from his classmates as the lone Negro in the academy."[29] In another 1967 dispatch she noted that two black soldiers were among thirteen Medal of Honor recipients, "a record hard to match anywhere."[30] In another, she quoted a white general who admired black soldiers who had the same "overall demeanor and outlook" as white cadets.[31]

Better Off in Vietnam

Dispatches also provided insight into how soldiers felt about the conflict and their status in the war. One soldier told Payne that attitudes depended on how strongly soldiers felt "about the freedom of these people."[32] Many soldiers thought freedom for the Vietnamese was worth fighting for. "The enemy is the enemy no matter what his skin is," a soldier said.[33]

Integration had a positive effect in the war zone, Payne reported. Many GIs believed that blacks were doing better in Vietnam than in America. She later recalled that the conflict had been "an equal opportunity employer."[34] She added, "That's a sad commentary on the whole societal system in this country, that blacks have to turn to war to find occupations and find a way of living—or dying."[35] As she wrote in the *Defender:*

> Looking at all these fresh young faces and seeing the comradeship of Negroes and whites together, all Americans, I wondered if the American people back home can really comprehend and appreciate what is going on here, if they realize that this is more than just guns and blood being spilled against a cunning adversary. . . . It is the battle to restore human dignity, to know that in this family of man, there is a responsibility as brothers, regardless of color of skin or language and custom.[36]

Payne frequently compared African Americans fighting for civil rights at home to black soldiers freed from racial barriers in Vietnam.[37] Life was improving for the fighters, but not for black Americans at home. One soldier told Payne, "Over here the Negro is a leader. He is known to have guts and is respected for it. Back home, we could die at the hands of some lynch mob, but if you die over here at least you die for a purpose."[38]

Payne left Vietnam on February 22, 1967, but her stories ran until April 11. The *Defender* continued to promote her in March and April as if she were still overseas. It was common practice for the black press to run stories with overseas datelines after the reporters were back on American soil.[39] Interestingly, Payne seems to have written only about "safe" subjects from Vietnam. She did not file controversial stories about race relations until after her return. A story dated March 20, 1967, asserted that black soldiers still faced discrimination and that soldiers self-segregated themselves in some villages. Soldiers told Payne they had been threatened in their barracks. "[S]ome instances of bigotry" eventually "threaten to spell trouble unless they are checked at the source," she wrote.[40] Even in these stories, Payne suggested that the real reason for racial hostility was long hours of boredom and loneliness. The *Defender*'s founder Robert Abbott had used a similar tactic when he traveled in South American and Europe in the 1920s. Intent on showing positive race relations abroad, he glossed over the racism he found. To have done otherwise might have damaged the black cause.

A 2,500-word story embodied Sengstacke's reason for sending Payne to Vietnam. Not only did the military personnel come alive, but the issue of integration was front and center. The editor introduced the piece by stating that reporting on the war was needed to boost the morale of the troops, especially because many civil rights leaders "were bitter about the war—in which soldiers of color were killing other soldiers of color."[41] Payne reported that GIs often pushed equal rights, antiwar protests, and the country's rationale for the war to the back of their minds. They were more concerned with staying alive. One soldier told her, "Up here on the line you gotta be together. Charlie doesn't know the difference between black and white. Either he kills you or you kill him." Other soldiers favored the civil rights movement but were divided on tactics. "Gone, too, is the type of individual who resigned himself to the system," Payne wrote, explaining that a "new breed" of "more aggressive, more militant" soldiers were more sure of themselves and their expectations of life once they returned home.[42]

Payne had reported similar remarks in previous stories, but now she included the name, rank, division, and hometown of each soldier. The troops were no longer nameless soldiers; they were men whose families and friends could recognize them. In one piece she quoted Robert Boudreaux, a twenty-one-year-old from San Francísco who was serving with the Fourth Infantry Division.

> I remember when President Johnson made his speech saying, "If a man is willing to fight and die for his country, his country should be willing to fight for him."
>
> This is the big question for Negro soldiers over here. They're laying it on the line and asking no quarter from anyone because of the way they've been treated back home.
>
> So, they're proving themselves. But what is America going to do when they get back, if they make it back, about giving them a fair shake? I mean a guy is going to feel pretty wasted if he comes back and somebody tells him he can't live in a certain neighborhood because that's for white only, or he can't get a job because they don't hire Negroes.
>
> He's going to be pretty mad inside to know he's fought one war against Communism over here and then he has to fight another war at home to get his rights.[43]

Payne concluded by stating that the black soldiers who had fought in an exceptionally cruel war would return "to claim their share of democracy" alongside "their white buddies who have been through the same baptism of fire and are convinced that the old attitudes of prejudice are wrong."[44] Even without that help, blacks would "demand a better deal from America. In the months and years ahead, the veterans of Vietnam will be banding together to achieve those rights."

The small number of journalists of color had concerned Payne when she was in Vietnam, and it remained on her mind as she concluded her assignment. She wished she had tapped additional sources to report more stories, especially about race relations. She wrote to Sengstacke that military authorities did not like the idea of concentrating on black soldiers because, in their words, "the services were so integrated there was no need for special reporting."[45] She urged her boss to send a reporter on a "quasi-permanent" basis to Vietnam, to follow up on the "incidents of racial prejudice" she had found. She suggested that the black press should consider stationing a pool correspondent in Thailand, Japan, and Formosa as well. At least one black weekly newspaper, *The Afro-American,* took up the challenge.

The Afro-American's Mike Davis

Less than a year after Ethel Payne's return, *The Afro-American* assigned Michael DeMond Davis to Vietnam. Davis had long wanted to become a foreign correspondent. His Harvard-educated activist father John P. Davis had founded *Our World* magazine. Mike Davis was a recent graduate of Morehouse College in Atlanta when Ralph McGill hired him as the *Atlanta Constitution*'s first black reporter in 1966. Under McGill's tutelage, Davis became a top-notch journalist, covering civil rights and other issues. But that was not enough to keep him in Georgia when black troops were fighting and dying half a world away. "That is what drew him back to black newspapers," Michelle Davis said of her father, who died in 2003.[46] Mike Davis contacted *The Afro-American* with a proposal to be its war correspondent.[47] He got the nod and left the mainstream press for the black press, bucking the trend of recent years.

"Advocacy was always a part of our family," Michelle Davis said. Her father had viewed journalism as a powerful tool of activism. Born in 1939 in Washington, D.C., he was educated at the New Lincoln School in New York, where he was yearbook editor and on the newspaper staff. Despite expectations that he would follow in his father's footsteps and attend Harvard or another Ivy League university, his desire to be involved in the civil rights movement in the South led him to choose the acclaimed all-male black college. There he captained the debate team, joined the Southern Christian Leadership Conference, and took part in sit-ins that led to the desegregation of Atlanta's department-store lunch counters. Before leaving for Vietnam in 1967, he filed several stories to *The Afro-American.*

One of them contrasted the small percentage of black officers in Vietnam with the high percentage of black deaths.[48] In another, Davis wrote that the black community was concerned about the large number of soldiers who were losing their lives overseas. Three weeks later, in its trademark treatment of foreign correspondents, *The Afro-American* ran a full-body photo of Davis, briefcase in one hand and camera in the other, to announce that he would cover Vietnam, the paper's new beat.

The Afro-American stated that Davis would go to Saigon first but would move to wherever black military personnel were stationed. As it had done during previous wars, the newspaper solicited from readers the names of loved ones in the war so Davis could find and report on them. Readers had been informed about the war by letters from soldiers whose family members shared them with the newspaper. This was now part of Davis's job.

While en route to Vietnam, Davis referred to the late publisher of *The Afro-American,* Carl Murphy, who believed that too little attention was paid to "the little things about the little people."[49] The ugly war in Vietnam was being fought by those little people, Davis wrote, adding, "I am sure that each of the men now stationed in Vietnam has a story to tell. And I am sure that each one will be anxious to know how the folks back home are getting along."[50] Davis's agenda was to focus not on the battles but on the people.

Like Ethel Payne, Davis was in the combat zone but did not report from the battlefield. The reports he filed were based on interviews with more than one hundred soldiers. The overwhelming focus of his dispatches was the troops, including their view that war was hell and their preoccupation with survival. How they felt about race relations was a theme in very few stories. Davis provided minute details about each soldier, including hometown, street address, education level, parents, wives, children, brothers, sisters, even cousins. Payne had suggested when she left Vietnam that the black press send a reporter back to write more human-interest stories. Davis did that in his articles and in a column called "Vietnam Notebook."

He often romanticized the soldiers, portraying them as distinguished, capable, educated men. In one story, he called Maj. Beauregard Brown III "one of the leading and outstanding characters in the drama of war."[51] The thirty-one-year-old college-educated second lieutenant from DeQuincy, Louisiana, was a key assistant on Gen. William Westmoreland's staff. A column in the same issue included the stories of Sfc. Carlton Jones of Miami, who was crew chief of an H-23 light-observation helicopter, and Capt. Barrett Coleman, a graduate of Howard University's medical school and a doctor with the Third Field Army Hospital, Twenty-fifth Infantry Division, the "Wolf Hounds."[52] Another piece quoted a white soldier who said black soldiers were as capable as any. "I've been in the Army eight years and I've never had any racial problems with any of the men I have met," he said.[53]

War Is Hell

Davis was not in the combat zone, but he filed stories about the horrific nature of the conflict, gleaned from experiences the soldiers told him about. His personal style of journalism gave his work a sense of immediacy. He wrote about barely escaping an enemy attack. He described the blood that trailed from a helicopter carrying two men who had been shot in the head. Mostly, he let the soldiers tell their own stories. One soldier said he felt like he was reloading and firing his weapon automatically during a firefight. Davis quoted an officer preparing his troops for a crash: "If you have to vomit, use your helmet. If you hear two short rings, prepare for an emergency landing. If you hear one long ring, grab something and hold on."[54]

Perhaps even more than Payne did, Davis suggested that survival trumped racial tensions at home and in the jungle. "PFC. James Bristol of Newark, N. J. didn't know anything about the recent racial disturbances in his home town. He wasn't even concerned about the Vietnam War. He was engaged in a private battle. A war all his own. A fight for his life."[55] Most troops he interviewed did not believe their treatment in Vietnam was based on race.

But the subject of race did sometimes surface. Pfc. Roland Sherwood of Seattle, Washington, was displeased with developments at home and wondered what blacks were trying to accomplish. "I know that everything isn't what it should be as far as race relations are concerned but rioting is no way to set things right.'"[56] *The Afro-American* ran Davis's firsthand observation of the interaction of black and white troops:

> For five days and four nights this reporter has lived with combat troops on the front line in Vietnam. For five days and four nights he has

> watched the patrols go out into the jungle in search of the enemy. He has watched them come back, tired, hungry, muddy, and hurt but still proud to be soldiers in the Army of the United States. He has watched white and black men kneel and pray together, share the same can of beans and drink from a common cup. If any lesson is to be learned in the classroom of Vietnam it is that democracy can work—that men can live together—even under the most trying circumstances. The mortars that sail over the 173rd Airborne Brigade's base camp here have no racial designations. They can kill white men and black men with equal facility. It happens all the time in Vietnam. Men who live within rifle range of the enemy's deadly Chinese-made AK 47 rifle quickly learn that the color of a man's skin or his family background is not important. . . . "We're in this thing together," a white private from Alabama remarked. "If we are going to get out of this thing together we have to get along. Internal differences don't help us to survive in Vietnam."[57]

One soldier told Davis that anyone who had been under fire by the enemy was automatically a member of a select and proud band. "He walks with his head held a little higher and when he meets another who has also been in combat, spontaneous mutual respect is evident."[58] A black man, Col. Preston Davis, told Davis that the army had been "in the forefront for integration" and had provided opportunities for black servicemen for the past twenty years.

But Thomas Jackson Jr. charged that racism still persisted and that white GIs were teaching the Viet Cong to be prejudiced. A staff sergeant complained of the lack of promotions for black soldiers, despite their distinguished service, and implied that the system was racist. Significantly, these stories did not run until Davis was back in the United States, just as Payne's negative assessment of integration did not appear in the *Chicago Daily Defender* until she returned. Davis himself addressed racism, writing that black troops were not going to tolerate discrimination at the war's end.

> If you think they are having a long hot summer back home, you just wait until some of these GIs get home. Then you are going to have some long hot winters too. . . . When the colored GI gets home, he is going back to his little town and when that same white man that has been calling him boy all his life calls him boy again, is he going to answer yes sir? . . . Pfc. Stanley Williams of Roanoke, Va. feels that many

> of the returning GIs will use their deadly combat skills in the streets. "I know fellows who have been taught to make nitro out of common household products. Some fellows can kill a man with a single blow and some can blow up a ten story building. Do you think they are going to take any stuff when they get home?"[59]

Davis interviewed only a handful of white soldiers. Although he rarely identified soldiers by race, all of his photos were of blacks. In this he differed from Payne, who frequently cited white sources to attest to the valor of race troops. Davis provided evidence in minute details, citing the educational backgrounds of his sources. He did not write about the possibly racist obstacles he faced in Vietnam. Although he tried to get to the front lines, he never did. Authorities told him repeatedly that there was no room for him on the crowded helicopters headed to the battlefield. Davis was the last foreign correspondent for the black media to cover black troops over a sustained period from Vietnam. *The Afro-American* sometimes ran as many as eight of his stories on a page. Writing for a weekly newspaper, he had to cover news that other papers ran daily.

Working for the White Media: The Turning Point

At least three other black journalists were assigned to Vietnam or Cambodia, but they worked for the white media. A few months before Davis went to Vietnam, and five months after Payne arrived, Wallace Terry was reporting for *Time* magazine, followed shortly by Thomas A. Johnson of the *New York Times* and Ed Bradley of CBS.[60] They represented the integration of the mainstream press and the virtual demise of foreign correspondence in the black press. It was a turning point for the black press as an institution in the black community. This major development in foreign reporting raised the question of whether pioneering journalists for the mainstream media would adhere to the traditional role of the black press as advocates for the race. Or would they be journalists first, committed to objectivity, balance, and fairness?

Terry had an extensive media background when he arrived in Vietnam in March 1967. As a reporter for the *Brown Daily Herald*, he had posed as a waiter to get an interview with Orval Faubus, the segregationist governor of Arkansas. A photograph of him shaking hands with Faubus made the front page of the *New York Times* and even ran in some international newspapers.

Later, at Brown University, Terry became the first black editor-in-chief of an Ivy League newspaper.[61] The *Washington Post* hired him when he was nineteen years old. He garnered major scoops while covering the civil rights movement and the rise of the black power movement. In fact, Martin Luther King Jr. was godfather to one of Terry's sons.[62] Terry left the *Post* in 1963 to take a job with *Time*, where he became the first black Washington correspondent for the mainstream media and the first of his race to work for a news magazine. Four years later, the twenty-nine-year-old correspondent became deputy bureau chief in Saigon and the first full-time African American reporter in Vietnam for the mainstream media. He was part of the team that reported a 1967 cover story on black troops in Vietnam. "This was my first experience reporting a war," Terry noted, "but not my first experience reporting violence. For nearly seven years I have followed the development of the Negro revolution in all corners of America."[63]

The story pointed out that, although the military was now fully integrated, there was still racial conflict off the battlefield. Troops preferred associating with members of their own race, and many black troops self-segregated in an area they called Soulsville. (Payne and Davis both mentioned Soulsville, and the positive reaction of the Vietnamese to the troops who congregated there, in their coverage.) The *Time* article also addressed possible discrimination, noting that only 5 percent of 11,000 officers were black and only 2 blacks out of 380 combat battalion commanders were black. A black captain told *Time* that some black officers and enlisted men occasionally complained about discrimination, but they were using race "as a crutch."[64] *Time* suggested that blacks were to blame for the discrimination that persisted in the military. The black press never presented such a perspective.

As *Time*'s deputy bureau chief in Saigon, Terry continued to cover the Tet Offensive for two years, reporting from the front lines, flying on missions with South Vietnamese and American pilots, and being embedded with the troops. He also wrote about the Vietnamese people and politics. He believed the troops had a still more compelling story to tell. He told it in his 1984 book *Bloods: Black Veterans of the Vietnam War: An Oral History*. Like Ethel Payne and Mike Davis, Terry came away from the war convinced that "of all the professional and admirable GIs in Viet Nam, African American soldiers appeared in the press as among the most dedicated and able, which was a decidedly new image for them."[65]

"I Saw the Story, and He Didn't"

Thomas A. Johnson's road to Vietnam as the *New York Times*'s first black foreign correspondent started long before he arrived in Southeast Asia. In fact, Johnson became a journalist almost by happenstance. He joined the army after high school, read voraciously, and, by the time he left three years later, knew he wanted a career in writing.[66] After finishing college in 1954, and unable to find a job in journalism, Johnson worked in public relations. He also wrote a column and several stories per week for the New York edition of the *Pittsburgh Courier*. He noted years later that he had "built up a huge list of bylines and a reputation."[67]

One day in 1962, Louie Martin, one of the top black newspapermen of the day, called Johnson at two in the morning and told him, "Hey man, I want you to get your resume over to *Newsday*. They're looking for one."[68] "One" meant a black reporter, which mainstream media found by asking other black journalists to recommend somebody. Johnson walked into the editor's office to find him sitting at a desk with a Confederate flag on the wall behind him. "Tom," the editor said, "we talk about integration around here, but we ain't got a single nigra in this place. We've been reading your stuff and we want to talk to you about coming over here."[69] Johnson accepted the job and later became good friends with the editor.

Two years later, Johnson landed a plum job with the *New York Times*. Relationships he had built with black leaders made him well prepared to cover civil rights, sit-ins, and riots. The self-described "action reporter" viewed his assignment to Vietnam as a natural next step, an assignment suited to his talents. In Vietnam, he covered the action, but he believed the story of black soldiers should be shared with mainstream readers. When he returned from Vietnam, he wrote three front-page stories of four thousand words each, inspired by the hours he had spent with black soldiers and civilians. "The foreign editor wasn't pleased when I told him what I was going to do," he recalled. "But I saw the story, and he didn't. Once he saw what I'd written he accepted it as it was."[70] Johnson wrote that black soldiers and civilians were better off in Southeast Asia. He articulated the soldiers' views of the war and of civil rights, and he addressed the war's impact on the Vietnamese people. He noted later that he had "observed relations between black and white servicemen" and traveled with them to Bangkok to watch them relax but had rarely "asked a direct question."[71]

On April 29, 1968, the *Times* published Johnson's first installment on page

1. The piece painted a vivid picture of soldiers who "were doing everything." Johnson wrote, "[T]hey were planning battles, moving supplies, baking bread, advising the South Vietnamese Army, practicing law, patrolling the Mekong Delta canals, repairing jets on carriers in the Tonkin Gulf, guarding the United States Embassy, drinking in sleazy bars and dining in the best French restaurants, running press centers, digging latrines, driving trucks and serving on the staff of William C. Westmoreland, the American commander."[72]

This passage conveyed what the black press had always sought to demonstrate, that blacks were multitalented and could function in a variety of situations if given the opportunity. Johnson acknowledged as much when he noted, "In this highly controversial and exhaustively documented war, the Negro, and particularly the Negro fighting man, has attained sudden visibility—a visibility his forefathers never realized while fighting in past American wars."[73]

Johnson's story the following day gave an overview of blacks' life in Southeast Asia. Because the military and government agencies were now integrated, black soldiers had greater opportunities to hold positions that had been denied them in the States but "had always been available to whites."[74] They were becoming career soldiers, taking on professional and technical roles in the military, and serving in civilian administrations. These opportunities accounted for the fact that the reenlistment rate among blacks that was three times that of whites. Black expatriates, Johnson wrote, were living "in the closest approximation of a fully integrated society that America has ever produced."[75] One source told Johnson that the war offered "the best potential for creating a democratic society and a high standard of living for all." In the words of one civilian, Vietnam represented "bread and freedom, man, bread and freedom."[76]

Johnson's second piece showed that total integration was a goal, not a reality. A black soldier explained that self-segregation sometimes occurred because "a man wants to relax, really relax, when he's off duty."[77] He also addressed the issue of what blacks wanted to be called; some chose the word "black," while others preferred "Negro." And Johnson noted that members of both races casually used derogatory names for Asians.

In his third piece, he addressed race relations at home. He quoted a speaker who had railed against America's duplicity—the nation's expectation of black loyalty and patriotism despite numerous racial inequities. To put the plight of the soldiers in context, Johnson noted that blacks made up almost 10 percent of all military personnel in Vietnam but accounted for 25 percent of the combat leaders on the battlefront and 14 percent of the men who died in action. Soldiers wrestled with the notion of fighting the Viet Cong while reading about the heavy-handed tactics used to quell outbreaks of racial violence at home. Most of the troops Johnson interviewed believed wearing the uniform prevented them from actively taking part in the civil rights movement, but many career soldiers argued that their decision to remain in the military was a fight for civil rights. An army corporal told him, "We were working our show the same as Negroes back home." Another soldier said he "couldn't care less" if a white person back home liked him, adding, "But he has no right that says he can keep me down, can deny me my rights."[78]

Johnson had the kind of access that Payne and Davis did not; he was at the battlefront. Rather than relaying what troops told him, he wrote about what he saw and experienced. He reported on a mission to rescue wounded American soldiers and the return of the chopper with the troops and several North Vietnamese prisoners. "Within six minutes after touchdown, the crew had unloaded the ammunition crates. From a nearby bunker, a group of marines, several heavily bandaged, ran to the plane crouched low. Others carried stretchers with wounded men."[79] In another dispatch, he described the streets of downtown Saigon, deserted because U.S. servicemen had been ordered to stay away during the three-day celebration of the lunar new year. Bar girls left the nightclubs early because of the lack of customers. Johnson did not see "the familiar sights of an American soldier leaning a rifle against a wall while snapping pictures of beggars or street vendors, or middle-aged colonels entering official buildings with briefcases and submachine guns."[80]

In the early years of the Vietnam War, two black newspapers, a major mainstream magazine, and a major newspaper sent black reporters to cover the war and to report on black troops. The reports they generated were vastly different. Payne and Davis focused almost solely on a racial agenda, practicing advocacy journalism. Terry reported while also guiding *Time*'s coverage of the war. Johnson filed stories about the daily action of the war. Both he and Terry had to wait until they returned home to write definitive stories about black troops—Johnson in his three-part series and Terry in his book. Payne and Davis did not report from the front, while Johnson and Terry provided eyewitness accounts of battles. Johnson was a reporter who happened to be black covering a major story. Terry was an African American who was directing the coverage of the war as well as accompanying troops on the front lines. Both men, working for mainstream media, were in the thick of things.

Whether from overseas or upon their return, the correspondents placed

African American soldiers and their role in the Vietnam War in the public sphere. The themes and perspectives of the correspondents were overwhelmingly alike. All portrayed black enlisted personnel, officers, and civilians as loyal to their country despite inequities at home.

During the crucial decade of the 1960s, and the transformation of the mass media as a result of integration, the black press was far ahead of mainstream media in bringing the story of black soldiers to the forefront. The Vietnam War was another milestone in black foreign reporting and the evolution of African American journalism. The white media now sent black journalists overseas, primarily to cover the war but also to write about black troops. If integration had not opened the doors for Terry and Johnson to become magazine and newspaper reporters, they would probably have become correspondents for black newspapers as their predecessors had done.

[14]

In the Mainstream

Africa and Beyond

Leon Dash of the *Washington Post* spent most of the early 1970s trekking through Africa with guerrillas who were trying to wrest Angola from Portuguese colonial rule. Dash was not viewed as a foreign correspondent but as a reporter who had seized the chance to have a front-row view of Angola's march toward independence. He made two private trips and one sanctioned by the colonial government before getting an official post as a foreign correspondent in 1978. That allowed him to crisscross the continent and tell its story.

Dash was one of the few black journalists working for the mainstream media after the integration of the nation's newsrooms. As their ranks increased, they were assigned to cover events all over the world. Simultaneously, foreign reporting in the black press virtually ceased. *The Afro-American* engaged in some foreign news gathering during the 1970s. Executive editor Moses James Newson covered Bahamian independence in 1973, South Africa in 1974, and Cuba in 1976. The *Chicago Daily Defender* ran foreign news supplied by United Press International (UPI). Most black foreign correspondents now worked for the mainstream media. They lived in the countries from which they reported and rarely spent much time in one spot. Their on-the-scene reporting was based on observation and on interviews with leaders and ordinary people. Their news organizations provided the resources they needed to work and live overseas. The black press, in contrast, lacked the financial means to base reporters abroad and had to rely on stringers or travelers.

The first assignment for some black reporters for the mainstream press was Africa. Jack White of *Time* magazine, Larry Olmstead of the *Detroit Free Press*, Sheila Rule of the *New York Times*, Nathaniel Sheppard of the *Chicago Tribune*, and Jerry Gray of the Associated Press were in Africa in the 1980s. During the following decade, the establishment media assigned more black correspondents to Africa, including Howard French of the *New York Times* and Keith Richburg and Lynne Duke of the *Washington Post*. It is interesting to compare what correspondents for the mainstream media wrote to what their counterparts in the black press reported a few decades earlier.

In 1968 Dash took a leave from his job at the *Washington Post* to volunteer for the Peace Corps and teach at a rural high school in Kenya. He had been editor of the school newspaper while a student at Lincoln University in Philadelphia; after two years there, he transferred to Howard University. In 1966, while still a student there, he got a job as a copy boy at the *Washington Post*. By the time he graduated in 1968, he had been promoted to reporter. That was the beginning of a career with the newspaper that would last for thirty years. In Kenya, Dash met foreign correspondents and decided he wanted to be one of those journalists and he wanted to cover Africa.[1] When his Peace Corps stint was over, Dash returned to the newspaper.

While working at the *Post*, Dash got a phone call from a Harvard University graduate student who asked if he would go to Angola with a liberation movement. The idea intrigued him—his great-uncle had been born in Angola to a Guyanese missionary—but he was not sure how the *Post* would react. This opportunity came not long after he had led a group of blacks who filed an Equal Employment Opportunity Commission complaint against the newspaper. But the *Post* gave its blessing, and soon Dash was "tramping around" with guerrillas from the National Movement for the Total Independence of Angola (UNITA).[2] Dash lived with UNITA guerrillas for three months and covered more than eight hundred miles with them as he gathered information about why they were fighting. He spent several days, and more than twenty hours, interviewing UNITA leader Jonas Savimbi, who told Dash that most journalists had spent only half an hour with him. Dash's four-part series on Angola ran in the *Post* in December 1973. His was the first comprehensive reporting on the conflict in Angola. He examined the reasons for the fighting, and he gave his personal observations on the warfare and his experiences with the fighters. Dash recalled that the mainstream media either were not covering Angola or were covering it from a Washington and Cold War perspective, reporting that Western-backed groups and Soviet Union-backed groups were clashing.[3]

Dash did not consider himself a foreign correspondent. He knew he would have to work on a variety of fronts and demonstrate that he could handle any kind of story before he would be given a foreign-correspondent post. He flew to Lisbon to obtain a visa and then flew to Angola, where he spent three months reporting on the Portuguese colonial government. He returned to the States to write a series that ran in August 1974. His reporting won Dash the George Polk Award and an award from the Washington-Baltimore Newspaper Guild.

The series, "Angola: Birth of a Nation," described concerns about how Angola would become independent in light of its ethnic, tribal, regional, political, and racial fractures. Guerrillas were fighting the government, but ethnic distinctions led to fighting among the three guerrilla groups. Despite 13 years of fighting, 80,000 Portuguese soldiers and 14,000 guerrillas had reached a stalemate. Some Portuguese criticized the government for trying to hold on to Angola. "I'm a school teacher, not a soldier," one officer told Dash. "What the hell am I doing in this hole?"[4] One commando described how government troops mowed people down as they fled their villages. "They shot women in the back because they fed the guerrillas. They shot children, too. Then they torched the villages."[5] Dash interviewed a former UNITA officer who was now tending bar in Angola for the Portuguese. He had been captured while fishing and forced to fight with the guerrillas for six years before he could escape.

In 1976, Dash was back in Angola. The Portuguese had granted Angola independence in 1975. The Cuban- and Marxist-backed Popular Movement for the Liberation of Angola (PMLA) had become the Angolan government. The PMLA invited Dash to report on the fighting, which was now a civil war. Instead, Dash chose to live with the UNITA guerrillas again. UNITA was considered a pariah because it was aligned with the American Central Intelligence Agency (CIA) and with South Africa. Dash met twenty guerrilla escorts on the Angola-Zambia border and began a seven-month journey through the bush. He battled foot sores, fever, and parasites and ate rancid hippopotamus meat. He hiked with the fighters through forests and swamps and up steep hills for hours without stopping. He interviewed guerrillas, peasants, and prisoners whom UNITA had captured.

The thirty-three-year-old reporter wanted to understand what motivated the men—some accompanied by their families—to fight in the long, arduous civil war. He wanted to tell the real story, not the story American newspapers told, which described the fighting as backed by the Soviet Union or Western countries. In the interest of balanced reporting, Dash interviewed the National Liberation Front of Angola (FNLA) and officials from the People's Movement for the Liberation of Angola (MPLA) as well as government sources. His seven-part series ran in August 1977. It maintained that ethnic fear was the motivation for the ongoing civil war in Angola. All factions feared that if one ethnic group came to power the others would suffer.

Dash explained that UNITA was primarily Jonas Savimbi's one-person operation. His followers had "an almost mythical allegiance" to him. A high-ranking UNITA official told Dash that if the leader were killed the group would disintegrate. Dash's prediction that the war would last many years was correct. It lasted until February 2002, when Savimbi was killed in a battle with Angolan government troops.

The *Post* sent Dash to Africa as a correspondent in October 1978. Based in Abidjan on the Ivory Coast, he was the newspaper's one-man African bureau from March 1979 until April 1984, covering West, East, and Central Africa. Dash was unlike correspondents for the black press, who had traditionally focused on Africa's commonalities with blacks in America. Africa had held great promise to the black press and the black community as independence movements swept the continent in the late 1950s and 1960s. By the mid-1970s the continent was in a state close to chaos. Idi Amin was infamous for his brutal regime in Uganda. Both Ethiopia's Haile Selassie, whom the black press had championed in the 1930s, and Jean-Bedel Bokassa, the self-styled emperor of Central Africa, had fallen from power. Apartheid continued in South Africa, and antiapartheid activist Steve Biko died under mysterious circumstances in 1977.

Dash believed that editors in the mainstream press hesitated to send black journalists to Africa as correspondents because they believed African Americans would not be objective. Once he was assigned to Africa, he found that, just as the black press had told only part of the story, white correspondents of the past had not told the whole story either. They, too, had glossed over or ignored anything negative. When Dash covered Zaire in the 1980s, he was shocked at the lack of economic development. He wrote about the problem despite being told that, if he did so, he would not be allowed back in the country. "White correspondents had given Zaire a pass so that they could go in and out," he later said. "All of that left me with a bad taste for the correspondents who had come before me. They hadn't told what was happening. White correspondents protected Zaire because it was an integral part of American foreign policy."[6] That assertion agrees with the views of correspondents for the black press, especially William Worthy, who consistently accused the mainstream media of having a government agenda.

Dash was not looking for positive stories. He went to report the facts objectively. His primary interest was the economic and political development of the continent, especially the models that African leaders were implementing. Some leaders looked to models that had a semblance of socialism, while others placed a strong emphasis on capitalism.

The manner in which heads of African states were addressing policy issues was also a common theme in Dash's dispatches. In September 1979, Nigeria's newly elected president, Shehu Shagari, planned to adopt a militant position against minority white government rule in Africa, and he was considering providing arms to guerrillas fighting in South Africa.[7] A year later, Dash reported allegations that Shagari had cheated the Unity Party of Nigeria out of the presidency. Noting that Nigeria had a population of 100 million comprising 250 ethnic groups, Dash stated that political antagonism could lead to civil disorder.[8]

In November 1981, Dash reported that in the aftermath of Idi Amin's rule in Uganda, Zaire and Sudan were in crisis. Thousands of refugees were flooding in, and the countries feared the effect that would have "on their already severely strapped economies and social and political stability."[9] Dash also wrote a series of articles about Kilibwoni, the Kenyan village where he had lived as a young Peace Corps teacher from 1968 until 1970. He went back in 1973, 1977, 1982, and 1983 because he believed the village was the one place where he could measure the impact of development. Kilibwoni's progressive attitude had resulted in progress.

Objective reporting was Dash's hallmark, so much so that it annoyed his friends. One friend who read his 1977 series told Dash it "was so objective it was frightening." An activist friend suggested Dash take sides. The reporter later recalled saying "That was never going to happen."[10] He saw himself as a reporter, not as a *black* reporter.

Dash left Africa in 1984 and returned to the *Washington Post*, where he did groundbreaking and award-winning reporting. His series on an urban underclass family won a Pulitzer Prize in 1995, and was the basis for one of several books he wrote. Today Dash is a professor of journalism and African American studies at the University of Illinois at Urbana-Champaign. He still believes that economic and political development will determine Africa's future.[11]

Howard W. French: A Decade Later, a Different Perspective

While reporting from a black perspective was not Leon Dash's goal, other journalists say they could not escape race in their foreign correspondence. Howard W.

French believed he was in a privileged position as a black foreign correspondent for the *New York Times*, and he was compelled to look for the story about Africa that had not been told. He covered civil unrest in Haiti, genocide in Rwanda, hope for progress in Africa, floods in China, and heated tennis matches at Wimbledon. He was a prolific writer who turned out thousands of articles during his two decades at the *New York Times*.

French's globetrotting preceded his days as a foreign correspondent. As a student at the University of Massachusetts in Amherst, he had visited his family in Abidjan, the capital of the Ivory Coast. His father, a doctor, ran a healthcare program for the World Health Organization.[12] The trip helped shape French's worldview. Decades later, he explained the pull of the continent: "The thrill of travel and discovery in this part of Africa—a civil war in Chad, a coup in Guinea, a stolen election in Liberia—would turn me away from an early, passing interest in becoming a lawyer and propel me instead into a career in journalism."[13]

French moved to the Ivory Coast after graduating and worked as an English interpreter. Eventually, he was able to earn a respectable living as a freelance writer. Dash, a friend of French's family, had recommended him as a stringer to the *Washington Post* foreign editor in 1984. A year later, with a wife and small child, French wanted the security of a staff job. He wrote to the *New York Times* and several other major publications. Although the *Wall Street Journal* offered him a job, he accepted an offer from the *Times*. French later said that he had applied in 1985 when the newspaper was becoming conscious of the need for diversity in the newsroom. The mainstream media complained that it was hard to find qualified blacks, but French knew he possessed the experience the *Times* sought in its reporters. "I had a rarer sort of . . . expertise that stemmed from living in West Africa since 1979 and writing from abroad. I think they saw me as a rare commodity and they jumped on it."[14]

While living in West Africa and reading the U.S. media, French was acutely aware of the inadequacy of American coverage of the continent. When the *Times* hired him, he had a dilemma. He had pushed for the paper to give him a foreign post, and he assumed that he would be assigned to Africa. He wanted to tell the real story about Africa, but he did not want "to be pigeon-holed or stereotyped or ghettoized" because "everything about the news industry viewed Africa as being less than the rest of the world."[15]

French's perception was that, with one or two exceptions, every African American foreign correspondent previously hired by the *Times* had been sent to Africa.[16] Correspondents for other media went there, too. Les Payne, a Pulitzer Prize–winning journalist, covered Africa for *Newsday.* In 1976, in the aftermath of the Soweto uprising in South Africa, Payne wrote an eleven-part series that was nominated for another Pulitzer. He returned to South Africa in 1985 and again in 1990, chronicling the impact of Nelson Mandela's release on the continent. From 1978 to 1980 he periodically visited Rhodesia-Zimbabwe. Ron Allen, a longtime CBS correspondent, received an Emmy and a Robert F. Kennedy Award for his work on Sudan in 1994 and numerous awards for his coverage of genocide in Rwanda in 1995. Earl Caldwell, writer-in-residence at the journalism school at Hampton University, was a columnist at the *New York Daily News.* He was assigned to report from Africa for a year in the late 1970s, covering the election of the first black government in Zimbabwe.

French believed that assigning black correspondents to Africa "was a way of pretending to allow African Americans to be a part of the process of covering the world, but only allowing them to cover that corner of the world for which the news organization felt we were properly suited." He believed Africa deserved more and better coverage, but he was determined not to be another black reporter relegated to that post and excluded from other places. He planned to work at the *Times* for three years before pushing for an overseas assignment. The newspaper sent French to the Caribbean. He had broken the mold, becoming one of the first blacks to have a foreign assignment that was not Africa. He took an ironic view of the situation. "There was no other part of the world less important than Africa in their scheme of things except for the Caribbean. So I had gotten my wish of not going to Africa by going to another place that was essentially in their minds a black place . . . of lesser importance than Africa."[17]

French covered major stories in the Caribbean and Central America and won awards for his reporting. The rise and fall of Jean-Bertrand Aristide in Haiti, one of the biggest stories anywhere, happened on French's watch. He won several awards and crisscrossed the world covering government meltdowns, social chaos, political corruption, powerless states, and violent struggles for power.[18]

After French had spent four years as a one-man Central America bureau, the *Times* asked him to go to Africa. He agreed, but with several conditions. He was determined that his coverage of the continent would be different from that of the mainstream media. The paper agreed to allow French to cover other subjects and, if French was not satisfied, to assign him to cover another part of the world.

He arrived in Africa in 1994 as violence escalated. In the midst of the fighting, French wrote about African culture, sports, and literature. Although he was writing for the dominant media, he had an Afrocentric agenda. He wanted to understand why the place he had known a decade earlier, "poor and politically backward to be sure, had now settled into a spiral of bloody traumas and chronic disorder."[19]

French reported as an objective journalist who cited the facts and examined what was happening in Africa with a critical eye. He had pointed out to his editors that a continent with half a billion people received no business coverage in the dominant media; the type of stories they ran was predictable, narrow, and negative. He was determined to change that.

In one article, French wrote about France's attempt to maintain economic control in Africa. France had devaluated the currency of its former colonies as they tried to open themselves up to foreign trade and investment. Decades of carefully cultivated relations and overseeing African affairs had virtually guaranteed French businesses an advantage when international contracts were awarded. France was even trying to prevent African pharmacists from buying lower-cost medicines from Europe and Asia.[20]

French reported on constant crises on the continent. There was "a long spree of very difficult experiences, stories that involved violence and disaster and tragedy in Africa that could be construed as bad news or negative, but . . . undoubtedly events that were newsworthy."[21] He covered the war in Zaire and the fall of its dictator of thirty years, Mobuto Sese Seko, a staunch ally of the United States. The conflict killed more than five million persons. Just as Dash had reported on guerrilla warfare from Angola, French provided from Sierra Leone a sobering account of rebel fighting. Dash had written that ethnic conflict was the rationale two decades earlier. He reported that Sierra Leone's mineral wealth—not politics—was the goal of the rebel Revolutionary United Front.[22]

French explored the role of the United States and other Western nations in Africa. He later explained why he had challenged U.S. policy toward Africa.

> I tried to help readers understand the stories around the stories about how things came to be, how the United States created situations that produced the crises. I think I had a fair amount of success. Previous white correspondents had looked at Africa's problems as if they were the fault of Africa. There was the assumption that the United States

and the West were by default on the side of the right and good of the situation at the moment. They didn't probe into the facts and the history of the situation. They didn't probe deeply into how the West was responsible.[23]

French wrote about subjects he deemed important—a film festival, the arrival of Chinese merchants—not the typical stories of brutality. He was interested in Africa's alternative story. He found hints of hope in a land many believed hope had abandoned long ago. He wrote about the first vaccine against malaria, especially important because 90 percent of the two million people who died yearly from the disease lived in tropical Africa.[24] Nelson Mandela's 1995 attempt to peacefully end tension with rivals exemplified hope that violent conflict might be a fading tradition.

French had sidestepped many landmines during his years on the continent, but it was a mosquito bite that convinced him to leave Africa in 1997. He decided he was not going to let the continent kill him. He had tolerated "years of bad roads and horrible flights, separation from family, arrests, unsafe water and contaminated food, and finally malaria."[25] But he knew he would miss so much that he loved about Africa: "the beauty and the unfussy grace of the people, the amazing food . . . music rich beyond comparison, the sheer immediacy of human contact," and the joy of living by his wits.[26] When he completed his assignment, he asked to go to a vastly different place—Japan. For the rest of his career with the *New York Times*, he reported on Asia as well as other places, people, and issues throughout the world.

For Leon Dash, the question of race or the black agenda at home was not a consideration in his foreign reporting. That was also the case with Keith B. Richburg, the Africa bureau chief for the *Washington Post* from 1991 to 1995. Richburg has written that he pondered, "Are you black first, or a journalist first?" Although he "constantly struggled with the dilemma of whether to report accurately or to push some kind of black agenda," he reported on societal chaos, violence, and governmental deterioration.[27] Referring to African American views of Africa, he wrote, "[W]hat came out was a nauseating outpouring of praise from black Americans for a coterie of some of Africa's most ruthless strongmen and dictators."[28] He was determined not to be part of that cohort.

Howard French also chose objectivity, but he made a conscious effort to find stories that did not fit the stereotype of crisis and chaos. Sheila Rule, a black woman who was the *New York Times* correspondent in Africa from

1984 to 1988, looked for the race angle as she reported from twenty-five countries on the continent. Rule said later that she had always preferred to write about black people and the black experience. Her reporting from abroad was an extension of what she was already doing. "I'm a journalist, but I'm also an Afro-American journalist. My perspective, my approach, my attitude—all are influenced by who I am."[29]

In some ways, French and Rule were like the journalists for the black press who held the actions of the United States—or in some cases the lack of action—partially responsible for conflict and societal deterioration in other countries. In 2004, French published *A Continent for the Taking: The Tragedy and Hope of Africa*. Not constrained by journalistic objectivity, French openly blamed the United States for Africa's tortuous conditions. He criticized the Clinton administration for not doing enough to aid the continent, and he chastised the United States for never having a policy that addressed chronic hunger, poverty, and preventable disease. "America remains numb to the suffering, and indeed often makes things worse," he wrote.[30]

Ebony's Perspective

Like French, *Ebony*'s John H. Johnson looked for the good news in Africa. During the 1990s, *Ebony* made up for its lack of coverage in the previous twenty years. A supplement to its February 1990 issue highlighted progress in Nigeria. "Modern Nigeria is the fascinating story of a people's determined and sustained hunt for an enduring democratic system," one article stated. As the magazine had done in 1966, it portrayed Nigeria as a country that was moving in a positive direction. A follow-up piece the following month called Nigeria the "African Giant" and a nation in transition. "No longer are the people content to be tied to the umbilical cord of foreign imports," the story stated, adding that the country was becoming more self-sufficient.[31] That perspective ignored the economic instability and political turmoil in the country, which had been a constant in the 1970s and 1980s and continued into the 1990s, but it adhered to *Ebony*'s goal of seeking out the positive.

Soon after the new decade began, *Ebony*'s attention turned to Nelson Mandela and South Africa. The black community had long identified with the struggles of South Africans because of similar historical circumstances, and *Ebony* redoubled its efforts to document events there. Of the thirty-one articles on South Africa that the monthly ran during the decade, fifteen appeared between 1990 and 1994, years that encompassed the freeing of Mandela and the first open elections in the country. Several major events coincided with the increased coverage, including Mandela's winning the Nobel Peace Prize, the dismantling of the apartheid regime in South Africa, the country's first democratic elections in which full enfranchisement was granted, and Mandela's 1994 election as president. South Africa emerged from the international isolation of apartheid and became a leading international factor.

The May 1990 issue featured an exclusive interview with Mandela, who shared his dream for a "free, democratic and non-racial South Africa," and drew parallels between the black battle for civil rights in America and South Africans' struggle for self-determination.[32] Coverage continued the following month with excerpts from Mandela's letters from prison. In the same issue, correspondent Hans Massaquoi wrote about Namibia's freedom from South Africa. "So when independence finally came to Namibia after 106 years under colonial rule, it sent ripples of euphoria throughout Africa and the African Diaspora while raising demands for a free South Africa to a new pitch."[33]

Beyond Africa

While black journalists overwhelmingly went to Africa during their early years of working for the mainstream press, they moved beyond those posts—although some were still sent to what Howard French described as countries populated by minorities. Paul Delaney of the *New York Times* was made head of its Madrid bureau. Ron Allen, the London-based correspondent for ABC in the 1990s, reported for a decade from seventy-five countries, including Pakistan, Israel, Palestinian territories, Afghanistan, Rwanda, and South Africa.[34] Ginger Thompson covered Cuba for the *Chicago Tribune* and Latin America for the *Baltimore Sun* before moving to the *New York Times;* she became its Mexico bureau chief in 2000.[35]

The mainstream media have continued to assign black journalists to cover stories abroad, but they are not based in a particular country. Instead they engage in parachute journalism, going overseas, like their white counterparts, to cover a specific news story. CNN's Bernard Shaw was an early example. People the world over sat glued to their television sets as Shaw, reporting with correspondents Peter Arnett and John Holliman in Baghdad, crouched under a desk as he reported cruise missiles flying past the window of their hotel room when the United States launched the first Gulf War in 1991.

In some ways, black foreign correspondence has come full circle from the days when travelers and freelance journalists reported from abroad. Howard French teaches at Columbia University's journalism school, but he is still a globetrotting foreign correspondent. He writes freelance articles for the *New York Times* and other publications; he also disseminates his foreign reporting on his Internet blog *A Glimpse of the World*. In the spring of 2010, he published online a major piece on China's current role in Africa.[36] In November 2010, his article in the *Columbia Journalism Review* explored how the Internet in China has given a voice to persons who were silent or invisible. A month later, French's blog documented his visit to Rangoon, where he noted the absence of traffic signals in the center of a city of five million people because "the regime's notorious police unit had banned these for security reasons."[37]

French is not unlike George Washington Williams, Mary Ann Shadd Cary, William Worthy Jr., and other pioneering black foreign correspondents who traveled on their own to tell what they called "the real story."

Epilogue

When I began this project, the names of only two black foreign correspondents came to mind—CBS's Ed Bradley and CNN's Bernard Shaw. Bradley's reports from Vietnam during that war and his subsequent reports from abroad, and Shaw's gripping reporting from under a hotel bed in Baghdad during Operation Desert Storm still conjure up images of daring and dogged pursuit of international news. Both men worked in television; therefore, their stories from abroad came to us in our living rooms. I did not know about the accidental foreign correspondents, Frederick Douglass and Mary Ann Shadd Cary, who left their country in the mid-1800s to escape slavery and intolerable conditions for blacks and started a genre of African American foreign correspondence; nor did I have much knowledge of Ralph Waldo Tyler's reports from World War I, or of Joel Augustus Rogers, who as the first correspondent the black press sent abroad, covered the Italian-Ethiopian War to tell that little African nation's side of the story in the 1930s. I had never heard of Nancy Cunard, the white British socialite who was disinherited because of her support of black causes. Such a lack of knowledge is understandable because although the body of literature on the black press continues to grow, hardly anything has focused on black foreign reporting.[1] This book fills that void, focusing primarily on African American foreign correspondence in black publications, for that is where the reporting was most prolific, and then on correspondence in some mainstream publications.

Media historians note that early in the genre, the *New York Herald* and *New-York Tribune* provided correspondence that was primarily episodic and rooted in accomplishments.[2] The foreign correspondence of African Americans was contemporaneous with that of those newspapers, occurring a decade before the Civil War. Foreign correspondence by African Americans and at least one white person was a conversation about race and government and race and media. The writers, most of whom were men, recognized that the ability to live, work, travel, and even eat and sleep anywhere in the country was not a permitted birthright for African Americans. Consignment to a permanent underclass in the United States and an intolerance of racism, exploitation, and injustice compelled African Americans to go abroad and gather and present information and perspectives that would not only enlighten, but would aid in pleading the cause of blacks in the United States and people of color worldwide. Thousands and thousands of stories constructed an alternative narrative grounded in advocacy and truth telling. That black perspective gave meaning and visibility to people and issues typically either marginalized or misrepresented in media and society.

As George Washington Williams wrote in 1890 when he challenged the rule of Congo by Belgium's King Leopold II and the foreign reporting of famed *New York Herald* correspondent Henry Morton Stanley, "And while I have an interest in the civilization of Africa equal to any person's, I cannot be silent, or suffer to pass unchallenged statements calculated to mislead and deceive the friend of humanity and civilization."[3] That desire to tell the truth or "our story" characterized the genre of African American foreign correspondence well into the twentieth century.

Providing foreign news took grit and determination. The men and women were unafraid to fight for the opportunity to go overseas. Once there, they objectively reported information that by its very nature challenged injustices. T. Thomas Fortune's reports in the *Voice of the Negro* used the words of Filipinos to challenge racism. The *Pittsburg Courier*'s Frank Whisonant and *The Afro-American*'s James Hicks exposed racism during the Korean War. Like other African American journalists, the foreign correspondents did the "leg work" for the black newspapers and the world community of color. Enoch Waters, who covered World War II and some of the African liberation movement, noted that black writers "faced racial barriers, ridicule, insults, and even violence in the efforts to carry out assignments," devising "techniques and stratagems to overcome and circumvent obstacles meant to prevent and discourage them from obtaining information needed to carry out the mission of the black press."[4]

No better example of this role exists than William Worthy Jr., who often went abroad at the behest of *The Afro-American* newspaper chain, or acted alone, with little more than a letter of introduction and copies of stories he had written, to gain entry to and report from foreign countries. Like the majority of black foreign correspondence, Worthy confronted the U.S. government and the mainstream media for excluding information about world developments that was vital to an enlightened public. He once wrote: "Our daily papers, giant weekly news magazines, radio and television networks will not and psychologically cannot report the hard facts and bitter truth from Latin America, Asia, and Africa. They can't because they have too much of a stake in the status quo—emotionally, financially, and socially . . . The colored press must assume this responsibility."[5]

The writers were stringers, travelers, quasi correspondents, and, as the years progressed, formally trained journalists. Some owned newspapers or news services, while others were editors, part-time staff members, and reporters for black publications and an occasional white publication. In the last half of the twentieth century, they were primarily correspondents for the mainstream media. All but three of the dozens and dozens of early foreign correspondents were men.[6] Nancy Cunard, Era Bell Thompson, and Ethel Payne are among the many women who followed and who produced award-winning work for print and broadcast media.[7] Virtually all of the correspondents were college-educated and were part of the black middle class. The fact that they had income allowed many travelers early on to bring information home from abroad. Correspondents such as Mary Ann Church Terrell, who was active in the black women's club movement, suffrage, and other issues, and Irene Diggs, a college professor, were some of the travelers. Even if the writers were not born into the black elite of their time, their work as correspondents propelled them to stardom—just as it did for white correspondents. They often went on speaking tours upon their return home, and their newspapers aggressively promoted them and their work.

When blacks in the United States decided they did not want to rely solely on clipping foreign correspondence from the establishment press and the publications committed to overseas news gathering in a more formal way at the beginning of the twentieth century, personal journalism was very much a part of the reportage, as it was in the mainstream press. That was the case with the *Chicago Defender*'s Robert S. Abbott, who traveled to South America and Europe to explore race relations in 1923 and 1929, respectively; *The Afro-American*'s Carl Murphy, who went to Germany in 1914 and to Haiti in the 1930s; and the Associated Negro Press's (ANP's) Carl Barnett, who sometimes traveled and sent stories to subscriber publications. Some newspapers also dispatched their editors to what they considered hot spots. By the end of 1920s, *The Afro-American* had reported on slavery in Liberia, and the *Defender* had established the black press's first foreign news service.

During World War I and World War II, letters from black soldiers in the field were the only way black readers obtained a sense of the experiences of their kin and friends. That type of correspondence sufficed until black leaders and editors convinced the government to allow them to send accredited correspondents abroad. While the Second Great War is more associated with reporting from abroad by African Americans, the 1930s was, indeed, a golden decade. News from all corners of the globe made its way to a reading public hungry to know about world events that affected people who shared their identity. Highlights include Jesse Owens's feats during the 1936 Olympics in Germany, which received extensive firsthand coverage, thanks to the *Pittsburgh Courier*'s Robert Vann; Langston Hughes's dispatches from the front during the Spanish Civil War for *The Afro-American;* and Nancy Cunard's evisceration of fascism during the conflict for the ANP. In 1937, *The Afro-American* dispatched Ralph Matthews to cover the coronation of Great Britain's King George VI because he would be ruler over three-fourths of the world's black population. For that same reason, the ANP sent Fay Jackson abroad. Adolf Hitler's march also received substantial coverage, as did Africa and the West Indies.

While the mainstream media presented information and enlightened readers, that was not the end point for African American foreign correspondence. The goal—the *why*—was social reform in the United States and global policy changes that eliminated oppression. African American foreign news gathering adhered primarily to a civil rights agenda, grounded in advocacy, protest, and pride. Guided by that mission, these journalists discredited the prevailing white ideology of blackness by creating and amplifying an alternative, more realistic, and positive identity for race members. Dispatches highlighted the achievement of people of color, especially during wars. Ralph Waldo Tyler reported on the experiences of black soldiers in World War I, and thirty black war correspondents chronicled the experiences and valor of the troops and black expatriates not only to illustrate black gallantry and loyalty, but with the hope that such information would lead to social justice and civil equity. Mike (Michael DeMonde) Davis humanized the soldiers during the Vietnam War for *The Afro-American,* providing such detailed information as the names of parents, siblings—even cousins—in addition to street addresses in their hometowns, education, and military rank. Still, negative images persisted in society.

The misrepresentation of darker people was prevalent in the mainstream media and still remains a throbbing memory in the black community. The late Frank Bolden, a World War II foreign correspondent who eventually worked for the *New York Times*, asserted as much before he died in 2003, stating that people read the black press "because the white newspapers did not carry positive news about blacks. All of them carried the pathological side of negro life, which was crime-crime-crime."[8]

At the core of the foreign reporting was the belief that America could be greater if it lived up to its stated democratic principles. Most African American foreign correspondents believed that they could gain equal rights and human dignity for blacks and oppressed if they provided credible, verifiable evidence of other nations' more egalitarian treatment of their black populations, and if they exposed the hypocrisy of the United States as it professed a doctrine of freedom and equality in its international involvement while denying basic human rights to blacks domestically. Metz Lochard, who served as the *Chicago Defender*'s foreign editor and editorial-page chief for years, wrote that the black press seized the opportunity and exploited "to the fullest" the fact that the world was watching the United States to see how it dealt with its "sore spot," the "negro problem," as it supported democracy around the world.[9]

The *other* stories and viewpoints that characterized foreign reporting by blacks were primarily about race relations and ethnic topics, as opposed to political, economic, and social issues in the countries that correspondents reported from. When they addressed those issues, they did so through the lens of race, examining how and why people in the African Diaspora fit into the fabric of a society and how transnational white supremacy robbed darker peoples of their natural birthright. Some might argue that black foreign correspondence did not adhere to the norms and routines of journalism because so much of it was advocacy. This book shows that overwhelmingly the writers successfully navigated their dual role as members of the black community and as journalists. Most objectively presented factual, verifiable information in the same way that white foreign correspondents did. They often interjected themselves in their reportage, just as mainstream correspondents did, often when providing war coverage. The difference is that the majority of black writers wrote to reposition the race.

This is not to say that all information was the *truth* the black press looked for. Robert Abbott educated readers by providing accounts about the places he visited, but he also inaccurately reported that Europe was racially inclusive. During the African independence movements, accomplished foreign correspondents first presented a positive storyline of economic and political progress in the newly freed nations, despite years of colonial rule and continuing obstruction by the former colonizers. The black press largely refrained from reporting on Africa when disorder characterized the continent because positive portrayal of darker peoples was seen as an avenue to black empowerment. Reporting stories to the contrary would have confirmed the prevailing and accepted notion of blacks as being unworthy of self-governing or social equality. Yet, as conditions deteriorated on the continent, the ANP's Enoch Waters reported the facts.

Integration of the nation's newsrooms during the 1960s was a virtual death knell for African American foreign correspondence in the black press, and it had a detrimental impact on black publications. The black press had begun to decline after World War II because of a chronic lack of advertising, mismanagement, and other factors.[10] Now, their star journalists gravitated to the white press, which offered them larger and steadier paychecks and a bigger audience for their work, among other incentives. Interestingly, large numbers of black foreign correspondents for the mainstream media were sent to Africa. This suggests that those media organizations might have felt that because the correspondents were black they would have a better understanding of race; or it could be that, Howard French said, "everything about the news industry viewed Africa as being less than the rest of the world."[11] This, of course, was a type of marginalization. Some of these correspondents relished the assignment. Lynne Dukes, who was the Johannesburg bureau chief for the *Washington Post* from 1995 to 1999, wrote in an autobiographical statement: "For 20 years, I wrote local, national, international and magazine articles for the *Washington Post.* But of all my beats, it is the African beat, the Africa stories, that are closest to my heart and that grip me to this day."[12] Shelia Rule, who wrote for the *New York Times* from Africa and Europe during the 1980s, said "race informed" all of her writing.[13] Still other blacks such as the *Post*'s Leon Dash indicate that race or the race story did not govern their reporting.

World War II was the last period in which blacks reported in large numbers over an extended period for the African American press. Only two African American publications—the *Chicago Daily Defender* and *The Afro-American*—fielded correspondents during the Vietnam War. Mike Davis, *The Afro-American*'s correspondent, went to work for a white newspaper when he graduated from college. He left that job as the first black reporter at the *Atlanta Constitution* when he saw an opportunity to go overseas for the black newspaper. If Davis had not volunteered for that assignment, *The Afro-American* probably would not have fielded a correspondent.

In recent history, reporting from abroad is almost nonexistent. Between 1969 and 2006, there is no indication that black publications engaged in foreign reporting. Foreign news came via the wire services. *The Afro-American* did manage to provide coverage from abroad, always with the goal of reporting on race troops. James Wright of the newspaper's Washington edition reported from Afghanistan for ten days in July 2006, while Leonard Sparks, Baltimore editor, was in Iraq from September to November of that year. George Curry, editor of *Emerge* magazine, reported briefly from Iraq for the National Newspaper Publishers Association. The work of Howard French, the former *New York Times* correspondent, operating alone, provides freelance foreign reports to the news media and posts his work on his website.[14] This type of episodic foreign news gathering is reminiscent of the genre in its early days.

The demise of African American foreign correspondence is indicative of a larger struggle for a black press that once was the primary voice for and source of news and information for the black community. Black publications were the eyes, ears, and voices. As the black press served as a watchdog of government and the mainstream media, it also was the bulletin board that relayed information about the doings of the race. And through its foreign correspondence, it provided the linkages between blacks at home and those with whom they shared a common heritage—all the while giving glimpses of life and the black experience in far-flung places. For much of the last half of the twentieth century and continuing today, blacks have a multitude of options from which to get their information. Thus, they largely do not turn to black publications,[15] instead opting for newspapers, broadcast and cable network programming, and new media technologies that provide direct, interactive information arrangements. Facebook, Twitter, and blogs often drive stories and action. While websites such as Blackamericanweb.com seek to directly reach black audiences, major mainstream news organizations have created websites tailored specifically to that audience. The *Washington Post*'s The Root DC and NBC's The Grio are two examples.

Ultimately, when we look at the history and role of the press, we try to determine the medium's impact. Whether it was from challenging American-inflamed racial oppression in South America, economic restrictions in England and France, caste distinctions in Italy, or Hitler-driven racial brutality in Germany, journalists reporting from abroad took on racism under every layer of purported freedom. Repression in America and oppression abroad was the common thread that ran through African American foreign correspondence for the black press. Racism prevented the college-educated Homer Smith (also known as Chatwood Hall) from getting a job; therefore, he moved to Russia in 1932 and remained there until 1946—even covering the Russian campaign during World War II—before moving to Ethiopia, where he stayed until 1966. Ollie Stewart, one of the star reporters during that same war, left the United States in 1949 because he could not stand being a second-class citizen in his home country. He filed articles and columns for *The Afro-American* and several other organs before returning home in 1977, shortly before he died. During the twenty-eight years Stewart was based in Paris, he did not make one visit back to the United States.

These reporters continued to present an alternative, positive aspect of blackness and otherness, all the while illustrating America's duplicity. Most of African American foreign correspondence tried to influence the dominant society, to change attitudes, and, thereby, reshape America into a more racially inclusive nation that guaranteed black rights protection and advancement. Some other writings urged blacks to leave America for Canada or Africa, as was the case with the *Provincial Freeman* and the *Negro World.* Thousands of blacks heeded Mary Ann Shadd Cary's call and moved to Canada, and it is estimated that as many as six million people read the *Negro World.* Despite the continuing presentation of the alternative, positive aspects of blackness, as well as the illustration of America's duplicity, for more than a century, except in a few instances, the status quo did not change. Laws and traditions kept blacks subjugated at home, and the United States and Western nations continued their policies in darker nations. There were some successes. Going beyond solely the issue of race, William Worthy's actions transformed foreign correspondence by gaining the right for correspondents to report from anywhere unimpeded. Substantive change in the condition of blacks in the United States came with the civil rights movement that some historians argue had its genesis when black soldiers returned from World War II determined that they would no longer tolerate inequality after having fought for freedom in a different land. Oddly enough, this was the same time African American foreign correspondence was waning; therefore, one cannot argue that black foreign reportage brought about change in race relations.

Despite failing to change the existing state of affairs, African American foreign correspondence succeeded in fulfilling the traditional role of the black press. As an argument for equality and democracy, it provided a depth of visibility for blacks that gave meaning and substance to their lives, thus shaping the discourse in the public sphere. It often stressed the values of hard work, saving, and good decision making, and seemed to ask blacks what they could learn from the information provided. Through the span of history, it informed current and future generations and preserved for posterity another story about those who shared a transnational black identity, thus, fostering pride among race members, and, arguably, their interpretation of what it meant to be black. African American reporting helped readers see blacks and people of color—and the world—in a new and different way. Without the concerted effort of those who wrote from abroad, a different view of the world and of history—or what they termed "our story"—would not have been told.

At its core, this book is about more than just African American foreign correspondence; it is about black, American, world, and media history. In examining how and why blacks used their pens and voices, this book should contribute to a broader conversation about navigating racial, societal, and global problems that persist today. This is even more important because as a voice for blacks, the traditional African American press is largely silent, and there is concern about the lack of diversity nation's newsrooms[16] where presentation of blacks and people of color of in the newsrooms still fits the historic pattern of marginalization or stereotype.[17]

Notes

INTRODUCTION

1. See John Maxwell Hamilton, *Journalism's Roving Eye: A History of Foreign Reporting* (Baton Rouge: Louisiana State University Press, 2009); Robert Desmond, *The Information Process: World News Reporting to the Twentieth Century* (Iowa City: University of Iowa Press, 1978); Robert Desmond, *Windows on the World: World News Reporting 1900–1920* (Iowa City: University of Iowa Press, 1980); Robert Desmond, *Crisis and Conflict: World News Reporter* (Iowa City: University of Iowa Press, 1982); Robert Desmond, *Tides of War: World News Reporting 1940–1945* (Iowa City: University of Iowa Press, 1984); Michael Emery, *On the Front Lines: Following America's Foreign Correspondents across the Twentieth Century* (Washington, DC: The American University Press, 1995).

2. Hamilton, *Journalism's Roving Eye*, 157.

3. See Lerone Bennett Jr., *Pioneers in Protest* (Chicago: Johnson Publishing Company, 1968), 61; Frederick Detweiler, *The Negro Press in the United States* (College Park, MD: McGrath Publishing Company, 1968 reprint of 1922 edition), 204; Roland Wolseley, *The Black Press, USA* (Ames: Iowa State University Press, 1990), 24; Armistead S. Pride and Clint C. Wilson II, *A History of the Black Press* (Washington, DC: Howard University Press, 1997), 13.

4. Carl Senna, *The Black Press and the Struggle for Civil Rights* (Danbury, CT: Scholastic Library Publishing, 1994), 32, 56.

5. Bernell Tripp, *Origins of the Black Press: New York, 1827–1874* (Northport, AL: Vision Press, 1992).

6. See Franklin, *From Slavery to Freedom*, 206–8. Franklin notes that following the end of slavery and as Reconstruction was underway, whites in the South passed these measures to regain control over blacks and assure their presence as a labor force necessary for the region's survival. Black Codes dictated where blacks could live, mandated whether they could own or rent property, and stripped them of the right to testify in court, to vote, and to participate in the affairs of government.

7. Pride and Wilson, *History of the Black Press*, 88.

8. J. Max Barber, "The Morning Cometh," *Voice of the Negro* 1 (January 1904): 38.

9. R. N. Jacobs, "Race, Media and Civil Society," *International Sociology* 14, no. 3 (1999): 355–72.

10. John H. Sengstacke, "From Soup to Citizenship," statement to the Publicity Club of Chicago, October 12, 1955, 9, Abbott-Sengstacke Papers, Series 13, Box 3, Folder 21, Vivian G. Harsh Research Collection of Afro-American History and Literature, Chicago Public Library, Chicago, Illinois.

11. Enoch P. Waters, *American Diary: A Personal History of the Black Press* (Chicago: Path Press, Inc., 1987), xxi.

12. Maxwell Brooks, *The Negro Press Re-examined: Political Content of Leading Negro Newspapers* (Boston: The Christopher Publishing House, 1959), 103.

13. See "Ollie Stewart, AFRO writer, Dies in Atlanta," undated clipping, Ollie B. Stewart File, Manuscript Division, Moorland-Spingarn Research Center, Howard University, Washington, D.C.

14. See "Our Monthly Review," *Voice of the Negro* (March 1904):587; "Why We Are for Japan," *New York Times*, March 1, 1904, 8.

15. Correspondence from Jacob Schiff to W. E. B. Du Bois, April 1905, quoted in Dan S. Green, "W.E.B. Du Bois: His Journalist Career," *Negro History Bulletin* 40 (1997): 64.

16. Linda Johnson Rice, "*Ebony's* African World—Magazine's Coverage of African Events—Fiftieth Anniversary Issue," *Ebony*, November 1995, 80–87.

17. Edward R. Bradley, oral interview in Wallace Terry, *Missing Pages: Black Journalists of Modern America: An Oral History* (New York: Carroll and Graf Publishers, 2007); Jinx C. Broussard interview of Leon Dash, November 22, 2010.

CHAPTER ONE

1. Frederick Douglass, letter to William Lloyd Garrison, October 24, 1945, in Philip Forner, ed., *Life and Writings of Frederick Douglass*, vol. 1 (New York: International Publisher, 1950), 120. Accessed at www.yale.edu/gld, June 26, 2008.

2. Ibid.

3. Ibid.

4. Fionnghuala Sweeney, *Frederick Douglass and the Atlantic World* (Liverpool: Liverpool University Press, 2007), 29.

5. Frederick Douglass, letter to William Lloyd Garrison, January 1, 1846, in Philip Forner, ed., *Life and Writings of Frederick Douglass*, vol. 1 (New York: International Publisher, 1950), 125. Accessed at www.yale.edu/gld, June 26, 2008.

6. Frederick Douglass, letter to Horace Greeley, written April 15, 1846, from Glasgow, and published in the *New-York Tribune*, in Philip Forner, ed., *Life and Writings of Frederick Douglass*. vol. 1 (New York: International Publisher, 1950), 144. Accessed at www.yale.edu/glc/archive/1096.htm, June 26, 2008.

7. Frederick Douglass, letter to William Lloyd Garrison, March 27, 1846, in Philip Forner, ed., *Life and Writings of Frederick Douglass*. vol. 1 (New York: International Publisher, 1950), 125. Accessed at www.yale.edu/glc/archive/1089.htm, January 26, 2009.

8. Frederick Douglass, letter to William Lloyd Garrison, May 15, 1849, in Philip Forner, ed., *Life and Writings of Frederick Douglass*. vol. 1 (New York: International Publisher, 1950), 149. Accessed at www.yale.edu/gld, June 26, 2008.

9. Ibid.

10. Richard Almonte, introduction to Mary Ann Shadd, *A Plea for Emigration: Or, Notes on Canada West* (Toronto: The Mercury Press, 1998), 15.

11. Jane Rhodes, *Mary Ann Shadd Cary: The Black Press and Protest in the Nineteenth Century* (Bloomington: Indiana University Press, 1998), 80. For additional information about Shadd Cary, see Rhodes's work on her life and career.

12. Ibid., xiv.

13. Ibid., 2, 4–5.

14. See John Hope Franklin and Alfred A. Moss Jr., *From Slavery to Freedom: A History of Negro Americans,* 6th ed. (New York: Alfred A. Knopf, 1988), 135–37; 152–53; Carl Senna, *The Black Press and the Struggle for Civil Rights* (New York: Franklin Watts, 1993), 23. These historians point out that during the 1830s, violence mounted as pro- and antislavery forces debated the status of blacks in both the North and the South. Fear and reprisal increased after the revolt led by Virginia slave Nat Turner killed fifty-seven whites on August 21, 1831, and revolts occurred in several other southern and northern states. In the ensuing decades, southern states strengthened Black Codes, depriving blacks of their right to vote, assemble, own or rent property, or work in the trades. Other statutes allowed for the arrest and forced labor of blacks accused of vagrancy, deprived blacks of the right to defend themselves in court, and made them vulnerable to being kidnapped and forced into slavery. Blacks fared little better in the North. Those migrating from the South were unwelcome and free blacks already there were often the victims of mob violence. Black and white abolitionists along the Eastern Seaboard were militant in their call for emancipation and improvement in the status of blacks, thus contributing to fear among whites.

15. Rhodes, *Mary Ann Shadd Cary,* 5, 26.

16. J. B. Y., "Miss Shadd's Pamphlet," *North Star,* June 8, 1849.

17. Ibid.

18. Mary Ann Shadd, letter to Frederick Douglass, *North Star,* March 23, 1849.

19. Ibid.

20. Ibid.

21. Shadd, *Plea for Emigration,* 4.

22. Shadd, *Plea for Emigration,* cited on page 44 of Altmonte's edited version.

23. Almonte, introduction to Shadd Cary, *Plea for Emigration,* 43, 52.

24. Ibid.

25. Ibid., 59.

26. Samuel Ringgold Ward's introduction on page 1 of the *Provincial Freeman,* as cited in Rhodes, *Mary Ann Shadd Cary.*

27. "ATTENTION!!!" *Provincial Freeman,* March 25, 1854.

28. Mary Ann Shadd, letter to Abraham McKinney, August 29, 1854, Mary Ann Shadd Cary Papers, Folder 3, Moorland-Spingarn Research Center, Howard University, Washington, D.C.

29. "Notice," *Provincial Freeman,* November 11, 1854. Accessed at www.accessible.com/accessible/print?AADocList=6&AADocStyle=STYLE&AA.com, April 22, 2009.

30. See I. Garland Penn, *The Afro-American Press and Its Editors* (New York: Arno Press, 1891), 367–427.

31. Chatham, Canada West, petition, March 4, 1858, Mary Ann Shadd Cary Papers, Folder 3, Moorland-Spingarn Research Center, Howard University, Washington, D.C.

32. "Brooklyn, N.Y. April 12th, 1854. MR. EDITOR," *Provincial Freeman,* May 6, 1854. Accessed at www.accessible.com/accessible/docButton?AAWhat=doc&AAWhere=69&AABean.com, March 26, 2010.

33. "Our Friend GAINES is Very Much Amused at the Honesty of Emigrationists," *Provincial Freeman,* January 20, 1854, Accessed at www.accessible.com/accessible/print?AADocList=6&AADocStyle=STYLE&AA.com, March 26, 2010.

34. "Newspapers by Colored People in the United States," *Provincial Freeman*, June 23, 1855, Accessed at http://www.accessible.com/docButton?AAWhat=doc&AAWhere=50&AABean.com, March 26, 2010.

35. "A Word about, and to Emigrationists," *Provincial Freeman*, April 15, 1854, Accessed at www.accessible.com/accessible/print?AADocList=6&AADocStyle=STYLE&AA.com, April 22, 2009.

36. M. A. Shadd, "Our Tour," *Provincial Freeman*, July 22, 1854. Accessed at www.accessible.com/accessible/print?AADocList=86&AADocStyle=STYLED&AA.com, March 26, 2010.

37. Rhodes, *Mary Ann Shadd Cary*, 99.

38. John Hope Franklin, "George Washington Williams and Africa," in *Africa and Afro-American Experience*, ed. Lorraine A. Williams (Washington, DC: Howard University Press, 1977), 68. For a detailed accounting of Williams's life and career, see also John Hope Franklin, *George Washington Williams: A Biography* (Chicago: University of Chicago Press, 1985). Williams did not write an autobiography and there are no special collections devoted solely to him, thus, I was unsuccessful in locating primary sources and accessing his writings.

39. George Washington Williams, "The Opening of Africa: Talk with King Leopold about the Congo Free State," *Boston Herald*, November 17, 1889, 23.

40. Lerone Bennett Jr., *The Shaping of Black America* (Chicago: Johnson Publishing Company, 1975), 208.

41. Franklin, *George Washington Williams*, 179–80.

42. Williams's biographer John Hope Franklin indicated that Williams's diaries and other papers could not be located, but the painstaking and highly regarded research the biographer did provides compelling evidence that Williams, indeed, went overseas and submitted reports that were published in the United States.

43. Ibid., xix, 22.

44. George Washington Williams, letter to Henry Wadsworth Longfellow, July 24, 1875, Longfellow Papers, Houghton Library, Harvard University, as cited in Franklin, *George Washington Williams*, 221.

45. Ibid., 66.

46. Ibid., 142–63, 310. Williams gained such stature in the party that Republican President Chester A. Arthur nominated him as minister to Haiti only hours before leaving office in the hands of Democrat Grover Cleveland. Although he was sworn in as the new minister, Williams never assumed the post because of fierce opposition from Democrats who resented Arthur's last-minute appointment, and from fellow Republicans and vocal black editors who had supported other Republican candidates. This latter group viewed the appointment as a reward for Williams's political support, and accused him of seeking the office while professing to work for the race.

47. Ibid., 18.

48. For reference, see Certificate of Disability for Discharge, July 27, 1868, U.S. Pension Office, National Archives, Record Group 15; Passport Application, No. 12282, Department of State, National Archives, Record Group 59. Williams's military discharge papers had the former description, while his June 30, 1884, passport application indicated the latter.

49. Franklin, "George Washington Williams," 178.

50. John Maxwell Hamilton, *Journalism's Roving Eye: A History of American Foreign Reporting* (Baton Rouge: Louisiana State University Press, 2009), 79.

51. For reference, see "Livingstone, Missionary Travels and Researchers in South Africa," in *Stanley's Despatches to the New York Herald, 1871–1871, 1874–1877*, ed. Norman Bennett (Boston: Boston University Press, 1970), xix. In the introduction to the compilation of Stanley's dispatches from abroad, Bennett noted that from 1854 through 1856, Livingstone provided detailed accounts of his travels from the west coast of Africa and across the continent. His exploits earned him the designation as the "greatest propagandist for Africa that the European world had yet known."

52. Henry Morton Stanley, *Through the Dark Continent or The Sources of the Nile Around the Great Lakes of Equatorial Africa and Down Livingstone River to the Atlantic Ocean* (New York: Harper & Brothers, 1878), 2.

53. See Henry Morton Stanley, *The Congo and the Founding of Its Free State: A Story of Work and Exploration*, vol. 1 (New York: Harper & Brothers, 1885).

54. The titles of Stanley's comprehensive books and other foreign correspondence framed the African continent. See, for example, Henry Morton Stanley, *Through the Dark Continent or The Sources of the Nile Around the Great Lakes of Equatorial Africa and Down Livingstone River to the Atlantic Ocean* (New York: Harper & Brothers, 1878).

55. Bennett, ed., *Stanley's Despatches to the New York Herald*, xxxii.

56. Beverly Ann Deepe Keever, "The Origin of a News Gap," in *U.S. News Coverage of Racial Minorities: A Sourcebook, 1934–1996*, ed. Beverly Ann Deepe Keever, Carolyn Martindale, and Mary Ann Westin (Westport, CT: Greenwood Press, 1997), 2.

57. Bennett, ed., *Stanley's Despatches to the New York Herald*, xxi.

58. Hamilton, *Journalism's Roving Eye*, 82.

59. *Buffalo Express*, December 27, 1871, as cited in Bennett, ed., *Stanley's Despatches to the New York Herald*, xxi.

60. *New York Herald*, April 13, 1872, November 5, 1872, cited in Bennett, ed., *Stanley's Despatches to the New York Herald*, xxv.

61. Franklin, "George Washington Williams," 70.

62. Ibid., 73.

63. George Washington Williams, "A Report on the Proposed Congo Railway by Colonel [sic] the Honorable Geo. W. Williams of the United States of America," July 16, 1890, cited in Franklin, *George Washington Williams*, Appendix 2, 255.

64. Franklin, *George Washington Williams*, 187. See also George Washington Williams, "A Report upon the Congo-State and Country to the President of the Republic of the United States of America," cited in Franklin, *George Washington Williams*, Appendix 3, 265–69.

65. George Washington Williams, "An Open Letter to the King of the Belgians," July 18, 1890, cited in Franklin, *George Washington Williams*, Appendix 1, 242–54.

66. Ibid.

67. Ibid.

68. Hamilton, *Journalism's Roving Eye*, 83.

CHAPTER TWO

1. T. Thomas Fortune, "The Filipino: A Social Study in Three Parts," *Voice of the Negro* (March 1904): 97.

2. Sherman Briscoe, "Executive Director's 25 Greatest Publishers," *NNPA Convention Journal* 32 (n.d.), 1974, Abbott-Sengstacke Papers, Series 13, Box 176, Folder 2, Vivian G. Harsh Research Collection of Afro-American History and Literature, Chicago Public Library, Chicago, Illinois.

3. Ibid.

4. T. Thomas Fortune, "The White Man's Burden," *New York Age*, April 1899. Accessed at www.nationalhumanitiescenter.org/pds/filded/empire, presented by the National Humanities Center, Research Triangle Park, North Carolina, 2005.

5. William G. Jordan, *African-American Newspapers and America's War for Democracy, 1914–1920* (Chapel Hill: University of North Carolina Press, 2001), 25.

6. Armistead Pride, "Register and History of the Negro Newspaper in the United States, 1827–1950" (unpublished dissertation, Northwestern University, 1950), 5; Armistead Pride and Clint C. Wilson, *A History of the Black Press* (Washington, DC: Howard University Press, 1997), 96, 98; Penelope Bullock, *The Afro-American Periodical Press, 1838–1909* (Baton Rouge: Louisiana State University Press, 1981), 3.

7. "Who Founded the *Voice*?" *Voice of the Negro* 2 (March 1905): 192–93.

8. Max J. Barber, "The Morning Cometh," *Voice of the Negro* 1 (January 1904): 38.

9. Ibid.

10. "Our Monthly Review," *Voice of the Negro* (March 1904): 85.

11. Michael Emery, *On the Front Lines: Following America's Foreign Correspondents across the Twentieth Century* (Washington, DC: The American University Press, 1995), xii.

12. "Our Monthly Review"; "Why We Are for Japan," *New York Times*, March 1, 1904, 8.

13. "Foreign Affairs," *New York Times*, January 1, 1904, 6.

14. "Why We Are for Japan."

15. "Armageddon in Tremor," *Chicago Defender*, May 10, 1913, 8.

16. Fortune, "The Filipino: A Social Study in Three Parts," 97.

17. Ibid, 99.

18. T. Thomas Fortune, "The Filipino: The Filipinos Do Not Understand the Prejudice of White Americans against Black Americans," *Voice of the Negro* (May 1904): 199.

19. Ibid.

20. Ibid., 197–203.

21. Ibid., 94, 95

22. Ibid., 99.

23. Archibald H. Grimke, "The Dominican Republic and Her Revolution," *Voice of the Negro* (April 1904): 134.

24. Ibid.

25. Mary Church Terrell, "The Berlin International Congress of Women," *Voice of the Negro* (October 1904): 457.

26. Theopolius Bolden Steward, "Social Distinctions in Porto [sic] Rico," *Voice of the Negro* (November 1905): 171–73.

27. Ibid.

28. See T. Thomas Fortune, "Haytian Revolutions, " *Voice of the Negro* (April 1904): 138; John S. Durham, "The Hidden Wealth of Hayti," *Voice of the Negro* (April 1904): 142; W. S. Scarborough, "From the Thames to the Tiber," *Voice of the Negro* (October 1904): 466; W. S. Scarborough, "In and Around Edinburgh," *Voice of the Negro* (August 1905): 548–52.

29. "The Congo Infamy," *Voice of the Negro* (December 1906): 541.

30. Richard Almonte, ed., *Mary Ann Shadd Cary's A Plea for Emigration: Or, Notes of Canada West* (Toronto: The Mercury Press, 1998).

31. Abby Arthur Johnson and Ronald M. Johnson, "Away from Accommodation: Radical Editors and Protest Journalism, 1900-1910," *Journal of Negro History* 62, no. 4 (1977): 332.

CHAPTER THREE

1. John H. Murphy was a former slave who merged three religious publications, the *Ledger*, the *Afro-American*, and the *Sunday School Helper*, to form *The Afro-American*.

2. "Glimpses of the Old World Cities: A Vivid Description of the Many Quaint and Strange Sights That Greet the Tourist in European Centres," *The Afro-American*, August, 15, 1914, 1; C. J. Murphy, "Travels by Rail in Germany; One Can Travel in the Land of the Kaiser at the Rate of One Cent a Mile; Gets Courteous Treatment," *The Afro-American*, August 29, 1914, 1.

3. "Marooned in the Europeans War District; Many Prominent Colored Men and Women Are Unable to Secure Passage to This Country," *Afro-American Ledger*, August 8, 1914, 1.

4. "Carl Murphy Returns from War Zone," *The Afro-American*, October 4, 1914, 1.

5. Ibid.

6. "Study the War," editorial, *The Afro-American*, July 14, 1917, 4.

7. See *The Afro-American*, June 28 and September 13, 1918.

8. Thomas M. Johnson, "2 Brave Colored Soldiers Rout 24 Germans," *The Afro-American*, May 24, 1918, 1.

9. "Colored Troops in Thick Fight," *The Afro-American*, July 19, 1918, 1.

10. "Stirring Letters from 'Over There,'" *The Afro-American*, August 9, 1918, 1.

11. Ibid.

12. "Letters from France," editorial, *The Afro-American*, August 9, 1918, 4.

13. Jas. W. Dorsey, "From the Trenches" column, *The Afro-American*, November 15, 1918, 4.

14. "From the Trenches" column, *The Afro-American*, September 27, 1918, 4.

15. Osceola McKaine, "From the Trenches" column, *The Afro-American*, October 11, 1918, 4.

16. Stanley R. Norvell, "From 'Over There,'" *Chicago Defender*, October 12, 1918, 5.

17. E. A. Tooke, "Chicago Hears From Eighth Regiment," *Chicago Defender*, August 10, 1918, 1.

18. August Meier, "Booker T. Washington and the Negro Press; With Special Reference to the Colored American Magazine," *Journal of Negro History* 38, no. 1 (January 1953): 68.

19. "The Black Soldier," *The Crisis*, June 1918, 60.

20. W. E. B. Du Bois, "The World Last Month," in *Crisis: A Record of the Darker Races*, vols. 15–16 (New York: Negro Universities Press, 1969), 215.

21. "The Black Soldier," 60.

22. Ibid., 9, 32–34; John Hope Franklin and Alfred Moss, *From Slavery to Freedom* (New York: McGraw Hill Publishing Company, 1988). Franklin's African American history indicates that some 200,000 African Americans were dispatched overseas primarily as noncombat laborers and stevedores in segregated units under the command of white officers. Forty-two thousand saw combat and at the war's end African Americans in 114 different units comprised approximately one-third of the American troops abroad. Also see Emmett J. Scott, *Scott's Official History of the American Negro in the World War* (New York: Arno Press, 1969). In his account of blacks during

World War I, Scott, special assistant to the secretary of war for black affairs, documented that of the more than 400,000 African American soldiers in the war, almost 368,000 were draftees and the others volunteered. According to Scott, based on their population, blacks were drafted in greater numbers than white men and were represented in almost all military branches.

23. "Advisor to War Department," *Official Bulletin*, the Committee on Public Information, October 5, 1917, cited in Scott, *Scott's Official History*, 40. The advisory describes Scott as the confidential secretary of Booker T. Washington and secretary of Tuskegee Institute.

24. Scott, *Scott's Official History*, 41.

25. Emmett J. Scott, letters to Julius Rosenwald, March 24 and April 16, 1917, cited in Scott, *Scott's Official History*, 42–43.

26. Franklin and Moss, *From Slavery to Freedom*, 307.

27. "To Educate the Colored American on the War Aims of the United States," editorial, *The Afro-American*, May 7, 1918, 4.

28. Franklin and Moss, *From Slavery to Freedom*.

29. *The Afro-American*'s coverage provided a list of editors present at the conference, including Tyler, and stated that the "conferees were given an opportunity to present their views, reflecting the state of mind of the colored people of the country, with the utmost freedom and frankness, unhampered by parliamentary restrictions or any effort to direct opinion in an particular channel." "Editors Discuss War Problems with Scott," *The Afro-American*, July 5, 1918, 1.

30. "Lighter Side of War," *Chicago Defender*, April 13, 1918, 4.

31. "Newspaper Men and Leaders in Important Conference," *Chicago Defender*, July 6, 1918, 4; "How Negroes Are Helping To Win the War," *New York Times*, July 7, 1918, 58.

32. Alfred Lawrence Lorenz, "Ralph W. Tyler: The Unknown Correspondent of World War I," *Journalism History* 31, no. 1 (Spring 2005): 4. Lorenz cites the following original source: "Address to the Committee on Public Information," undated ms., Emmett J. Scott Papers, Record Group 107, No. 96, Box 2, National Archives.

33. W. E. B. Du Bois, "Closed Ranks," editorial, *The Crisis*, July 1918, 111.

34. Committee of Public Information Bulletin, September 16, 1918, cited in Scott, *Scott's Official History*, 284–85.

35. Ibid.

36. Lorenz, "Ralph W. Tyler," 3.

37. "Tyler, Ralph Waldo," in *American National Biography*, ed. John A Garry and Mark C. Carmer (New York: Oxford University Press, 1999), 22.

38. See Ralph W. Tyler, letters to Emmett J. Scott Jr., October 8, 1917, November 27, 1918, December 5, 1917, January 9, 1919, March 18, 1918, March 26, 1918, March 28, 1918, and June 6, 1918, Emmett J. Scott Collection, Morgan State University, Baltimore, Maryland. Tyler was primarily intervening for his sons who were being discriminated against in the military, and for other troops in segregated training camps. A concerned Tyler wrote in the October letter about his son being given an HONORABLE DISCHARGE from the military just as he hoped to deploy overseas. Tyler reminded Scott that his family members had served as privates in every war dating back to the Revolutionary War and that the family deserved a commission—especially the one that Harold Tyler had earned. Scott's replies were on November 28, 1917, December 10, 1917, March 28, 1918, and April 17, 1918. Scott also followed up with military officials by calling to their attention the concerns Tyler raised. For reference, see Emmett J. Scott "Memorandum—for

The Adjutant General," November 28, 1917, Emmett J. Scott Collection, Morgan State University, Baltimore, Maryland.

39. "Tyler to Write War News 'Over There,'" *The Afro-American,* September 20, 1918, 1; "Our News Correspondent at the Front," *The Afro-American,* September 20, 1918, 4.

40. "Tyler to Write War News 'Over There.'"

41. Ibid.

42. Ralph Tyler, letter to Carl Byoir, October 9, 1918, Emmett J. Scott Collection, Morgan State University, Baltimore, Maryland.

43. Ralph Tyler, letter to Carl Byoir, October 21, 1918, Emmett J. Scott Collection, Morgan State University, Baltimore, Maryland.

44. Ibid.

45. Emmett J. Scott, letter to Col. A. L. Singleton, January 25, 1919, Emmett J. Scott Collection, Morgan State University, Baltimore, Maryland.

46. Emmett Scott, letter to Ralph Waldo Tyler, November 20, 1918, Emmett J. Scott Collection, Morgan State University, Baltimore, Maryland.

47. Scott, *Scott's Official History,* 130, 134, 163, 168. Scott indicates that the staff and field officers were largely white, and that the division received its orders to join the American Expeditionary Forces in France in May 1918. The first contingent sailed from Hoboken, New Jersey, on June 10 and reached Brest (Finisterre) in June 1918. The soldiers returned from overseas on March 12, 1919, after having fought in the last battle of the war.

48. Ralph W. Tyler, "Ralph W. Tyler Arrives in France," *The Afro-American,* November 8, 1918, 1.

49. Ibid., 6.

50. Ralph W. Tyler, "Colored Boys Held Till Turned Over by French," *The Afro-American,* November 15, 1918, 1.

51. Ralph W. Tyler, "Tyler Makes Trip to Base Hospital," *The Afro-American,* November 29, 1918.

52. Ralph W. Tyler, letter to Emmett J. Scott, November 5, 1918, Emmett J. Scott Collection, Morgan State University, Baltimore, Maryland.

53. Ibid.

54. R. H. Leavitt, Memorandum from Headquarters, Ninety-second Division, September 11, 1918. Despite that assertion, another memorandum offered as Exhibit B from T. T. Thompson, a black first lieutenant who had been acting division personnel officer and had "systematized and built up the operation," was demoted to statistical officer and placed under a white officer when they arrived overseas. (See T. T. Thompson, 1st Lt. Inf., U. S. A., Memorandum to Commanding General, Ninety-second Division, A. E. F., Emmett Scott Collection, Morgan State University, Baltimore, Maryland). Exhibit D from the Ninety-second Division Headquarters explained that the War Department did not allow Lt. Thompson to remain in the position "on the ground that the personnel should be white."

55. Ibid.

56. Ralph Waldo Tyler, "92nd Division Makes Fine Record in France," *The Afro-American,* December 6. 1918, 1.

57. Roi Ottley, *The Lonely Warrior: The Life and Times of Robert S. Abbott* (Chicago: Henry Regnery Company, 1955), 22, 152.

58. Roscoe C. Simmons, "Roscoe Tells of Pan-African Meet," *Chicago Defender,* May 10, 1919,

1. The article states that Simmons wrote this account in March 1919, but it was not printed until May. "*Defender's* Foreign Representative Writes of Racial Activities in Paris," *Chicago Defender*, April 5, 1919, 20. This article also stated the original date was January 25.

59. "Col. Simmons Is Back Home Again; Roscoe Welcomed Home by Chicagoans; Noted Journalist Back From France, Brimful of Information," *Chicago Defender*, April 12, 1919, 1.

60. "Col. Simmons Speaks to 4,000 Chicagoans," *Chicago Defender*, May 3, 1919, 1.

CHAPTER FOUR

1. W. E. B. Du Bois, *Dusk to Dawn* (New York: Schocken, 1968), 260–61; *The Crisis*, May 1919, 17.

2. Metz T. P. Lochard, *The Negro Press*, unpublished ms., chapter 2, page 26, Metz. T. Z. Lochard Papers, Box 137–2, Folder 12, Moorland-Spingarn Research Center, Howard University, Washington, D.C.

3. Ibid.

4. Herbert Aptheker, ed., *The Correspondence of W. E. B. Du Bois*, vol. 1 (Boston: University of Massachusetts Press, 1973), 232. Aptheker notes that the government did not bar Du Bois from the *Orizaba* because Wilson was sending to France another prominent black, Tuskegee Institute President Robert R. Moton. Aptheker also points to government distrust of Du Bois, as evidenced by a secret memo that called for tracking Du Bois's movements and actions while he was abroad.

5. For reference, see "Minutes of the Board of Directors of the NAACP," September 9, 1918, and October 14, 1918, Records of the NAACP, Library of Congress.

6. W. E. B. Du Bois, letter to Newton D. Baker, November 27, 1918, Emmett J. Scott Collection, Box 112, Morgan State University, Baltimore, Maryland.

7. J. P. Tumulty, letter to W. E. B. Du Bois, November 28, 1918, cited in Aptheker, ed., *Correspondence of W. E. B. Du Bois*, 232.

8. Du Bois, "My Mission," *The Crisis*, May 1919, 7.

9. W. E. B. Du Bois, "On Board the *Orizaba*, December, 1918," *The Crisis*, February 1919, 1.

10. Robert Desmond, *World News Reporting: 1900–1920* (Iowa City: University of Iowa Press, 1980), 410.

11. W. E. B. Du Bois, "The Peace Conference," *The Crisis*, January 1919, 111–12.

12. W. E. B. Du Bois, "The Pan-African Congress," *The Crisis*, April 1919, 271–74.

13. Du Bois, "My Mission."

14. Ibid.

15. W. E. B. Du Bois, "Vive La France," *The Crisis*, April 1919, 215.

16. "Wilson Is to Explain League to Senators; Cables His Invitation," *Washington Post*, February 16, 1919, 1; "Wilson Lands Today," *Washington Post*, February 24, 1919, 1.

17. See the following articles: "Wilson Endeavors to Mediate on Claims of Italy and Jugoslavs," *Washington Post*, February 7, 1919, 1; Albert W. Fox, "Wilson Plan at Test," *Washington Post*, February 8, 1919, 1; "Course of Peace Congress Forces France to Rely Upon Her Armies For Safety," *Washington Post*, February 9, 1919, 1.

18. Lawrence Hogan's history of the ANP states that the *Chicago Defender* withheld its support of the ANP because the newspaper was essentially serving as a news agency for the rest of

the black press. In addition, the "sense of insecurity coupled with excessive pride limited" the black publishers' involvement, although they recognized how such a cooperative venture would benefit them. Lawrence Hogan, *A Black News Service: The Associated Negro Press and Claude Barnett, 1919–1945* (Rutherford, NJ: Farleigh Dickinson University Press, 1984), 46.

19. Hogan, *Black News Service,* 48; Claude A. Barnett, *Fly Out of Darkness,* chapter 1, page 13, unpublished autobiography, CAB Papers, Box 406, Chicago Historical Museum, Chicago, Illinois.

20. Hogan, *Black News Service,* 85.

21. The Jamaican-born Garvey was one of the most influential black leaders in America from his arrival in the country in 1917 throughout the 1920s. His newspaper remained an influential institution in the black community even after Garvey was sentenced to prison in 1925 for alleged mail fraud in connection with his Black Star shipping line that was to transport blacks to Africa.

22. Further elaboration on Garveyism and the Harlem Renaissance can be found in Lawrence W. Levine, *Black Culture, Black Consciousness: Afro-American Folk Thought from Slavery to Freedom* (New York: Oxford University Press, 1977); Arna Bontemps, *The Harlem Renaissance Remembered* (New York: Dodd, Mead and Company, 1972); Nathan I. Huggins, *Voices from the Harlem Renaissance* (New York: Oxford University Press, 1996); Chidi Ikonne, *From Du Bois to Van Vechten: The Early New Negro Literature, 1903–1926* (Westport, CT: Greenwood Press, 1981); Cary D. Wants, *The Harlem Renaissance: 1920–1940: The Emergence of the Harlem Renaissance* (New York: Garland Press, 1996). Race periodicals such as the NAACP's *The Crisis* and the National Urban League's *Opportunity: A Journal of Negro Life,* ran the artistic output of the era and illuminated the cultural phenomenon and its impact.

23. James H. Cone, *Martin and Malcolm and America: A Dream or a Nightmare* (Maryknoll, NY: Orbis Books, 1991), 10.

24. Amy Jacques Garvey, handwritten notation in scrapbook, Marcus Mosiah Garvey Memorial Collection, Box 12, Fisk University Library Special Collections, Nashville, Tennessee.

25. Amy Jacques Garvey, "Have a Heart," *Negro World,* August 2, 1924.

26. Amy Jacques Garvey, "Be Prepared," ms., Marcus Mosiah Garvey Memorial Collection, Box 5, Folder 11, Fisk University Library Special Collections, Nashville, Tennessee.

27. W. E. B. Du Bois, "The African Roots of War," *Atlantic Monthly* 115 (May 1915): 707–8.

28. Clennel W. Wickham, "Strong Analysis of Garveyism and Potentiality; 'Cheap' Critics Scored; West Indian Writer Says Depth of Solidity of Foundations Will Surprise the World," *Negro World,* October 27, 1923, 1. The *Chicago Defender* and the *Pittsburgh Courier* were often Garvey's harshest critics, as an editorial cartoon in the September 6, 1924, issue of the *Defender* illustrated. Titled "The Quitter," the cartoon depicted Garvey running down a road, bag of money in hand, leaving a cloud of dust that read "Our Fight for Constitutional Rights in America." Abbott biographer Roi Ottley maintained that the publisher believed Garvey was a fraud and that he and his followers were agitators who disrespected and were disloyal to the United States. See Roi Ottley, *The Lonely Warrior: The Life and Times of Robert S. Abbott* (Chicago: Henry Regnery Company, 1955), 215–16.

29. Additional information about Rogers can be found in the sixteen books and pamphlets he wrote.

30. J. A. Rogers, "No Color Prejudice in England, Says J. A. Rogers; American Writer Finds Dol-

lars," *New York Amsterdam News,* July 25, 1925, 1; J. A. Rogers, "J. A. Rogers Tells of Distinguished White and Colored Londoners; George Lansbury, M. P., Dr. Theophilus Scholes, Prof. A. A. Chinappa and Miss Ira Aldridge Entertain Him While in London," *New York Amsterdam News,* August 26, 1925, 9.

31. During Rogers's more than fifty-year career, leading black periodicals such as the NAACP's *The Crisis* magazine, the *Messenger,* and *Survey Graphics* published his exhaustive research on people of African descent throughout the world. Because he was unable to find a mainstream publisher for his work, Rogers self-published sixteen books and pamphlets that circulated in the black community.

32. J. A. Rogers, "Arrives in Paris," *Pittsburgh Courier,* September 26, 1925, 9.

33. J. A. Rogers, "Rogers Writes Final Article, Analyzing Mussolini," *Pittsburgh Courier,* October 29, 1925, 2.

34. J. A. Rogers, "I Find Italy a Land of Art—Writes J. A. Rogers," *Pittsburgh Courier,* May 14, 1937, A-1; "Ethiopia and Egypt Made Nordic Civilization Possible," *Pittsburgh Courier,* April 30, 1927, 5.

35. J. A. Rogers, "Paris Gives Cuban Taste of Fairness," *Chicago Defender,* July 2, 1927, 1.

36. "Rogers Meets 'Homesick' American Negroes in Marseilles, France," *Pittsburgh Courier,* July 2, 1927, 5.

37. Ibid.

38. Ibid.

CHAPTER FIVE

1. Robert S. Abbott, "My Trip through South America, Installment 1; Personal Motives," *Chicago Defender,* June 2, 1923, 5.

2. "The *Chicago Defender,*" unpublished brief history, 1, Abbott-Sengstacke Papers, Series 9, Box 111, Folder 21, Vivian G. Harsh Research Collection of Afro-American History and Literature, Chicago Public Library, Chicago, Illinois.

3. Roi Ottley, *The Lonely Warrior: The Life and Times of Robert S. Abbott* (Chicago: Henry Regnery Company, 1955), 7.

4. *The Weekly Chicago Defender and the Daily Defender, May 5, 1905–February 6, 1956,* pamphlet, Abbott-Sengstacke Papers, Series 9, Box 111, Folder 21, Vivian G. Harsh Research Collection of Afro-American History and Literature, Chicago Public Library, Chicago, Illinois.

5. John H. Sengstacke, "From Soup to Citizenship," statement to the Publicity Club of Chicago, October 12, 1955, 3, Abbott-Sengstacke Papers, Series 9, Box 112, Folder 21, Vivian G. Harsh Research Collection of Afro-American History and Literature, Chicago Public Library, Chicago, Illinois.

6. Metz T. Z. Lochard, "History of the Negro Press," chapter 4, page 15, unpublished ms., Metz T. Z. Lochard Papers, Box 137–2, Folder 18, Moorland-Spingarn Research Center, Howard University, Washington, D.C.

7. Sengstacke, "From Soup to Citizenship," 4.

8. Armistead Pride and Clint C. Wilson, *A History of the Black Press* (Washington, DC: Howard University Press, 1997), 136–37.

9. Ibid.

10. Lochard, "History of the Negro Press," 19, 20.

11. *Chicago Defender,* unpublished ms., 1.

12. "Abbott and Wife to Tour South America," *Chicago Defender,* January 13, 1923, 1. Accessed at www.proquest.com, January 22, 2009.

13. No title, *Chicago Defender,* March 17, 1923, 1.

14. Roscoe Simmons, "This Week" column, *Chicago Defender* (National Edition), May 19, 1923, 13. Accessed at http://www.proquest.com, January 22, 2009.

15. Ibid.

16. Ottley, *Lonely Warrior,* 229–31.

17. "South Americans Get Prejudice from the South; Mr. Abbott Tells Appomattox Club Members Interesting Stories of His Travels," Accessed at www.proquest.com, January 22, 2009.

18. Ibid.

19. Robert S. Abbott, "My Trip through South America," *Chicago Defender,* August 11, 1923, 1. Accessed at www.proquest.com, January 22, 2009.

20. Robert S. Abbott, "My Trip through South America," *Chicago Defender,* September 29, 1953, 13. Accessed at www.proquest.com, January 22, 2009.

21. Robert S. Abbott, "My Trip through South America," *Chicago Defender,* August 18, 1923, 13. Accessed at www.proquest.com, January 22, 2009.

22. Ibid.

23. Ibid., 14.

24. "Mr. Abbott Returns to Home Town; Friends Greet Mr. Abbott at Englewood Station," *Chicago Defender,* May 26, 1923, 1. Accessed at www.proquest.com, January 22, 2009.

25. See Robert S. Abbott, "My Trip through South America: Head of Engineering Dept of the City of Rio de Janeiro," *Chicago Defender,* September, 1, 1923, 13; Robert S. Abbott, "My Trip through South America, Article 5," September 29, 1953, 13. Accessed at www.proquest.com, January 22, 2009.

26. Ottley, *Lonely Warrior,* 240.

27. Ibid., 241.

28. Ibid., 241, 245–46.

29. Metz T. Z. Lochard, "History of the Negro Press," chapter 4, pages 15–17, unpublished ms., Metz T. Z. Lochard Papers, Box 137–2, Folder 18, Moorland-Spingarn Research Center, Howard University, Washington, D.C.

30. Carlos Hechos, "Story of the Virgin Islands of the United States: Land Where Dark People Dwell and Are Ruled Under the American Flag Yet Are Not Considered U. S. Citizens," *Chicago Defender,* June 14, 1924, 1.

31. Ibid.

32. Robert S. Abbott, "My Trip Abroad: Paris," *Chicago Defender,* November, 9, 1929, 1. Accessed at www.proquest.com, January 22, 2009.

33. Ottley, *Lonely Warrior,* 271.

34. Robert S. Abbott, "My Trip Abroad: The Colored American in Paris," *Chicago Defender,* November 23, 1929, 1. Accessed at http://www.proquest.com, January 22, 2009.

35. Robert S. Abbott, "We Arrive in England," *Chicago Defender,* January 4, 1930, 1. Accessed at www.proquest.com, January 22, 2009.

36. Ibid.

37. Robert S. Abbott, "Rome—The Eternal City," *Chicago Defender*, January 25, 1930, 1. Accessed at www.proquest.com, January 22, 2009.

38. Robert S. Abbott, "The Congo Museum," *Chicago Defender*, December 7, 1929, 1. Accessed at www.proquest.com, January 22, 2009.

39. Abbott, "My Trip Abroad: The Colored American in Paris," 1.

40. Robert S. Abbott, "My Trip Abroad: Across the Alps," *Chicago Defender*, January 18, 1930, 1. Accessed at www.proquest.com, January 22, 2009.

41. Robert S. Abbott, "My Trip Abroad: Kojo of Dahomey," *Chicago Defender*, February. 1, 1930, 1. Accessed at www.proquest.com, January 22, 2009.

42. Ibid.

43. Ibid., 10.

44. Ibid.

45. Ottley, *Lonely Warrior*, 287–89.

46. Ibid.

CHAPTER SIX

1. Dan Burley, "Black People Saw the Light in 1935; Learned They Had a True, Great History; Stirring Events of the Year Drew Back Curtain of History and Let Them Know Their Past Glories; Foreign News Dept. Led Way," *Chicago Defender*, January 4, 1936, 24.

2. Metz T. Z. Lochard, "History of the Negro Press," chapter 1, page 34, unpublished ms., Metz T. Z. Lochard Papers, Box 137–2, Folder 12, Moorland-Spingarn Research Center, Howard University, Washington, D.C.

3. Ibid., 31, 32.

4. Robert S. Abbott, letter to John H. Sengstacke, February 17, 1938, Abbott-Sengstacke Papers, Series 3, Box 8, Folder 33, Vivian G. Harsh Research Collection of Afro-American History and Literature, Chicago Public Library, Chicago, Illinois.

5. Minutes of the Annual Meeting of the Directors of the Robert S. Abbott Publishing Company, January 28, 1933, Abbott-Sengstacke Papers, Series 3, Box 8, Folder 33, Vivian G. Harsh Research Collection of Afro-American History and Literature, Chicago Public Library, Chicago, Illinois.

6. Ibid., 36.

7. Andrew Buni, *Robert L. Vann of the Pittsburgh Courier: Politics and Black Journalism* (Pittsburgh: University of Pittsburgh Press, 1974), 236.

8. Ibid.

9. Homer Smith, *A Black Man in Red Russia* (Chicago: Johnson Publishing Company, 1964), 56–57.

10. Maxim Matusevich, "Journeys of Hope: African Diaspora and the 'Soviet Identity,'" *African Diaspora* 1 (2008): 55.

11. Ibid.

12. Smith, *Black Man in Red Russia*, 67.

13. Ibid.

14. See, for example, Chatwood Hall, "Paul Robeson Jr., Elected Member of Russian Football Team," *Atlanta Daily World*, October 19, 1937, 5; and Chatwood Hall, "'For All Citizens,' Read Signs in Georgia, Russia," *The Afro-American*, March 13, 1937, 1.

15. For reference, see Chatwood Hall, "A Column from Russia," *Chicago Defender*, April 6, 1936, 11; Jim Crow Is Unknown in Soviet Russia," *Chicago Defender*, April 2, 1938,1; "Moscow Has No Housing Segregation," *Chicago Defender*, April 23, 1938, 24.

16. Chatwood Hall, "Russia Discovers Solution of Race Problem; Country Under Old Czar; Regime Catered to All Forms of Discrimination; But New Order Has Brought New Deal to Minority Groups," *Chicago Defender*, October 14, 1933, 10.

17. Ibid.

18. Chatwood Hall, "Correspondent Compares 'Red' Russia with 'White' America," *Chicago Defender*, February 2, 1935, 11.

19. Chatwood Hall, "While American Farmers Are Starving, Look at Moscow," *Chicago Defender*, April 1, 1933, 11.

20. Ibid.

21. Ibid.

22. For reference, see Chatwood Hall, "Young Race Artist Stirs Moscow with Her Songs; Corretti Arle Proves That Real Talent Has No Color Limitations," *Chicago Defender*, June 23, 1934, 12; "Celeste Cole, Charming Young Soprano, Now Red Army Darling," *Chicago Defender*, November 11, 1934, 12; "Here's How One Race Technician Fares in Soviet City; As Russian Sees Us!" *Chicago Defender*, September 15, 1934, 1.

23. Chatwood Hall, column from Moscow, *Chicago Defender*, March 4, 1933, 10.

24. John Maxwell Hamilton, *Journalism's Roving Eye: A History of American Foreign Reporting* (Baton Rouge: Louisiana State University Press, 2009), 177.

25. Chatwood Hall, "Jobs Beg for Workers in Soviet Russia; Color Line in Employment is Unknown; Situation Amazes Urban League Visitors," *Chicago Defender* (National Edition). Accessed at www.proquest.com, January 29, 2008.

26. Hamilton, *Journalism's Roving Eye*, 177.

27. Chatwood Hall, "Why I Went to Russia and Why I Left," Chatwood Hall's story in *The Afro-American*, magazine section, September 27, 1955, 6.

28. Hayward Farrar, *The Baltimore Afro-American: 1892–1950* (Westport, CT: Greenwood Press, 1998), 159.

29. "Liberian Chief's Tales Cites Woes of Read Bondage; Native Leader Flogged for Failure to Furnish Slaves," *The Afro-American*, June 14, 1929, 1.

30. For reference, see articles that ran in *The Afro-American* during the following time periods: January to September 1922, January 15, 1927. Coverage continued until the early 1930s.

31. "Bootlegging in Men Still Goes on in Africa," *The Afro-American*, November 2, 1929, 1.

32. William N. Jones, "No Dictator for Liberia, Says Grimes; Se. of State Recommends Refusal of the League's Plan," *The Afro-American*, November 18, 1933, 1.

33. William N. Jones, "Liberian Legislature Puts Future Up To U. S.," *The Afro-American*, December 2, 1933, 1.

34. "Jones Returns from Liberia on the Bremen; Afro's Editor Home Friday after 3-Mo. Goodwill Tour; Finds Liberia Looking to U. S.," *The Afro-American*, December 23, 1933, 1.

35. John Hope Franklin, *From Slavery to Freedom: A History of Negro American*, 3rd ed. (New York: Vintage Books, 1969), 496.

36. Wm. Jones, "Liberia Today, Tomorrow," *The Afro-American*, December 30, 1933, 1.

37. Ibid.

38. "Liberian Legislature Okeys [sic] Goodwill Mission," *The Afro-American*, January 6, 1934, 3; "Movement Is Started to Aid Liberia; Afro-American Will Call Group to Study Immediate Action," *The Afro-American*, January 6, 1934, 3.

39. For reference, see "Haitian Commission to Sail When Forbes Group Returns," *The Afro-American*, March 15, 1930, 1. The article explained that the commission would sail to Haiti in April after the return of a commission that was currently on the island to study the political situation and the extent to which the U.S. treaty with Haiti was being implemented, as well as to explore a timetable for ending the U.S. occupation of the nation. President Herbert Hoover charged the Moton Commission with mapping "a comprehensive and constructive educational program" for Haitians that would enable them "to advance educationally and economically."

40. Percival Prattis, letter to Claude A. Barnett, Percival Prattis Papers, Series C., Box 144-16, Folder 1, Moorland-Spingarn Research Center, Howard University, Washington, D.C. See also Percival Prattis, letter to Claude A. Barnett, July 8, 1930, CAB Papers, Chicago Historical Museum, Chicago, Illinois. Barnett had secured assistance from Robert R. Moton for Prattis to join the mission.

41. See Carl Murphy, "1923 Survey Recommended Use of Colored Teachers There: Three Factors: Race, Religions and Language Involved," *The Afro-American*, June 21, 1930, 1; Carl Murphy, "Haitians Cordial But View U. S. with Suspicion," *The Afro-American*, June 28, 1930, 1; Carl Murphy, "Pomp and Color Feature Routine of Moton Group; Commission Gets Down to Serious Study of Educational and Social Affairs of Republic," *The Afro-American*, June 28, 1930, 1.

42. Murphy, "Pomp and Color Feature Routine of Moton Group."

43. Carl Murphy, "Members of Moton Commission Work Hard and Work Together," *The Afro-American*, July 12, 1930, 1; Carl Murphy, "Heard and Seen in Haiti," *The Afro-American*, July 12, 1930, 17; Carl Murphy, "Chauffeurs Eat with Commissioners and Shock Haitian Teachers," *The Afro-American*, July 5, 1930, 1; Carl Murphy, "Moton Acts to Avert Haitian School Strike; Commission Head is Mediator in Damien College Tilt," *The Afro-American*, July 5, 1930, 1.

44. "Get Out of Haiti," editorial, *The Afro-American*, July 26, 1930, 6.

45. Ibid.

46. "*Defender* Popular in Berlin," *Chicago Defender*, September 4, 1932, 3.

47. Ibid. The short article was primarily the student's quote, without any refutation or comment by the *Defender*.

48. "The Moral of Hitlerism," *Pittsburgh Courier*, May 27, 1933, 10.

49. Ibid.

50. See "How Jews Fare Under Hitler Regime; Noted English Correspondent Reveals Inside Facts of Horrors Perpetrated by Germans on Defenseless Minority Groups; Nazis Stop at Nothing in Their Campaign of Barbarous Cruelties; A New Reign of Terror," *Chicago Defender*, June 16, 1934, 10.

51. "This Week," column, *Chicago Defender*, June 10, 1933, 10.

52. William Jones, "300 Families Affected by Hitler Ban," *The Afro-American* December 30, 1933, 1.

53. Pembroke Stephens, *Chicago Defender* (National Edition) (1921–1967), June 16, 1934. Accessed at www.proquest.com, January 28, 2008.

54. "*Courier* 'Scooped' Nation on Inquiry about Germany's Attitude toward Negroes in Olympics," *Pittsburgh Courier*, September 7, 1935, 1.

55. Most accounts say Hitler did not congratulate any athletes after the first day of the Games, but he actually congratulated German athletes only.

56. Robert L. Vann, "Hitler Salutes Jesse Owen," *Pittsburgh Courier*, August 8, 1936, 1.

57. Ibid.

58. Joe Jefferson, "Olympic Stars Given Welcome In Berlin; Prejudice Missing As Athletes Arrive," *Chicago Defender*, August 1, 1936, 1.

59. "Owens 'Takes' Olympics," *Chicago Defender*, August 8, 1936, 1.

60. "Deny Owens 100 Meters Mark; Officials Claim Wind Slightly in Favor of Runner," *Chicago Defender*, August 8, 1936, 13.

61. Ibid.

62. "ADOLF HITLER—JUST POOR WHITE TRASH," editorial, *Pittsburgh Courier*, August 4, 1936, 4.

63. "What Can We Expect under Fascism," editorial, *Chicago Defender*, November 27, 1937, 16.

64. "French, British Feared Black Troops Loyalty," *Pittsburgh Courier*, October 8, 1938, 1.

65. Ibid.

66. Ralph Matthews, "Carl Murphy Was a Newspaperman's Newspaperman—A Tribute," *The Afro-American*, March 11, 1967, 5.

67. Ibid.

68. Ralph Matthews, "England Snubs Africa at Big Show; India's Visiting Princes Get Kid Glove Treatment," *The Afro-American*, May 15, 1937, 8.

69. Ralph Matthews, "Matthew Sees All England in Arms; AFRO Editor in London Sees Behind Coronation; Show Feverish Preparation for Coming War," *The Afro-American*, May 8, 1937, 1.

70. "African Revolt Feared; Rigid Rule Proclaimed," *The Afro-American*, May 22, 1937, 8. The article did not have a byline, but Jackson was the only ANP correspondent on the scene.

71. "400 Million Have Only 2 Proxies at Crowning," *The Afro-American*, May 8, 1937, 8.

72. Ibid.

73. Fay Jackson, letter to Claude Barnett, CBA Papers, Box 166, Folder 3, Chicago Historical Museum, Chicago, Illinois.

CHAPTER SEVEN

1. "Abyssinia Ready for Coronation," *Chicago Defender*, October 25, 1930, 1; "To Crown Ras Taffari King on Sunday, Nov. 2," *Chicago Defender*, 1930, 1.

2. J. A. Rogers, "J. A. Rogers Writes on the Coronation of a King; *Courier* Columnist Gives 'Inside Story' of Ethiopia's Big Day Coronation Ceremonies of Ras Tafari," *Pittsburgh Courier*, December 13, 1930, A-7.

3. J. A. Rogers, "Getting Inside News From the Front," *Pittsburgh Courier*, November 9, 1935, 1.

4. See Brenda Gayle Plummer, *Rising Wind: Black Americans and U.S. Foreign Affairs, 1935–1960* (Chapel Hill: University of North Carolina Press, 1996), 51.

5. Ibid., 120.

6. Claude A. Barnett, letter to Malaka Bayen, February 5, 1935, and September 6, 1935, CAB Papers, Series 2, Box 170, Folder 9, Chicago Historical Museum, Chicago, Illinois.

7. P. L. Prattis, letter to Claude A. Barnett, CAB Papers, Series 2, Box 170, Folder 9, Chicago Historical Museum, Chicago, Illinois.

8. See Claude A. Barnett, letters to Percival L. Prattis, C. A. Scott, and P. B. Young Jr., November 23, 1935, CAB Papers, Series 2, Box 170, Folder 9, Chicago Historical Museum, Chicago, Illinois.

9. P. L. Prattis, letter to Claude A. Barnett, December 3, 1935, CAB Papers, Series 2, Box 170, Folder 9, Chicago Historical Museum, Chicago, Illinois.

10. Claude A Barnett, letter to Colonel J. C. Robinson, October 19, 1935, CAB Papers, Series 2, Box 170, Folder 9, Chicago Historical Museum, Chicago, Illinois.

11. "Ethiopian Air Unit Hopeless, Says U. S. Pilot; Robinson Says Plane Combat with Italy Would Be Murder," *The Afro-American*, October 12, 1935, 3.

12. Claude A. Barnett, letter to Colonel J. C. Robinson, December 31, 1935, CAB Papers, Series 2, Box 170, Folder 9, Chicago Historical Museum, Chicago, Illinois.

13. Claude A. Barnett, letter to Colonel J. C. Robinson, April 16, 1935, CAB Papers, Series 2, Box 170, Folder 9, Chicago Historical Museum, Chicago, Illinois.

14. Ibid.

15. J. C. Robinson, letter to Claude A. Barnett, June 3, 1935, CAB Papers, Series 2, Box 170, Folder 9, Chicago Historical Museum, Chicago, Illinois.

16. Ibid.

17. Nancy Cunard, "Maran Says Discrimination Is Growing Fast in France," *New York Amsterdam News*, December 7, 1935, 11.

18. Nancy Cunard, "Paris in Rally for Ethiopia," *Chicago Defender*, December 21, 1935, 24.

19. Untitled editorial, *Pittsburgh Courier*, November 23, 1935, 4.

20. Rogers wrote more than 2,500 newspaper articles for the black press between 1923 and 1950. Much of that work was from abroad, as we will see later.

21. The following stories provide detailed accounting of the *Pittsburgh Courier*'s rationale. J. A. Rogers, "Good-bye America! I'm Ethiopia Bound," *Pittsburgh Courier*, October 26, 1935, 1; J. A. Rogers, "Rogers' Stories to be Exclusive for the *Courier*," *Pittsburgh Courier*, October 26, 1935, 1; J. A. Rogers, "Rogers in Cairo Getting the 'Inside Story,'" *Pittsburgh Courier*, November 9, 1935, 1.

22. Floyd Calvin, "Hundreds Awaiting Truthful Reports," *Pittsburgh Courier*, November 30, 1935, 1.

23. See, for example, Rogers, "Rogers in Cairo Getting 'Inside' News from Front."

24. See, for example, "France to Fight Use of Force against Italy," *Chicago Daily Tribune*, August 29, 1935, 2. The unknown author wrote that officials had explained that "France must subordinate her sympathy for Ethiopia's plight to her concern for endangered Europe." See also "France Bids for 'Gibraltar' of Red Sea Gate," *Chicago Daily Tribune*, February 3, 1936, 14.

25. "Italy Is Found Guilty of War; Faces Boycott," *Chicago Daily Tribune*, October 8, 1935, 1. Below the headline, the newspaper ran a subhead titled: "Nation Outlawed by League Council."

26. Charlotte O'Kelly, "Black Newspapers and the Black Protest Movement: Their Historical Relationship, 1827–1945," *Phylon* 43, no. 1 (1982): 1–14.

27. "Editor's Note," *Pittsburgh Courier*, October 26, 1935.

28. For treatment of the black press, see Armistead S. Pride and Clint C. Wilson II, *A History of the Black Press* (Washington, DC: Howard University Press, 1997); Bernell Tripp, *Origins of*

the African-American Press: New York, 1827–1847 (Northport, AL: Vision Press, 1992); William G. Jordan, *African American Newspapers and America's War for Democracy, 1914–1920* (Chapel Hill: University of North Carolina Press, 2001); Charles A. Simmons, *The African American Press: With Special Reference to Four Newspapers, 1827–1965* (Jefferson, NC: McFarland, 1998); Henry Lewis Suggs, ed., *The Black Press in the Middle West, 1865–1985* (Westport, CT: Greenwood Press, 1996); and Roland E. Wolseley, *The Black Press, U.S.A.* (Ames: Iowa State University Press, 1990).

29. *Courier* correspondent, "Hundreds Die in Italian Air Raid on Adawa," *Pittsburgh Courier*, October 5, 1935, 1.

30. J. A. Rogers, "Warriors Crash Italian Lines, 30,000 on March," *Pittsburgh Courier*, November 23, 1934, 1.

31. J. A. Rogers, headline not legible, *Pittsburgh Courier*, November 9, 1935, 1.

32. J. A. Rogers, "Don't Be Fooled!—Ethiopia Welcomes Your Assistance," *Pittsburgh Courier*, November 16, 1935, 1. See also J. A. Rogers, "Ethiopians Are Negroes, Rogers Writes America," *Pittsburgh Courier*, November 30, 1935, 1.

33. J. A. Rogers, "J. A. Rogers Gets Exclusive Interview with Emperor," *Pittsburgh Courier*, March 7, 1936, 1.

34. See, for example, two page 1 articles: J. A. Rogers, "Rogers Leaves Ethiopia; French and English Interpreter for Haile Selassie to Take His Place," *Pittsburgh Courier, April 4, 1936*, and headline missing, *Pittsburgh Courier*, April 4, 1936, 1.

35. J. A. Rogers, "Ethiopian War Has Cost," *Pittsburgh Courier*, April 25, 1936, 1.

36. W. E. B. Du Bois, *The World and Africa: An Inquiry into the Part Which Africa Has Played in World History* (New York: International Publishers, 1946), xi.

37. The *Pittsburg Courier* had a circulation of 176,000 at the end of 1936.

38. "ABYSSINIAN GIVES VERSION OF WAR PERIL; Clash with Italian Troops Discussed DAUNTLESS ABYSSINIANS," *Chicago Defender*, December 29, 1934, 1. Accessed at www.proquest.com, January 28, 2008.

39. Carl Nelson, "Doom and Destruction Await Italy in Ethiopia, Says Expert; Mussolini's Troops Can Never Conquer African Warriors," *Chicago Defender*, March 9, 1935, 1.

40. Ibid.

41. For examples of the *Defender*'s coverage, see also the May 18, 1935, issue as well as "See Mussolini Forcing a War with Ethiopia," *Chicago Defender*, June 13, 1935, 1.

42. "Arabs Profit as Italians Plot Warfare," *Chicago Defender*, August 10, 1935, 12.

43. "*Defender* Foreign News Experts Forecast Attack on Ethiopia, Scooping World on Developments in African Empire; Intelligent Grasping of War Situation Allowed Defender Staff to Take This Step," *Chicago Defender*, January 4, 1936, 24.

44. Ibid.

45. Ottley, *Lonely Warrior*, 348.

46. For reference, see "Ethiopia's Artillery Readies for Mussolini—Volunteers Pour in for War" and "Ethiopian Conflict Stirs World; Nations Aroused as Italy Continues Its War Plans," *Chicago Defender*, July 20, 1935, 1.

47. Ibid.

48. Ibid.

49. Martin Dwyer, "Italy Pushes War Planes in Ethiopia," *Chicago Defender*, August 19, 1935, 1.

50. "Familiarity with Questions Enabled Staff to Describe Ultimate Steps in Plot; War in Ethiopia," *Chicago Defender*, January 4, 1936, 24.

51. Plummer, *Rising Wind*, 80.

52. Ibid.

CHAPTER EIGHT

1. Nancy Cunard, "Weekly Topics," *New York Amsterdam News*, January 8, 1938, 12.

2. Nancy Cunard, "Africans in Spanish War," *Atlanta Daily World*, August 12, 1936, 1.

3. Ibid.

4. Nancy Cunard, "Call on Africans to Fight for Loyalist," *Atlanta Daily World*, October 19, 1936, 1.

5. Nancy Cunard, "Moroccan Troops Hate Their Role in Spain's War, Nancy Cunard Declares," *Pittsburgh Courier*, December 12, 1936, 5.

6. Nancy Cunard, "Girl Writer Visits Spanish Morocco and Finds Hotbed of Fascist Hatred," *New York Amsterdam News*, January 23, 1937, 4.

7. Nancy Cunard, "Tells of League's Behind the Scenes Attitude on Ethiopia," *New York Amsterdam News*, July 19, 1937, 24.

8. Ibid.

9. Nancy Cunard, "Black Moors, Fighting for Spanish Fascists, Mistreated, Demoralized," *Pittsburgh Courier*, July 17, 1937, 11.

10. Nancy Cunard, "Spain's War Has Group Fighters," *Atlanta Daily World*, January 24, 1938, 1.

11. Nancy Cunard, "Africans Take Firm Stand against Fascist Movement," *Atlanta Daily World*, May 15, 1939, 1.

12. Nancy Cunard, "Black Men Flock to the Aid of France against Hitlerism," *Atlanta Daily World*, October 4. 1939, 1.

13. "Exclusive!!!" *The Afro-American*, October 23, 1937.

14. For reference, see Langston Hughes, *I Wonder as I Wander* (New York: Octagon Press, 1981, c. 1956), 307–17. Hughes wrote on page 308 of his autobiography that he sent most of his "very minor income from writing" and most of his newspaper royalties from Spain to his mother.

15. Ibid., 327.

16. Hughes, "Hughes Bombed in Spain," *The Afro-American*, October 23, 1937, 1.

17. Hughes, "Hughes Finds Moors Used as Pawns by Fascists in Spain," *The Afro-American*, October 30, 1937, 1.

18. Hughes, "Madrid's Flowers Hoist Bloom to Meet Raining Fascist Bombs," *The Afro-American*, November 27, 1937.

19. Hughes, "Hughes Finds Moors Used as Pawns by Fascists in Spain," 1.

CHAPTER NINE

Parts of this chapter appeared in *American Journalism* in 2005 as an article John Maxwell Hamilton and I wrote.

1. "America's Fighting Men," *Pittsburgh Courier,* July 18, 1942, 1.

2. "Prejudices Disappear in Face of Disaster," *Pittsburgh Courier,* April 18, 1942, 12.

3. Edgar T. Rouzeau, "Courier's Edgar T. Rouzeau Cables Exclusive Story from Far-Off Egypt," *Pittsburgh Courier,* September 26, 1942, 1. Thanks to a news-sharing arrangement between the *Courier,* the *Norfolk Journal and Guide,* and *The Afro-American,* a similar version of this story also appeared on page 1 of the *Guide* on the same day. That piece indicated that Rouzeau found race troops from all over the world playing vital roles in the Mideast Theater. The newspaper also explained that Rouzeau would provide detailed accounts "of the amazing accomplishments of our Negro engineer units, for whom that war provides a great opportunity for the black soldier to make use of his mechanical aptitudes."

4. "Pool News from Correspondents," *Norfolk Journal and Guide,* July 31, 1943, 1.

5. Homer Smith, *A Black Man in Red Russia* (Chicago: Johnson Publishing Company, 1964), 172.

6. Enoch Waters's letter to someone whose name was Doris indicated that this was a more accurate list of black correspondents who wrote from overseas during the war. EPW Papers, Box 176–2, Folder 3, Moorland-Spingarn Research Center, Howard University, Washington, D.C. Correspondents and their news organizations included Art Carter, Elizabeth Murphy Phillips, Herbert Frisby, Max Johnson, Vincent Tubbs, Ollie Stewart, and Frances Yancey of *The Afro-American;* Deton Brooks, David Orro, Edward Toles, and Enoch Waters of the *Chicago Defender;* Haskel Cohen, Randy Dixon, Collins George, Ollie Harrington, Billy Rowe, and Ted Stanford of the *Pittsburgh Courier;* John "Rover" Jordan, Thomas Young, and Lem Graves of the *Norfolk Journal and Guide;* Charley Loeb, Frank Bolden, and Fletcher Martin of the National Newspaper Publishers Association pool; and Rudolph Dunbar, who joined Hall and Padmore for the Associated Negro Press. James Hicks and Daniel Day were not accredited but were members of the armed forces who wrote stories for the black press. The NAACP's Walter White also was not an accredited correspondent, but he wrote several articles for the organization's *The Crisis* magazine after several fact-finding trips abroad. All told, thirty blacks wrote war stories for the black press during the war. Roi Ottley covered the war for *Liberty* magazine and *PM,* as well as the *Pittsburgh Courier.* Allan Morrison was a correspondent for *Stars and Stripes.* Phillips became ill in London on her way to Paris and never made it to the war front.

7. For additional information, see John D. Stevens, "Correspondents in World War II," *Journalism Monographs* 27 (February 1973): 12–13.

8. John Hope Freedom and Alfred A. Moss Jr., *From Slavery to Freedom: A History of Negro Americans,* 6th ed. (New York: McGraw-Hill Publishing Company, 1988), 389–90.

9. Enoch P. Waters, ms. for *American Diary: A Personal History of the Black Press,* EPW Papers, Box 176–1, Folder 1, Moorland-Spingarn Research Center, Howard University, Washington, D.C. *American Diary: A Personal History of the Black Press* was published by Path Press in Chicago in 1987.

10. Metz T. Z. Lochard, unpublished history of the black press, Metz T. Z. Lochard Papers, Box 137–2, Folder 12, Moorland-Spingarn Research Center, Howard University, Washington, D.C.

11. Levi Pierce, letter to Harry H. Woodring, October 19, 1939, CAB Papers, Chicago Historical Museum, Chicago, Illinois.

12. "Chance in U.S. Army Sought," *Norfolk Journal and Guide,* May 5, 1940, 1.

13. Awake White America, The Hour Is at Hand," editorial, *Chicago Defender,* December 13, 1941, 1.

14. Walter White, letter to Claude A. Barnett, January 31, 1942, CAB Papers, Series 2, Box 312, Folder 6, Chicago Historical Museum, Chicago, Illinois.

15. "Speak Out, Mr. President: Tell the Minority Groups What They Are Fighting for; Define Democracy as It Applies to Them," editorial, *The Afro-American*, October 17, 1942, 4.

16. Walter White, *A Man Called White* (New York: Viking Press, 1948), 206–07.

17. See, for example, Patrick Washburn, *A Question of Sedition: The Federal Government's Investigation of the Black Press during World War II* (New York: Oxford University Press, 1986), 9.

18. Federal Bureau of Investigation United States Department of Justice to Claude A. Barnett, May 22, 1943, CAB Papers, Series 2, Box 318, Folder 4, Chicago Historical Museum, Chicago, Illinois.

19. Percival L. Prattis, "The Function of a Minority Press in a Nation at War," undated typed ms., Percival L. Prattis Papers, Series C, Box 144–16, Folder 12, Moorland-Spingarn Research Center, Howard University, Washington, D.C.

20. "Leaders of Race Pledge Support As War Comes," *Chicago Defender*, December 13, 1941, 3.

21. James G. Thompson, "Should I Sacrifice to Live 'Half American'?" *Pittsburgh Courier*, January 31, 1942, 5.

22. W. W. B. Du Bois, *Souls of Black Folk* (Chicago: A. C. McClung and Company, 1903), 2.

23. Claude A. Barnett, "The Negro Press in America's War Effort," Special Release, March 7, 1942, over Columbia Broadcasting System, CAB Papers, Series 2, Box 318, Folder 4, Chicago Historical Museum, Chicago, Illinois.

24. Enoch P. Waters, ms., *American Diary: A Personal History of the Black Press*, EPW Papers, Box 176–1, Folder 1, Moorland-Spingarn Research Center, Howard University, Washington, D.C.

25. Truman K. Gibson, letter to John H. Sengstacke, May 11, 1942, Abbott and Sengstacke Papers, Series 9, Box 58, Folder 1, Vivian G. Harsh Research Collection of Afro-American History and Literature, Chicago Public Library, Chicago, Illinois.

26. Enoch P. Waters, ms., *American Diary*, 371.

27. For reference, see Enoch P. Waters, letter to President Franklin D. Roosevelt, January 19, 1941, Abbott and Sengstacke Papers, Series 9, Box 58, Folder 1, Vivian G. Harsh Research Collection of Afro-American History and Literature, Chicago Public Library, Chicago, Illinois.

28. John H. Sengstacke, letter to Henry L. Stinson, February 5, 1941, and Henry L. Stinson, letter to John H. Sengstacke, February 11, 1941, Abbott and Sengstacke Papers, Series 9, Box 58, Folder 1, Vivian G. Harsh Research Collection of Afro-American History and Literature, Chicago Public Library, Chicago, Illinois.

29. John H. Sengstacke, letter to Frank Knox, April 11, 1942, Abbott and Sengstacke Papers, Series 9, Box 58, Folder 1, Vivian G. Harsh Research Collection of Afro-American History and Literature, Chicago Public Library, Chicago, Illinois. See also letters on the same date to Uric Bell of the Office of Facts and Figures, Abbott and Sengstacke Family Papers, Series 9, Box 58, Folder 1, Vivian G. Harsh Research Collection of Afro-American History and Literature, Chicago Public Library, Chicago, Illinois.

30. For reference, see John H. Sengstacke, letter to Frank Knox, John H. Sengstacke, letter to Steve Early, John H. Sengstacke, letter to Byron Price, April 11, 1942, Abbott and Sengstacke Papers, Series 9, Box 58, Folder 1, Vivian G. Harsh Research Collection of Afro-American History and Literature, Chicago Public Library, Chicago, Illinois.

31. Waters, ms., *American Diary*, 314–15.

32. "Black Press Confers with War Officials," *Norfolk Journal and Guide*, July 24, 1943, 2.

33. Ibid.

34. Ollie Stewart, "Soldiers Meet Color Bar in London," *The Afro-American*, September 19, 1942, 1.

35. Edward B. Toles, "Black Troops Made Path for Invasion; Storm French Coast; Block Enemy Lines; Hammer German Troops in Fight to Establish Beachheads," *Chicago Defender*, June 17, 1944, 1.

36. Ibid.

37. Edward B. Toles, "Toles Lands on Normandy Beachhead as Thousands 'Sail' against Nazis," *Chicago Defender*, July 15, 1944, 1.

38. Harry McAlpin, "Two Negroes among 450 Correspondents in Invasion," *Chicago Defender*, June 17, 1944, 1.

39. John "Rover" Jordan, "92nd Division Opens Offensive to Crush Nazis," *Norfolk Journal and Guide*, September 9, 1944.

40. Patrick Washburn, "George Padmore of the Pittsburgh Courier and the Chicago Defender: A Decidedly Different World War II Correspondent," *The Mary Junck Research Colloquium Series*, Spring 2008.

41. George Padmore, "Nazi Bombs Blast Racial Prejudice in Big Convoy," *Chicago Defender*, December 26, 1942, 1.

42. Ibid.

43. Art Carter, "25 Days to Africa on North Atlantic Convoy," *The Afro-American*, December 11, 1943, 1.

44. Ollie Stewart, "Sicily Battle Ends; Afro's Stewart Gets to Front Line Riding in Hay Wagon; Big Guns Shake Earth, Causes Ears to Ring; Bridges Dynamited; Everywhere Burnt Tanks, Trucks," *The Afro American*, August 21, 1943, 1.

45. Introduction to Enoch Waters, *American Diary: A Personal History of the Black Press* (Chicago: Path Press, Inc., 1987), xii–xiv.

46. Edgar T. Rouzeau, "Says Troops Doing Well in North Ireland," *Norfolk Journal and Guide*, October 10, 1942, 1.

47. Jinx Coleman Broussard and John Maxwell Hamilton, "Covering a Two-Front War: African American Foreign Correspondents during World War II," *American Journalism* 22, no. 2 (Winter 2005): 45.

48. Fletcher Martin, "Capt. Jenkins, His Gun Blazing, Leads Attack," *Chicago Defender*, May 6, 1944, 2.

49. Ibid.

50. Ollie Stewart, "99th Flyers Suffer First Losses," *The Afro-American*, July 17, 1943. 1.

51. Ibid.

52. Ollie Stewart, "Race Share Same Bottle; Eat from Same Dish and Sleep in Same Trench in Sicily—Color Lines Vanish," *The Afro-American*, August 7, 1943, 1.

53. "The *Guide* Sets the Record Straight," *Norfolk Journal and Guide*, November 1, 1943, 1.

54. Ollie Stewart, "Guns Shell Rommel; All Hell Breaks Loose; Our Boys in Battle," *The Afro-American*, April 10, 1943, 1.

55. Ollie Stewart, "Our First Battle of the War," *The Afro-American*, April 10, 1943, 1.

56. Ibid.

57. *Norfolk Journal and Guide*, April 15, 1944, 1.

58. Edgar T. Rouzeau, "Unable to Find Negroes Manning Gun On Frontline," *Pittsburgh Courier*, January 1, 1944, 1.

59. Ibid.

60. Ibid., 4.

61. Fletcher Martin, "93rd Won't Be Used in Philippines Fight," *Chicago Defender*, December 16, 1944, 2.

62. Edward Toles, "Yanks Building Best Airfield in England," *Chicago Defender*, July 1, 1944, 6.

63. Art Carter, "Forgotten QM Battalion Nears Anniversary Abroad," *The Afro-American*, April 29, 1944, 1.

64. For reference, see "Life's War Book Editions Blundered Says Wilkins: IMP!!! ATTEMPTS TO GET BLACK NEWS IN WHITE PRESS," undated clipping, CAB Papers, Series 2, Box 318, Folder 4, Chicago Historical Museum, Chicago, Illinois.

65. Charles van Devander and William O. Player Jr., "Washington Memo," *New York Post*, February 10, 1944, clipping, CAB Papers, Series 2, Box 318, Folder 4, Chicago Historical Museum, Chicago, Illinois.

66. "The Negro Flyer," in "Other Papers Say" column, *Chicago Defender*, June 17, 1944, 10.

67. Armistead S. Pride, *A History of the Black Press* (Washington, DC: Howard University Press, 1997), 188.

CHAPTER TEN

1. Linda Johnson Rice, "Ebony's African World," *Ebony*, November 1995, 88.

2. John H. Johnson, "Publisher's Statement," *Ebony*, November 1945, 4.

3. John H. Johnson, *Succeeding Against the Odds* (New York: Warner Books, 1989), 162, 200.

4. Ibid.

5. Ibid.

6. Henry Lee Moon, "Beyond Objectivity: The 'Fighting Press,'" in *Race and the News Media*, ed. P. L. Fisher and R. Lowenstein (New York: Praeger, 1967), 139.

7. Rice, *Ebony's* African World."

8. "The World's Worst Slums," *Ebony*, November 1947, 39.

9. Era Bell Thompson, *Africa: Land of My Fathers* (Garden City, NY: Doubleday and Company, Inc., 1954), 10.

10. Ibid., 197.

11. Ibid.

12. Ibid., 193.

13. Ibid., 17.

14. Ralph E. Kliesch, "The U.S. Press Corps Abroad Rebounds: A 7th World Survey of Foreign Correspondents," *Newspaper Research Journal*, 12, no. 1 (Winter 1991): 24–33.

15. Era Bell Thompson, "Garden of Eden," *Ebony*, September 1953, 60.

16. John Bowles, "Market Report from Nigeria," *Ebony,* November 1962, 78.

17. Ibid.

18. Era Bell Thompson, "Ghana's Industrial Revolution," *Ebony,* May 1964, 154.

19. See David Rooney, *Kwame Nkrumah* (New York: St. Martin Press, 1988).

20. Ibid.

21. Era Bell Thompson, "Tshombe's Spanish Hideaway: Kantaga Leader Planned Comeback in Madrid," *Ebony,* August 1964, 100.

22. Charles L. Sanders, "Kwame Nkrumah: The Fall of the Messiah," *Ebony,* September 1966, 139.

23. Era Bell Thompson, "Jim Crow South African Style: American Bucks Apartheid," *Ebony,* May 1964, 123.

24. Era Bell Thompson, "Are Black Americans Welcome in Africa?" *Ebony,* January 1969, 44.

25. Walter Leavy, "African Giant," *Ebony,* March 1990, 80.

26. D. Michael Cheers, "A Special Message to Black Americans," *Ebony,* May 1990, 180.

27. For reference, see Magazine Publishers of America, "Average Circulation for Top ABC Magazines," September 2009. Accessed at www.magazine.org/Circulation/circulation trends and magazine handbook/1359.cfm, October 1, 2007.

28. Johnson, *Succeeding Against All Odds,* 160.

29. The June 18, 1946, letters are in the CAB Papers, Series 2, Box 168, Folder 5, Chicago History Museum, Chicago, Illinois.

30. "Liberian Workers Strike Against 40c Per Day Wage," *Pittsburgh Courier,* January 12, 1946, 12. Accessed at www.proquest.com, December 20, 2008.

31. I. Roland, letter to Milton A. McCaulay, March (n.d.) 1948, CAB Papers, Series 2, Box 166, Folder 2, Chicago History Museum, Chicago, Illinois.

32. Clifton S. Hardy, letter to Claude A. Barnett, February 5, 1958, CAB Papers, Series 2, Box 168, Folder 5, Chicago History Museum, Chicago, Illinois.

33. Claude A. Barnett, letter to Clifton S. Hardy, May 5, 1958, CAB Papers, Series 2, Box 168, Folder 5, Chicago History Museum, Chicago, Illinois.

34. For reference, see letters between Claude A. Barnett and Clifton S. Hardy, July 5, 1958, December 14, 1958, February 24, 1960, May 7, 1961, December 3, 1962, and December 29, 1962, CAB Papers, Series 2, Box 168, Folder 5, Chicago History Museum, Chicago, Illinois.

35. See Claude A. Barnett, letter to Nick Aaron Ford, April 4, 1961; Claude A. Barnett, letter to Dr. Charles A. Ray, April 8, 1961, CAB Papers, Series 2, Box 163, Folder 3, Chicago History Museum, Chicago, Illinois,

36. See February 20, 1969, form letter, CAB Papers, Series 2, Box 167, Folder 7, Chicago History Museum, Chicago, Illinois.

37. Claude A. Barnett, letter to "Whom It May Concern," April 22, 1961, CAB Papers, Series 2, Box 172, Folder 2, Chicago History Museum, Chicago, Illinois; Claude A. Barnett, letter to David Talbot, December 14, 1961, CAB Papers, Series 2, Box 166, Folder 2, Chicago History Museum, Chicago, Illinois.

38. Claude A. Barnett, letter to David Talbot, March 25, 1964, CAB Papers, Series 2, Box 166, Folder 2, Chicago History Museum, Chicago, Illinois. The seventeen undated clippings that Talbot wrote are also in that folder.

39. The manuscript for Enoch Waters's *Book of Enoch* is located in the EPW Papers, Box

172–2, Folder 19, Moorland-Spingarn Research Center, Howard University, Washington, D.C. That title, taken from the biblical reference of the same name, appears to have been a working title for Waters's book on the black press titled *American Diary: A Personal History of the Black Press* (Chicago: Chicago Review Press, 1984).

40. Enoch Waters, "Summary of Journalistic Career," ms., EPW Papers, Series 1, Box 176–11, Folder 10, Moorland-Spingarn Research Center, Howard University, Washington, D.C.

41. See the following: Enoc Waters, "Royal Titles Abundant in Democratic Nigeria," *Norfolk Journal and Guide* clipping; Enoc Waters, "Ex-sergeant Holds Important Position at Nigerian Airport," and Enoc Waters, "Speak of Spectaculars: Nigeria's 'Dubar' Tops All," *Norfolk Journal and Guide*, n.d., 9, EPW Papers, Box 176–7, Folder 45, Moorland-Spingarn Research Center, Howard University, Washington, D.C.

42. Enoc P. Waters, "An Innocent in Africa," column from Lagos, Nigeria, clipping, EPW Papers, Box 176–7, Folder 45, Moorland-Spingarn Research Center, Howard University, Washington, D.C.

43. Enoc P. Waters, "Nigerian Premier Feels U.S. Negros Don't Regard Africans As Brothers," undated clipping, EPW Papers, Box 176–7, Folder 45, Moorland-Spingarn Research Center, Howard University, Washington, D.C.

44. Enoc P. Waters, untitled typescript with a Lagos, Nigeria, dateline, EPW Papers, Box 176–8, Folder 45, Moorland-Spingarn Research Center, Howard University, Washington, D.C. See, also Enoc P. Waters, "Nigeria's Fabulous State Ball Was International, Interracial, Interesting: Champagne Flows; VIP's Enjoy 4 Bands, Reporter Dances with Princess, Etc.," *Norfolk Journal and Guide*, October 15, 1960 (page number not indicated), EPW Papers, Box 176–8, Folder 45, Moorland-Spingarn Research Center, Howard University, Washington, D.C.

45. Waters, "Nigeria's Fabulous State Ball Was International, Interracial, Interesting."

46. Enoc P. Waters Jr., "Nigerian Independence Activities," clipping, EPW Papers, Box 176–8, Folder 45, Moorland-Spingarn Research Center, Howard University, Washington, D.C.

47. Enoc P. Waters Jr., "Pros and Cons on Nigeria's Future as a Nation," *Cleveland Call and Post*, December 9, 1961, 7c, EPW Papers, Box 176–8, Folder 45, Moorland-Spingarn Research Center, Howard University, Washington, D.C.

48. Ibid.

49. Enoc P. Waters Jr. "Just 13 Months Ago . . . Pros and Cons of Nigeria's Future as Independent Nation," typescript dated November 15, 1961, EPW Papers, Box 176–8, Folder 45, Moorland-Spingarn Research Center, Howard University, Washington, D.C.

50. "Mann on the Job," undated typescript, EPW Papers, Box 176–8, Folder 43, Moorland-Spingarn Research Center, Howard University, Washington, D.C.

51. Enoc P. Waters, "Is It True What They Say about Liberia?" EPW Papers, Box 176–7, Folder 44, Moorland-Spingarn Research Center, Howard University, Washington, D.C.

52. Enoc Waters, "Learning from Oil," undated ms., EPW Papers, Box 176–9, Folder 27, Moorland-Spingarn Research Center, Howard University, Washington, D.C.

53. Enoch Waters, untitled ms., EPW Papers, Box 176–7, Folder 7, Moorland-Spingarn Research Center, Howard University, Washington, D.C.

54. Ethel Payne, "France Steps Up Military Aid to Biafran Rebels," *Chicago Daily Defender*, February 13, 1969, 10.

55. Ibid., 25.

56. Ethel Payne, "Deadly Power Game Behind Nigerian Strife," *Chicago Daily Defender,* February 3, 1969, 6.

57. Ethel L. Payne, "U.S. Relations with Nigeria Threatened," *Chicago Daily Defender,* February 4, 1969, 7.

58. For reference, see Ethel L. Payne, "Selassie's Problem: Unrest," *Chicago Daily Defender,* February 18, 1970, 14.

CHAPTER ELEVEN

1. For reference, see Lewis W. Jones, ed., *Negro Yearbook: A Review of Events Affecting Negro Life, 1952* (Tuskegee, AL: Tuskegee Institute, Department of Records and Research, 1952), 46.

2. "Assign Ace Defenderman To Korean War," *Chicago Defender,* July 15, 1950, 1.

3. Gene Roberts and Hank Kilbanoff, *The Race Beat: The Press, the Civil Rights Struggle, and the Awakening of a Nation* (New York: Random House, 2006).

4. For reference, see William T. Bowers, *Black Soldiers, White Army: The 24th Infantry Regiment in Korea* (Center for Military History, U.S. Army, 1996).

5. "First with the Facts," *Chicago Defender,* August 12, 1950, 1.

6. Ibid.

7. "More Negro Troops into Korean War," *Chicago Defender,* July 15, 1950, 1.

8. Carl Murphy, letter to Wilda Raines, September 22, 1930, Box 6, Folder R-1, Carl J. Murphy Papers, Moorland-Spingarn Research Center, Howard University, Washington, D.C.

9. James Hicks, "Your Letter Can Cheer GI's at Battle Front," *The Afro-American.* September 2, 1950, 1.

10. James Hicks, "What to Put in Letters Mailed to Soldiers Overseas," *The Afro-American,* September 30, 1950, 1.

11. James Hicks, "Personal," *The Afro-American,* August 12, 1950, 1. See also James Hicks, "Morale Universally High," *The Afro-American,* August 12, 1950, 1, and James Hicks, "Hicks Jumps Off with Marines in First Full-Scale Offensive," *The Afro-American,* August 12, 1950, 1.

12. See, for example, Ollie Stewart, "Soldiers Meet Color Bar in London," *The Afro American,* September 19, 1942, 1; George Padmore, "Nazi Bombs Blast Racial Prejudice In Big Convoy," *Chicago Defender,* December 26, 1942, 1; Jinx Broussard and John Maxwell Hamilton, "Covering a Two-Front War: Three African American Correspondents during World War II," *American Journalism,* 22, no. 2 (2005): 45.

13. James Hicks, "24th Soldiers Do Impossible," *The Afro-American,* August 12, 1950, 1.

14. L. Alexander Wilson, "Along the Korean War Front," *Chicago Defender,* August 26, 1950, 2.

15. L. Alexander Wilson, "Tan Yanks Recapture Korea's 'Battle Mountain,'" *Chicago Defender,* September 30, 1950, 4.

16. Frank Whisonant, "Tan GIs Kill 200," *Pittsburgh Courier,* September 2, 1950, 1, 4.

17. James Hicks, "Counts Rows of Wounded," *The Afro-American,* August 19, 1950, 1.

18. James Hicks, "24th Hit Hard," *The Afro-American,* August 19, 1950, 1.

19. Frank Whisonant, "Hint Move On To Discredit Negro Troops," *Pittsburgh Courier,* September 16, 1950, 1.

20. Frank Whisonant, "Is the 24th Being Framed?: Is Army Attempting to Make Tan Unit Scapegoat of War?" *Pittsburgh Courier,* September 23, 1950, 1.

21. James Hicks, "Army Passes Buck," *The Afro-American,* August 26, 1950, 1.

22. Frank Whisonant, "Gilbert's Exclusive Interview," *Pittsburgh Courier,* October 21, 1950, 1.

23. Frank Whisonant, "Courier Had Story; Couldn't Break It," *Pittsburgh Courier,* September 30, 1950, 1, 5;.

24. James Hicks, "Lt. Gilbert Will Not Die!" *The Afro-American,* November 18, 1950, 1.

25. "National Grapevine: Give Us Eyes to See," editorial, *Chicago Defender,* July 29, 1950, 6.

26. L. Alex Wilson, "Here're Some Bad Gunmen To Make You Proud—The 159th in Korea," *Chicago Defender,* September 9, 1950, 14; "'Just Lucky I Guess,' Says Yank After Bullet Dances In His Helmet," *Chicago Defender,* September 23, 1950, 4.

27. L. Alexander Wilson, "Does Integration Work In Korea?" *Chicago Defender,* September 16, 1950, 1.

28. L. Alexander Wilson, "Integration Is Forced to Test by War in Korea," *Chicago Defender,* February 3, 1951, 1.

29. Alexander Wilson, "Wilson Tells Story Of A Decision To Bring Democracy To Battlefield," *Chicago Defender,* October 28, 1950, 4.

30. Alexander Wilson, "Southern Whites, Negroes Give Jim Crow Hard Time in Mixed Tank Group," *Chicago Defender,* September 2, 1950, 4.

31. L. Alex Wilson, "Reveals Facts About North Koreans' Alleged Contempt For Negro GIs," Chicago Defender, March 3, 1951, 2. See also "Integration Is Forced To Test By War in Korea"; "General Traces High Casualties Among Troops To Army Jim Crow," *Chicago Defender,* February 10, 1951, 1; "Wilson Says Mixed Army Big Gain of Korean War," *Chicago Defender,* August 8, 1953, 1.

32. Frank Whisonant, "Chaplain in Korea Admits Race Prejudice," *Pittsburgh Courier,* September 9, 1950, 5.

33. "Abolish 'Negro' Units," editorial, *Pittsburgh Courier,* September 9, 1950, 6.

34. Ibid.

35. Frank Whisonant, "GIs Gone 'Sour' On White Officers Slandering Outfit," *Pittsburgh Courier,* September 2, 1950, 5.

36. Ibid.

37. James L. Hicks, "24th Division Gets Integrated Rifle Unit," *The Afro-American,* August 12, 1950, 1.

38. James Hicks, "Integration a Fact as we Fight Koreans," *The Afro-American,* August 19, 1950, 1.

39. "Matthews Off to Korean War," *The Afro-American,* July 21, 1952, 1; and "He's Off to Korea, With His Camera, Typewriter and Bag," *The Afro-American,* July 28, 1951.

40. "ARMY JC TO END: 24th Infantry Regiment to be Disbanded," *The Afro-American,* July 28, 1951, 1.

41. "Segregation Allowed under His Command: Tan Yanks Won't Shed Any Tears Over His Removal," *The Afro-American,* April 21, 1951, 1.

42. Ralph Matthews, "Korea Has Taught Us You Can't Win War with JC Units," *The Afro-American,* August 4, 1951.

43. Ralph Matthews, "Integration Complete in Tokyo, Matthews Finds," *The Afro-American,* August 11, 1951, 3.

44. Ralph Matthews, "Japanese Jim Crow Ended by Treaty," *The Afro-American*, September 22, 1951, 1; Ralph Matthews, "Colored Personnel In All Units of Service in Korea," *The Afro-American*, December 15, 1951, 3.

45. Ralph Matthews Sr., "White Soldiers Pleased With Korean Integration," *The Afro-American*, December 29, 1951, 13.

46. See, for example, William Worthy Jr., "Signing of Truce Leaves Soldiers in Korea Cold" and "Names of 40 on First War Prisoners List," *The Afro-American*, August 8, 1953, 1 .

47. "Korean Debacle Bound to Open Eyes of US GIs," *The Afro-American*, August 15, 1953, 1.

48. Ibid.

49. "Some POWs Desert Land of Jim Crow," *The Afro-American*, August 15, 1953, 1–2.

CHAPTER TWELVE

Parts of this chapter appeared in *Journalism Studies* in 2009 as an article Skye Chance Cooley and I wrote.

1. McCarran Internal Security Act, 50 U.S.C., Section 781.

2. Robert Wright interview of William Worthy Jr., February 28, 1970, William Worthy Jr. Folder, Moorland-Spingarn Research Center, Howard University, Washington, D.C.

3. Jinx Coleman Broussard interview of Raymond Boone, October 9, 2007.

4. Ibid.

5. Jinx Coleman Broussard interview of Michael Meyer, February 22, 2008.

6. "Reporter Defies China-Visit Ban," *Washington Post and Times Herald*, December 25, 1956, 12; Milton Bracker, "Defiant Newsman Back from China," *New York Times*, February 11, 1957, 8.

7. Jinx Coleman Broussard interview of Sarah-Ann Shaw, February 22, 2008. Shaw was the first African American reporter for Boston's NBC affiliate; Worthy was a commentator on her show during the early 1970s.

8. Ibid.

9. Ibid.

10. Jinx Coleman Broussard interview of Ruth Worthy, March 17, 2008.

11. *Mirror*, Bates College Yearbook (Lewiston, ME: Bates College, 1942), 79.

12. William Worthy, "Defense without Armament," *The Garnett*, February 1941 (Winter Issue), 33.

13. William Worthy Jr. ,"Worthy Assails Fascists Tendency in Country," *Bates Student*, November 26, 1941, 12.

14. William Worthy Jr., quoted in Adrian Walker, "Reclaiming a Gallant Voice," *The Boston Globe*, February 22, 2008, B-1.

15. Wright interview of Worthy, 2.

16. Broussard interview of Boone.

17. See, for example, William Worthy Jr., *Our Disgrace in Indo-China* (Self-Published, 1956); William Worthy Jr., *Interview with Prince Sihanouk* (Self-Published, 1965); Eric Norben, Andrew March, Mark Land, and William Worthy Jr., *The Silent Slaughter: The Role of the United States in the Indonesian* Massacre (Self-Published, 1967).

18. William Worthy Jr., *The Progressive*, April 1952, 26.

19. Ibid.

20. Broussard interview of Boone.

21. Ibid.

22. See "Some POWs Desert Land of Jim Crow," *The Afro-American*, August 15, 1953, 1–2; "Korean Debacle Bound to Open Eyes of US GIs," *The Afro-American*, August 15, 1953, 1.

23. Broussard interview of Ruth Worthy.

24. William Worthy Jr., "In One Ear and Out the Other," *The Afro-American*, October 23, 1954, 1.

25. William Worthy, "The Asian-African Conference: Bandung in Retrospect," *The Afro-American*, June 11, 1955, 1.

26. Ibid.

27. William Worthy Jr., "Diplomatic Service in the Far East," *The Afro-American*, July 2, 1955, 1.

28. Ibid.

29. For reference, see *Jet*, January 6, 1955, 51.

30. William Worthy, "A Window in Moscow," *The Afro-American*, magazine section, September 17, 1955, 1. Worthy was not the first African American person to report from Russia. Homer Smith, who used the pen name Chatwood Hall, lived in and reported from Russia for the *Chicago Defender* and other black publications. The introduction to a story that Hall wrote in 1955 for *The Afro-American* magazine section indicated that Smith was "irked" by segregation in the United States, so he "set out in 1932 to find a country where there was no jim crow." He lived there fourteen years and even covered the Russian campaigns during World War II. For additional reference, see Chatwood Hall, "Why I Went to Russia and Why I Left," *The Afro-American*, magazine section, September 24, 1955.

31. See Whitman Bassow, *The Moscow Correspondents: Reporting on Russia from the Revolution to Glasnost* (New York: William Morrow and Company, Inc., 1988).

32. Worthy, "Window in Moscow," 6.

33. Ibid.

34. William Worthy Jr., "Louisiana Senator Makes Bad Impression in Moscow," *The Afro-American*, October 1, 1955, 1.

35. "Follow William Worthy into Red China . . . in Your *Afro-American*," *The Afro-American*, February 2, 1957, 8.

36. William Worthy, Jr., "Worthy Visits Prisoners in Red China," *The Afro-American*, January 26, 1957,1.

37. Ibid.

38. "Racial Arrogance Gave Birth to Red China: Bill Worthy Reports," *The Afro-American*, February 2, 1957, 1.

39. Ibid.

40. William Worthy Jr., "No Campus Romances in Red China Universities," *The Afro-American*, March 23, 1957, 1.

41. William Worthy, "Some Day, They'll Come Home," *The Afro-American*, April 12, 1957, 1.

42. William Worthy, "Bill Worthy Talks to Red Premier Chou En-Lai," *The Afro-American*, January 12, 1957, 1.

43. William Worthy Jr., letter to the editor, *New York Times*, April 25, 1982, 20.

44. "Nation's Press Backs Worthy's China Trip," *The Afro-American*, January 12, 1957, 1.

45. See "Pulitzer Prize for Worthy?" *The Afro-American*, January 26, 1957, 1; "Report Labels Red China Ban to Newsmen Unconstitutional," *The Afro-American*, February, 2, 1957, 1; "Publishers Protest U. S. Travel Ban," *The Afro-American*, February 16, 1957, 1.

46. See "Passport Plea Made," *The Afro-American*, March 30, 1957; "An Apology to Worthy," *The Afro-American*, April 6, 1957; "Worthy to be Witness," *The Afro-American*, February 23, 1957, 1; "Bill Worthy Faces Passport Battle," *The Afro-American*, February 16, 1957, 1.

47. "Worthy to Face Passport Showdown: Bill Worthy Faces Passport Battle," *The Afro-American*, February 16, 1957, 1.

48. "Worthy to be a Witness," *The Afro-American*, February 23, 1957, 1.

49. "Ask Apology to Worthy," *The Afro-American*, April 6, 1957, 1. A federal official had testified that Worthy was jailed during World War II for refusing to go to a conscientious objector camp. Worthy countered that he refused to go to the camp because it was segregated, and, more important, he never faced draft-dodging charges.

50. "Worthy Calls Minority Group Custodian of U.S. Democracy," *The Afro-American*, May 11, 1957, 1.

51. *William Worthy v. Christian v Herter*, 270 F.2d 905, June 1959. Retrieved from personal collection of Ruth Worthy, March 17, 2008.

52. Wright interview of William Worthy, 1.

53. See Pedro Teichert, "Latin America and the Socio-Economic Impact of the Cuban Revolution," *Journal of Inter-American Studies* (January 1962): 105–120.

54. William Worthy Jr., "Our Man in Iran: Carrying on an AFRO Tradition," *The Afro-American*, February 16, 1980, 1.

55. "Bill Worthy Uncovers US Bias in Cuba," *American*, September 17, 1960, 1.

56. "Writer Sees No Need to Stay Out of Cuba." *The Afro-American*, October 8, 1960, 1.

57. Ibid.

58. Alvin White, "Fidel Calls Harlem 'An Oasis in Desert,'" *The Afro-American*, September 24, 1960, 1.

59. Steven Duncan, "Exclusive: Castro Interview: Premier Talks to *AFRO* in 929," *The Afro-American*. September 24, 1960, 1.

60. William Worthy Jr., "CUBA STORY NOT TOLD—WORTHY," *The Afro-American*, January 13, 1962, 1.

61. Max Frankel, "Angry Castro Switches Hotels and Moves to Harlem after Protesting to the U.N.," *New York Times*, September 20, 1960, 16.

62. Max Frankel, "Cuban Delegation Is Pleased By Attentions from Russia," *New York Times*, September 21, 1960, 1.

63. "Adam Clayton Powell Raps Castro's Stay in Harlem," *Chicago Daily Defender*, September 6, 1960, 25. See also "Harlem Labels Castro's Visit as Propaganda," *Chicago Daily Defender*, October 2, 1960, 2.

64. "Stretching the Law," editorial, *Chicago Daily Defender*, May 16, 1962, 11.

65. "Worthy Condemns Press Blackout," *The Afro-American*, June 30, 1962, 1–3.

66. *William Worthy Jr., Appellant v. United States of America, Appellee*, 328F.2d.386, February 20, 1964.

67. William Kuntsler, *My Life as a Radical Lawyer* (Secaucus, NJ: Carol Publishing Group, 1994).

68. Worthy, "Our Man in Iran," 1.

69. Ibid.

70. See Worthy, *Interview with Prince Sihanouk*; Norben, March, Land, and Worthy, *Silent Slaughter*.

71. See William Worthy, "The Black Power Establishment," *Esquire*, November 1967, 131; William Worthy, "Max Stanford: Profile of a Black Revolutionary," *Boston Sunday Globe*, June 16, 1968, 30; William Worthy, "Sostre in Solitary," *Boston Sunday Globe*, September 3, 1968, 44; William Worthy, "South End Memories," *Boston Sunday Globe*, December 5, 1971, 10.

72. William Worthy Jr., "Occupation of Haiti," Roots—Resources—Communications column, *The Afro-American*, August 27, 1976, 3.

73. William Worthy Jr., "Chairman Mao's Death," Roots—Resources—Communications column, *The Afro-American*, September 21, 1976, 3.

74. William Worthy Jr., Now the Truth will Come Out; If We Insist," Roots—Resources—Communications column, *The Afro-American*, September 28, 1979, 3.

75. Broussard interview of Goodman.

76. William Worthy, Jr., "To Outrage Iranians, The Shah Is What Hitler Was to the Jews," *The Afro-American*, November 3, 1976, 8.

77. William Worthy Jr., "Anti-Iranian Mood in America Reveals Ugly Face of Fascism," *The Afro-American*, December 1, 1979, 1.

78. Worthy, "Now the Truth Will Come Out; If We Insist," 3.

79. Broussard interview of Boone.

80. William Worthy Jr., "Hostages Give Views," *The Afro-American*, February 16, 1980, 1.

81. The following appeared in *The Afro-American:* William Worthy Jr., "Our Man in Iran: Carrying on an *AFRO* Tradition," February 16, 1980, 1; "Hostages Give Views," February 16, 1980. 1; "Why Iran Wants United States to Apologize," *The Afro-American*, March 1, 1980, 1.

82. Worthy "Why Iran Wants United States to Apologize." ,

83. Broussard interview of Goodman.

84. Ibid.

85. Ibid.

86. Scott Armstrong, "Iran Documents Give Rare Glimpse of a CIA Enterprise," *Washington Post*, January 20, 1982, 1.

87. Media Advisory, Civil Liberties Union of Massachusetts, January 20, 1982. Retrieved from the personal files of Ruth Worthy, March 17, 2008.

88. Broussard interview of Goodman.

89. Broussard interview of Boone.

90. Broussard interview of William Worthy, February 22, 2008.

91. Ibid.

92. Broussard interview of Meyer.

CHAPTER THIRTEEN

1. "*Daily Defender* to Have Its Own 'Man' In Viet Nam," *Chicago Daily Defender*, December 17, 1966, 1.

2. Kathleen Currie interview of Ethel Payne, Washington Press Club Foundation, August 25, 1987. Accessed at www.npc.press.org/wpforal/payn1.htm, September 20, 2008., 92.

3. "*Daily Defender* to Have Its Own 'Man' In Viet Nam."

4. Press release, October 21, 1966, Abbott-Sengstacke Papers, Series 13, Box 134, Folder 2, Vivian G. Harsh Research Collection of Afro-American History and Literature, Chicago Public Library, Chicago, Illinois. The press release announced Sengstacke *and* Sengstacke Publications' acquisition of the *Pittsburgh Courier* chain of weeklies, excluding the *Chicago Courier*. The purchase included the name, circulation, advertising, accounts, and "good will" of the *Pittsburgh Courier* Publishing Company. The paper was renamed the *New Pittsburgh Courier* and had offices at 315 E. Carson Street in Pittsburgh. See also the Bill of Sale and Assignment, which also spelled out the terms.

5. Ethel Payne, memorandum to Barry Zorthian and John Stuart, December 28, 1966, Ethel L. Payne personal folder, *Chicago Defender* archives, Chicago, Illinois.

6. Currie interview of Payne.

7. Norma Libman, "Ethel Payne: 'I had a very deep sense of concern for people,'" *Chicago Tribune*, July 31, 1988, Accessed at www.articles.chicagotribune.com/1988–07–31/features/8801190588_1_chicago-defender-ethel-payne-black, February 5, 2011.

8. Ethel Payne oral interview published in Wallace Terry, *Missing Pages: Black Journalists of Modern America: An Oral History* (New York: Carroll and Graf Publishers, 2007), 21. Payne did not write an autobiography, but she granted oral interviews for Terry's book, as well as to the Washington Press Foundation, among others. Those and the articles she wrote for various publications provided insight into her career and her perspectives on national and international issues and events.

9. Ibid., 20–21.

10. Ibid., 25.

11. An obituary and other documents in Payne's personal folder, *Chicago Defender* archives, Chicago, Illinois, indicated that the correspondent was known as the "first lady of the press." Such a designation came about because, among other reasons, Payne received national attention in 1954 when she asked President Dwight D. Eisenhower when he planned to ban segregation in interstate travel.

12. Ibid.

13. Currie interview of Payne.

14. Ibid.

15. Carolyn Martindale and Lillian Rae Dunlap, "The African American," in *U.S. Coverage of Racial Minorities: A Sourcebook, 1937–1996*, ed. Beverly Anne Deepe Keever, Carolyn Martindale, and Mary Ann Weston (Westport, CT: Greenwood Press, 1997), 131.

16. See Frank D. Russon, "A Study of Bias in TV Coverage of the Vietnamese War: 1969 and 1970," *Public Opinion Quarterly* 35 (Winter 1971–72): 539–43; Andrew J. Heubner, "Rethinking American Press Coverage of the Vietnam War, 1965–68," *Journalism History* 31 (2005): 150. Heubner examined previous scholarship, as well as print and television coverage, and concluded that "journalists, in fact, produced a body of work that faithfully reflected the complexities and perplexities of the American fighting man and the war in Vietnam," 159.

17. Whitney Young, "To Be Equal," *Chicago Daily Defender*, April 2, 1966, 15.

18. John H. Sengstacke acquired the *Pittsburgh Courier* in 1965 after the paper fell on hard times as a result of poor management and lack of financial resources. During the *Courier*'s heyday in the 1930s, its circulation reached 185,000, thanks to its coverage of the Italian-Ethiopian War. Circulation grew to 300,000 over the next two decades as the newspaper covered civil rights and waged battles on behalf of the race. The paper was grossing two million dollars a year, but the changes that integration brought in the 1960s, coupled with the management void left by the retirement of long-time editor Percival Prattis, put the paper in jeopardy of folding. See sales documents and press releases in the Abbott-Sengstacke Papers, Series 13, Box 134, Folder 1, Vivian G. Harsh Research Collection of Afro-American History and Literature, Chicago Public Library, Chicago, Illinois.

19. Gordon B. Hancock, "Viet Nam Protesters Are Called Stooges, Cowards," *Chicago Daily Defender*, March 12, 1966, 7.

20. "The Negro and Viet Nam," editorial, *Chicago Daily Defender*, March 26, 1966, 10.

21. "Negro Causalities," editorial, *Chicago Daily Defender*, March 17, 1966, 17.

22. Ethel Payne, "First Impressions in Viet Nam," *Chicago Daily Defender*, January 3, 1967, 4.

23. Ethel Payne, "'Brown Babies' Still Facing Japanese Scorn," *Chicago Daily Defender*, March 28, 1967, 4.

24. Ethel Payne, "USS Enterprise Crew Members Ask For Letters From Stateside," *Chicago Daily Defender*, January 16, 1967, 5.

25. Ethel Payne, "The People We Are Fighting and Dying For," *New Pittsburgh Courier*, January 14, 1967, 2.

26. Currie interview of Payne.

27. Ibid.

28. Ibid.

29. Ethel Payne, "B.O. Davis Says Merit Will Make More Gen'ls," *New Pittsburgh Courier*, March 25, 1967, 2.

30. Ethel Payne, "173d Airborne Brigade: The Heroes' Address," *Chicago Daily Defender*. March 23, 1967, 4.

31. Ethel Payne, "General Hails Negro GIs' Viet Performance," *Chicago Daily Defender*, March 14, 1967, 4.

32. Ethel Payne, "Memorable Days with the 'Famous Fourth,'" *Chicago Daily Defender*, February 6, 1967, 7.

33. Ethel Payne, "Crowded Saigon is Lonely Black GIs Find," *Chicago Daily Defender*, February 7, 1967, 6.

34. Currie interview of Payne.

35. Ibid.

36. Ethel Payne, "The Ramparts Marines Watch in Vietnam," *Chicago Daily Defender*, January 26, 1967, 4.

37. Ethel Payne, "Racism 'Out' for GIs in Cong Fire," *Chicago Daily Defender*, page number not visible, clipping in Payne's personal folder, *Chicago Defender* archives, Chicago, Illinois.

38. Ethel Payne, "Anti-War Demonstrators Not Concern of 7th Fighter Wing," *New Pittsburgh Courier*, March 4, 1967, 2.

39. For reference, see Ethel Payne, "Our 'Man' in Saigon Closes Out Her Vietnam Diary," *Chicago Daily Defender*, March 27, 1967, 4; "Vietnam Diary: Memorable Days with the Famous

Fourth," *Chicago Daily Defender,* February 2, 1967, 7; "It's a Big Job, Paying the Troops," *Chicago Daily Defender,* February 11, 1967, 1; "The Puzzling Adventure of Mildred Harrison: Negro Star Entertains Troops," *Chicago Daily Defender,* February 11, 1967, 1; "Negro Air Fighters Think about Home," *Chicago Daily Defender,* February 28, 1967, 6; "Third Field Hospital Called Nation's Best: 99 Percent of Patients Taken to Facility Survive," *Chicago Daily Defender,* March 9, 1964, 4; "Air Base in Japan Plays Role in Vietnam War: 554 Negro Troops Serve at Facility," *Chicago Daily Defender,* March 29, 1967, 4.

40. Ethel Payne, "Negro Soldiers Still Face Discrimination," *Chicago Daily Defender,* March 20, 1967, 4.

41. Ethel Payne, "GIs Tell How They Stand on the Viet War," *Chicago Daily Defender,* April 11, 1967, 2.

42. Ibid.

43. Ibid.

44. Ibid.

45. Ethel Payne, letter to John Sengstacke, March 30, 1967, Ethel Payne's personal folder, *Chicago Defender* archives, Chicago, Illinois.

46. Jinx Coleman Broussard interview with Michelle Davis, August 30, 2010.

47. Ibid. See also "Vietnam is New Beat for AFRO," *The Afro-American.*

48. Mike Davis, "Few Colored Officers in Command," *The Afro-American,* June 3, 1967, 1.

49. Mike Davis, "Davis to Tell AFRO Readers of Role of Our Men in Vietnam," *The Afro-American,* June 24, 1967, 2.

50. Ibid.

51. Mike Davis, "Your Decisions Have to be Right," *The Afro-American,* August 4, 1967, 1

52. Mike Davis, "Vietnam Notebook," *The Afro-American,* August 5, 1967, 14.

53. Mike, Davis, "He Works with People in Vietnam," *The Afro-American,* September 9, 1967, 12.

54. Mike Davis, "20 Minutes to Save Three Lives, *The Afro-American,* October 14, 1967, 1.

55. Mike Davis, "We Walked into an Ambush," *The Afro-American,* August 12, 1967, 12.

56. Mike Davis, "GIs Shocked by U.S. Riots," *The Afro-American,* August 12, 1967, 12.

57. Mike Davis, "Mud Erases Color in Jungle of Viet 'Front,'" *The Afro-American,* October 7, 1967, 1.

58. Mike Davis, "Togetherness Is Key as Men of 173rd Fight to Stay Alive," *The Afro-American,* November 11, 1967, 12.

59. Mike Davis, "Wait Till These GI's Come Home," *The Afro-American,* August 12, 1967, 1.

60. Because the book only addresses the print media, Bradley's reports are not examined.

61. Jinx Broussard interview of Janice Terry, February 22, 2011.

62. Terry, *Missing Pages,* 321.

63. "The Negro in Vietnam," *Time,* May 27, 1967, 15.

64. Ibid., 17.

65. Ibid.

66. Tom Johnson, oral interview in Wallace Terry, *Missing Pages,* 95.

67. Ibid.

68. Ibid.

69. Ibid., 93.

70. Ibid.

71. *Ibid.*, 97.

72. Thomas A. Johnson, "The U. S. Negro in Vietnam," *New York Times*, April 29, 1968, 1.

73. Ibid.

74. Thomas A. Johnson, "Negro Expatriates Finding Wide Opportunity in Asia," *New York Times*, April 30, 1968, 1.

75. Ibid., 18.

76. Ibid.

77. Ibid.

78. Ibid.

79. Thomas A. Johnson, "Stop and Khesanh: A Perilous Rescue," *New York Times*, February 4, 1968, 4.

80. Thomas A. Johnson, "Saigon Marks TET, But without G.I.'s," *New York Times*, January 30, 1967.

CHAPTER FOURTEEN

1. Jinx Coleman Broussard interview of Leon Dash, November 23, 2010. See also Leon Dash oral history in Wallace Terry, *Missing Pages: Black Journalists of Modern America: An Oral History* (Carroll and Graff Publishers: New York, 2007), 180. Dash became interested in Africa through his church when he was in junior high school. The youngster stuffed envelopes and ran errands for Operation Crossroads Africa, an organization his pastor founded.

2. Ibid.

3. Ibid.

4. Leon Dash, "After 13 Years, Angola War Remains a Stalemate," *Washington Post*, August 5, 1974, A-16.

5. Dash oral interview in Terry, *Missing Pages*, 186.

6. Broussard interview of Dash.

7. Leon Dash, "New Nigerian Leader Vows to Continue Role of Militant Leadership," *Washington Post*, September 14, 1979, A-23.

8. Leon Dash, "Nigerian Election Recriminations Revive Sensitivities of Civil War," *Washington Post*, December 28, 1980, A-27.

9. Leon Dash, "Refugees Set in Motion by Amin Disrupt Uganda, Zaire, Sudan: Zaire Takes in 632,800 Refugees but Fear Raising Border Tensions," *Washington Post*, November 13, 1981, A-42.

10. Broussard interview of Dash.

11. Ibid.

12. Howard W. French, *A Continent for the Taking: The Tragedy and Hope of Africa* (New York: Vintage Books, 2004), 3.

13. Ibid., xiii–xiv.

14. Jinx C. Broussard Interview of Howard French, November 1, 2010.

15. Ibid.

16. Ibid.

17. Ibid.

18. Howard W. French, "'We're Going to Vote Anyway,' Haitians Insist," *New York Times*, November 26, 1987; Howard W. French, "Voodoo Politics," *New York Times*, June 25, 1989; "The World; When Neighbors Aren't Friends," *New York Times*, July 10, 1994; "Slash Ties, Apartheid

Foes Urge," *New York Times*, February 9, 1987; "The French Keep Africa Under Wing," *New York Times*, September 11, 1994; "Nigeria, Strikers Reject Military Offer," *New York Times*, August 7, 1994; "Bandit Rebels Ravage Sierra Leone," *New York Times*, February 17, 1995.

19. French, *A Continent for the Taking*, 50.

20. French, "The French Keep Africa Under Wing."

21. Broussard interview of French.

22. Howard W. French, "Bandit Rebels Ravage Sierra Leone," *New York Times*, February 17, 1995.

23. Broussard interview of French.

24. Howard W. French, "Sept. 18–24: Hope in Africa; Anti-Malarial Vaccine May be Breakthrough," *New York Times*, September 25, 1994.

25. French, *A Continent for the Taking*, 50.

26. Ibid.

27. Keith B. Richburg, "American in Africa," *The Post Magazine*, March 26, 1995.

28. Ibid.

29. Jinx C. Broussard interview of Sheila Rule, July 12, 2005.

30. French, *A Continent for the Taking*, xv–xvi.

31. Walter Leavy, "African Giant," *Ebony*, March 1990, 80.

32. D. Michael Cheers, "A Special Message to Black Americans," *Ebony*, May 1990, 180.

33. Hans J. Massaquoi, "Namibia: Free At Last!" *Ebony*, June 1990, 124.

34. "Ron Allen: NBC News Correspondent," biographical sketch. Accessed at www.msnbc.msn.com/id/3080793/ns/nightly_news-about_us/, January 6, 2011.

35. See "Ginger Thompson Cabot Prize Citation," *Columbia News*. Accessed at www.columbia.edu/cu/news/06/06/thompson.html, July 28, 2010. In 2006, Columbia University awarded Thompson the Cabot Prize, noting: "Her piercing curiosity and keen sense of human rights have produced unusually dramatic and tightly woven stories on U.S.-backed death squads in Central America, the mysterious disappearances and murders of women on the U.S.-Mexico border, anarchy in Haiti, the growing threat of U.S.-based Latino gangs in Central America and the pathetic plight of smuggled illegal aliens making their way to the United States in dangerous sea voyages."

36. Howard W. French, "The Next Empire: All Across Africa, New Tracks are Being Laid, Highways Built, Ports Deepened, Commercial Contracts Signed, All On an Unprecedented Scale, and Led by China, Whose Appetite for Commodities Seems Insatiable," Accessed at www.howardwfrench.com/2010/04/the-next-empire-all-across-africa-new-tracks-are-being-laid-highways-builtports-deepened-commercial-contracts-signed%E2%80%9Aaiall-on-an-unprecedented-scale-and-led-by-china-whose-appetite-for/, January 26, 2011.

37. Howard W. French, "It's Not Convenient to Speak of Such Things: Notes from Rangoon." Accessed at www.howardwfrench.com/archives/2010/12/14/its_not_convenient_to_speak_of_such_things_notes_frof_rangoon/, January 11, 2011.

EPILOGUE

1. John Maxwell Hamilton, *Journalism's Roving Eye: A History of American Foreign Reporting* (Baton Rouge: Louisiana State University Press) 2009; Michael Emery, *On the Front Lines: Following America's Foreign Correspondents Across the Twentieth Century* (Washington, DC: The American

University Press, 1995); Patrick Washburn, "George Padmore of the Pittsburgh Courier and the Chicago Defender: A Decidedly Different World War II Correspondent," *The Mary Junck Research Colloquium Series*, Spring 2008.

2. Hamilton, *Journalism's Roving Eye*, 157.

3. George Washington Williams, "A Report on the Proposed Congo Railway by Colonel [sic] the Honorable Geo. W. Williams of the United States of America " July 16, 1890, cited as Appendix 2 of John Hope Franklin, *George Washington Williams: A Biography* (Chicago: University of Chicago Press, 1985), 255.

4. The manuscript for Enoch Waters's *Book of Enoch* is located in the EPW Papers, Box 172–2, Folder 19, Moorland-Spingarn Research Center, Howard University, Washington, D.C. That title, taken from the biblical reference of the same name, appears to have been a working title for Waters's book on the black press titled *American Diary: A Personal History of the Black Press* (Chicago, Illinois: Chicago Review Press, 1984).

5. "Worthy Condemns Press Blackout," *The Afro-American*, June 30, 1962, 1–3.

6. Black male correspondents for the mainstream media over the past fifty years are too numerous to name here, but include such *New York Times* correspondents as Paul Delaney, who was a Madrid bureau chief, and Calvin Sims, whose stints for the *Times* included Latin America, Japan, and Korea; Les Payne, who reported from Africa, the Caribbean, and Europe during a forty-year career at Newsday; Keith Richburg, who has been a bureau chief in Paris, Manila, and Hong Kong, among other places, and at this writing is reporting from China; CBS's Byron Pitts, who covered the refugee crisis in Kosovo and is now a correspondent on CBS; and Bill Whitaker, who was a CBS Tokyo correspondent covering stories throughout Asia, including the Tiananmen Square incident.

7. Some of these women include Sheila Rule, who reported from Africa and Europe during the 1980s for the *New York Times;* Charlayne Hunter-Gault , who won two Emmys and a Peabody award for her work on apartheid while bureau chief from Johannesburg for National Public Radio, and later was bureau chief from there for CNN; Lynn Duke, who covered Africa for the *Washington Post;* Jerri Eddings, who did the same for the *Baltimore Sun* in the early 1990s; and Ginger Thomas, who covered Latin America for that newspaper before becoming a foreign correspondent for the *New York Times*.

8. National Public Radio interview of Frank Bolden. Accessed at www.pbs.org/blackpress/film/transcripts/bolden.html, November 1, 2011.

9. Metz T. Z. Lochard, "History of the Negro Press," chapter 1, page 34, unpublished ms., Metz T. Z. Lochard Papers, Box 137–2, Folder 12, Moorland-Spingarn Research Center, Howard University, Washington, D.C.

10. Patrick S. Washington, *The African American Newspaper: Voice of Freedom* (Evanston, IL: Northwestern University Press, 2006), 188–89.

11. Ibid.

12. Lynne Duke, author's biography. Accessed at www.lynneduke.com, April 2, 2012.

13. Jinx Coleman Broussard interview of Shelia Rule, July 8, 2005.

14. See, for example, French's website at www.howardwfrench.com/ and his blog, "A Glimpse of the World."

15. Even *Ebony* magazine has suffered circulation, missing its guarantee to advertisers in

parts of 2009, 2010, and 2011. For reference, see "*Ebony* Aims to Rebound with Redesign and Circulation Consultants," *Advertising Age,* Accessed at www.adage.com, April 2, 2012.

16. Juan Gonzales and Joseph Torres, *News for All People: The Epic Story of Race and the American Media* (New York: Verso, 2011).

17. For reference, see Christopher P. Campbell, Kim LeDuff, Cheryl D. Jenkins, and Rockell A. Brown, *Race and News: Critical Perspectives* (New York: Routledge, 2012).

Index

www.ingramcontent.com/pod-product-compliance
Lightning Source LLC
LaVergne TN
LVHW091117080826
845145LV00008B/1953

* 9 7 8 0 8 0 7 1 8 8 3 9 2 *